Between Two Worlds

Between Two Worlds

Young Women in Crisis

by Linda Gray Sexton

William Morrow and Company, Inc.
New York   1979

Library of Congress Cataloging in Publication Data

Sexton, Linda Gray, 1953–
 Between two worlds.

 Bibliography: p.
 CONTENTS: Hallie Parrish.—Julie Fowler.—Lisa Matthews.—[etc.]
 1. Young women—United States—Interviews. 2. United States—Social conditions—1960– I. Title.
HQ1229.S45   301.41′2   79-17356
ISBN 0-688-03545-0

Book Design by Michael Mauceri

Printed in the United States of America.

First Edition

1 2 3 4 5 6 7 8 9 10

Because he was watchdog of the word
and a real mensch

for John

Acknowledgments

My thanks go to the many who helped me with *Between Two Worlds:*

Ed Forman and Amy Levine, who lit the fire under my tail; Bella Brodzki, Louise and Loring Conant, Charmian and Seelig Freund, Stanley King, Doug Schoen, Deborah Trustman, and especially my family, who bolstered me up along the way; Laura Burns and Kitty Kelly, who put me on the track and kept me there; all those anonymous people who hooked me up with my interview subjects; Mary Goggins, the master of nuts and bolts.

Many at William Morrow gave generously of their time and inspiration, especially Larry Hughes, Jane Lewis, Thelma Sargent, Gale McGovern, Honi Werner, Michael Mauceri; Pat Berens and Sterling Lord helped me refine my ideas, and then played a mean game of poker; Julie Houston, my editor, skillfully diagnosed and treated the book's many diseases.

John Freund, my partner in crime, suggested that instead of kvetching I write a book. Taking on the duties of assistant maniac for this marathon, he put his own work aside for mine, helping edit, shape, create, and even type. Best of all, never once did he complain about the lack of home-cooked meals, or the heap of unwashed laundry residing behind the bathroom door.

Most especially I thank the thirty women who let me and my tape recorder into their lives and into their hearts. They must remain nameless, but their gift can be found on the following pages.

LINDA GRAY SEXTON
April 1979

Contents

Part I: The Feminist Mystique *13*

Part II: Like Mother, Like Daughter *31*
One: Hallie Parrish *35*
Two: Julie Fowler *52*
Three: Lisa Matthews *68*

Part III: The Waiting Game *83*
Four: Katherine Townsend *87*
Five: Karin Blake *100*
Six: Sarah Suskind *113*
Seven: Andrea Shapiro *124*

Part IV: Mavericks *137*
Eight: Rebecca Madison *141*
Nine: Judith Habib *155*
Ten: Elaine Magdaal *168*
Eleven: Alexis Whitmer *180*
Twelve: Rachel Fielding *192*

Part V: Self-Made Women *205*
Thirteen: Amy Wheeler *209*
Fourteen: Brenda Cyndar *225*
Fifteen: Chris Hastings *238*

Part VI: Taking Risks, Making Choices *251*

Appendix *257*

Notes *260*

Bibliography *261*

Nothing requires a rarer intellectual heroism than willingness to see one's equation written out.

—GEORGE SANTAYANA

Part I

The

Feminist Mystique

> The identity crisis in men and women cannot be solved by one generation for the next; in our rapidly changing society, it must be faced continually, solved only to be faced again in the span of a single lifetime. . . . No woman in America today who starts her search for identity can be sure where it will take her. No woman starts that search today without struggle, conflict, and taking courage in her hands.
>
> —BETTY FRIEDAN
> *The Feminine Mystique*

Depression settled in. It was 1975, our senior year at Radcliffe College. Sitting on the industrial gray carpet of our concrete high-rise dorm, my three roommates and I glumly agreed that the future looked bleak, very bleak indeed. Katharine Hepburn, in a magazine article, had just announced to the world that she had sacrificed marriage and motherhood for her movie career. We had modeled ourselves on this classy, independent female; she was the lawyer, the athlete, the something of our dreams—and she always got Spencer Tracy in the end. Now she was telling us we had to choose? "A cop-out," we asserted vehemently.

Surrounded by professors, peers, and news media who all endorsed the idea of careers for women, we simply weren't interested in hearing about necessary choices. We needed to believe it was all possible—career, marriage, and motherhood. It would not be until two years later, long after I had forgotten Hepburn's pronouncement, that my viewpoint on this touchy subject changed radically.

It was the fifth wedding I'd been to in 1977, and as far as I was concerned, it was the fifth too many. When I turned twenty-four that year, still single, I had begun to feel increasingly uncomfortable with the square cream-colored envelopes which appeared in my mailbox month after month. As I watched my peers fall into formation one by one, like Canada geese lining up in a V wedge, I dreaded the arrival of their marriage announcements even more than the bill from New England Telephone.

Sitting at the wedding-supper table, with bride and groom

presiding from either end, I kept thinking how much we had
all changed in the two short years since college. This particular woman had made enormous career sacrifices to stay in
close proximity to her fiancé—sacrifices we would have found
unthinkable during our college years. The conversation at
my end of the table moved from the subject of marriage to
the prospect of children. Smiling, the groom reassured us
that they weren't planning to start their family for about five
years.

I thought privately that this would be just the wrong time
from Karen's point of view—with a new Ph.D. hot in her
hand, she would be tramping around looking for a job.
Then, from an entirely different conversation at the other
end of the table, her voice came drifting down past coffee
cups and dessert plates: "Oh no, I don't intend to have
children for at least ten years."

The timing of the remark was purely coincidental, and yet
it could not have been more perfect for provoking a confrontation. Mark picked up the discrepancy in their time sched-
ules immediately. He set his jaw and stared straight into her
eyes. "If you wait that long, my dear," he announced icily, "I
will have *sorely* misjudged you, and I will be gravely
disappointed."

Everyone fell silent. The day was supposed to be a joyful
joining of two lives, but it seemed that the long expanse of
wedding table was one of the smaller things coming between
these two. Karen's new husband, I thought cynically, must
believe she is one of the new line manufactured under the
brand name "Superwoman"—a species capable of cooking,
cleaning, raising children, and entertaining his clients—all
while simultaneously pursuing a full-time career of her own
that would interfere with none of the above.

The entire incident took me aback: as a single woman, I
hadn't had to do much compromising—yet. What scared me
most was a gut feeling that in all probability Mark was not
that different from most men I knew. As I started to look
around at other women, I realized that many of us were in a

quandary, waging a recurrent power struggle with our mates, lovers, or ourselves. Our unwillingness to admit the need to compromise was becoming more and more problematic.

The problem put down roots when we were young, and, initially, it was not limited to women alone. My friends and I grew up with parents who gave us everything we asked for, in addition to everything they thought we needed. A generation of children raised on TV, movies, airplanes, summer camps, ten million games, college, Europe—things which had been luxuries to our parents were the status quo to us

Making choices was never an issue, at least not until later on—not until it was almost too late. Never needing to choose left us nearly incapable of setting priorities. But society expected us, as adolescents, to enter the adult arena by making decisions. Again, we were offered a full spectrum of choices, a selection which our parents—and certainly our mothers—had never even dreamed of. It all provoked a crisis. Not having developed the requisite skills in culling one course from alternatives, many of us developed a self-protective reflex: a curious lack of interest in anything specific, a void where career drive and ambition were supposed to be champing at the bit. Soon it became a social commonplace not to know what you "wanted to do after college."

We got no sympathy from our parents, who simply could not understand what our problem was, who could not see that all our options had created a first-class prison. Of course, at the time, we attributed our uncertainty to a chic freewheeling approach to the future. "Let it be, let it be" was the refrain from a popular Beatles song of the early 1970s, and that's exactly what we did.

Meanwhile, just when my female peers and I were reaching early adulthood in the late 1960s, the Women's Movement began to draw big headlines. Our impressionable young minds absorbed the new ideology and rhetoric and incorporated it in our growing conception of ourselves as individuals. Feminism allayed our fears of having too many options. A liberated woman shouldn't have to choose, we were told. She could do everything.

My grandmother taught me that the only fulfilled woman was a devoted wife and mother. My mother had countered that the only fulfilled woman was a career woman. At twelve, I watched her move excitedly through Betty Friedan's *Feminine Mystique,* saying it was the most important book she had read in a decade. Then she gave it to me. I still have that first edition, filled with her penciled notations from 1965, as well as my own from 1971, when I finally read it. Friedan was a reassuring comfort, a friendly girder of support for my efforts to compromise between these two worlds. Later, I would find that if my college friends had read any one book of feminist instruction, this was invariably the primer.

> Women do not have to choose between marriage and career, that was the mistaken choice of the feminine mystique. In actual fact it is not as difficult as the feminine mystique implies to combine marriage and motherhood and even the kind of lifelong purpose that was once called "career"—it merely takes a new life plan—in terms of one's whole life as a woman. . . . It is wrong to keep spelling out unnecessary choices that make women unconsciously resist either commitment or motherhood—and that hold back recognition of the needed social changes. It is not a question of women having their cake and eating it too.[1]

Friedan persuaded me that I could please both my grandmother and my mother at once. Still, at that time, if I had had to make a choice, it certainly would not have been to give up a career. Awakening simultaneously to womanhood and to the new literature on the "condition" of the American woman, I was appalled by the tragedy, the crime, the inexcusable waste of being only a wife and mother.

> It is urgent to understand how the very condition of being a housewife can create a sense of emptiness, non-

existence, nothingness, in women. . . . I am convinced there is something about the housewife state itself that is dangerous. In a sense that is not as far-fetched as it sounds, the women who "adjust" as housewives, who grow up wanting to be "just a housewife" are in as much danger as the millions who walked to their own death in the concentration camps—and the millions more who refused to believe that the concentration camps existed.[2]

Even worse, Friedan told us that one out of every three of our mothers experienced depression or psychotic breakdown after bearing us. Other feminist authors kept pounding us with the idea that bringing new life into the world would be the last nail in our coffins. Kate Millett wrote in *Sexual Politics* (1971):

In terms of activity, sex role assigns domestic service and attendance upon infants to the female, and the rest of human achievement, interest and ambition to the male. The limited role allotted to the female tends to arrest her at the level of biological experience. Therefore nearly all that can be described as distinctly human rather than animal activity (in their own ways animals also give birth and care for their young) is largely reserved for the male.[3]

Later in the book, Millett put it even more strongly: "So long as every female, simply by virtue of her anatomy, is obliged, even forced, to be the sole or primary caretaker of childhood, she is prevented from being a human being." [4]

In 1970, *The Dialectic of Sex,* by Shulamith Firestone, warned that "the heart of woman's oppression is her childbearing and childraising roles." [5]

I responded to this pressure by *assuming* I would have a career, although I was never sure what it would be, and by exiling marriage and motherhood to the back of my mind. When I was a senior in high school, my social-science teacher ran a class poll. Out of fifty possible options, the ten pre-

ferred careers were all professional—medicine, law, architecture—for men and women alike. At the time, none of us
could foresee that very few of the women would be prepared
for such options.

In a technical sense, one of the crucial areas in which we
would be unprepared was math. My nemesis in high school,
I hated it and it hated me. I didn't feel particularly uncomfortable about this—because somewhere deep inside me, in-
bred before the advent of women's liberation, was the notion
that women weren't supposed to be good at it. I elected to
abstain from senior calculus, and got no argument from
either parents, guidance counselors, or teachers. Inability to
deal with logarithms did not shake an overall confidence in
my intelligence—and, sure enough, my theory was borne out
when, to my joy, Radcliffe College accepted me despite my
D in Algebra II and my abysmal SAT scores in math.

Many years later, in 1978, an article in *Time* magazine [6]
showed me the fallacy of this reasoning. According to a
survey conducted at the University of California at Berkeley,
students who had not completed calculus before they entered
college were ineligible, ipso facto, for 75 percent of the major
fields of study. Only 8 percent of the females in the study had
actually taken that fourth year of high school math, compared to 57 percent of the males. Thus, 92 percent of the
women—like myself—were automatically slotted into the humanities or a few social-science concentrations before they
ever reached the college of their choice.

Later in 1978, I also discovered, to my shock, that the
Educational Testing Service uses different percentile rank-
ings in evaluating SAT math scores for men and women. The
Department of Labor projects that within the next ten years
the job market will demand great numbers of workers with
mathematical training, while having little use for those
skilled only in the humanities. "Women's low participation
rates are highly dysfunctional in a nation that would like to
believe in a sexual equality within the job sphere, for they
suggest a clear inequality in preparation for the job mar-

ket." [7] The article concluded by saying, "Women need mathematical training to compete in that job market of the future." [8]

When my roommates and I got to Radcliffe in 1971, few of us worried actively about the practical aspects of careers. Our attitude didn't change over the next four years, either. We weren't at college to prepare, we told ourselves, but to experiment, to enjoy. Of my roommates, three, including myself, majored in English, one in art history, one in visual studies, two in history and literature, and one in social relations. In 1977, only 0.6 percent of the upper-class Radcliffe women were math majors, compared to 2.4 percent of Harvard men.[9]

We sat around and joked that we had no training except reading literature and analyzing art, never willing to deal with the fact that the job market might have no place for intelligent women with B.A.s in general education—from Harvard or anywhere else. The ivy-covered walls kept all reality at a distance, and our four-year vacation from the facts of everyday living enabled us to procrastinate and dream dangerously when it came to our own futures. We simply assumed that we were going to be the most dynamic group of young women ever to hit the job market. The media were running story after story on the powerful young woman executive, the intern, the government administrator. But on graduation day, very few of my women friends felt comfortable with the all too familiar refrain: "What are you going to do now?"

It was different for my male friends. To graduate from college and still take support from your parents was an acceptable norm for women but an embarrassment for men. So, pushed by social pressure and economic necessity, most of my male peers directed themselves—even if quite unhappily—toward traditional money-making roles in medicine, law, and business. Their role models were etched clearly in the historical ranks of Harvard graduates. Meanwhile, two of my roommates joined the Peace Corps to take a break from immediate decision making. Another, a brilliant young woman who, throughout college, had been trying to get a foot in the door of the communications industry, gave up on looking for a job before she began, and enrolled in a Parisian mime school.

Of course, I had planned just as ineffectively as everyone else. However, I was lucky enough to have an opportunity fall right in my lap with no pavement-pounding required—editing a book of letters. Not until I began looking at the plight of others during the year after our graduation did I realize my good fortune. My Radcliffe classmates, despite their Harvard degrees, had rapidly found that they were required to start at the bottom—as glorified secretaries—of whatever field they were interested in: a lot of typing, phone answering, and brownnosing. Many grew angry at being asked whether they took shorthand, and tried to hold out for "better things." It gradually dawned on us all that there were no "better things" accessible to us. As an employment agent said to someone I knew, "That's the trouble with you college girls. You all want interesting jobs, when you've got no experience."

Where had we gone wrong?

After college, I had occasion to reread *The Feminine Mystique,* and there it was in black and white:

> Educators at every women's college, at every university, junior college, and community college, must see to it that women make a lifetime commitment (call it a "life plan," a "vocation," a "life purpose" if that dirty word *career* has too many celibate connotations) to a field of thought, to work of serious importance to society . . . liberal education must be planned for serious use, not merely dilettantism or passive appreciation. As boys at Harvard or Yale or Columbia or Chicago go on from the liberal arts core to study architecture, medicine, law, and science, girls must be encouraged to go on and make a life plan.[10]

In point of fact, Radcliffe—peers, professors, deans, advisers—had prepared me for nothing more practical than Garland Junior College had my mother thirty years before—I would make a terrifically intelligent, well-informed wife and parent. But the standard, automatic mooring of a woman's life around the solidity of marriage and motherhood was no longer an accepted notion. By the time of my graduation from college, anyone committing this crime of "insecurity" received scorn in lieu of congratulations. Marriage was no longer an honorable estate.

Of course, some of my friends did major in the hard sciences and started out toward careers or graduate school. A number went into law or medicine, banking or business. But as I have talked with them since our graduation, I have found them to be no less conflicted than those who did not find such a well-defined niche. Their sacrifice for success is proving to be total and immense, and they have had the disturbing experience of watching their social lives either evaporate or become impossible to handle. Rarely can they find a man willing to put up with the demands of their work. In the final analysis, something has to give: either they follow their men, taking on the doubly taxing demands of being "Superwomen," or they live in a state of self-imposed isolation as they continue in their professions.

In any case, they are unhappy, torn. What a shock after college days, when men seemed completely a second consideration. We naïvely believed that personal relationships would simply fall into line when our careers were established. There was a standard assumption that we did not need to put men before all else as had former generations of women. Our careers were of number-one importance. It rarely occurred to us that career might turn out to be all we had. And so we whiled away our college years dressing only in Levi's and man-tailored shirts; makeup-less, with long unstyled hair which required no care, we ensured that men would be attracted to us for who we were, not what we looked like. We could never understand why all the Harvard men dated the less strident and better-dressed Wellesley and Pine Manor girls.

Much of the feminist rhetoric at that time inspired us to the call of battle. Friedan had made clear our duty—to make a scene.

> It is time to stop giving lip service to the idea that there are no battles left to be fought for women in America, that women's rights have already been won. It is ridiculous to tell girls to keep quiet when they enter a new field, or an old one, so the men will not notice they are there. In almost every professional field, in business and in the arts and sciences, women are still treated as second-class citizens. It would be a great service to tell girls who plan to work in society to expect this subtle, uncomfortable discrimination—and to tell them not to be quiet and hope it will go away—but fight it.[11]

Taking Friedan extremely literally, we washed our sense of humor down the drain, while an inability to let anything slide off our back flourished. We made a point of picking verbal fights with anyone we viewed as "sexist"—taking offense at the mildest and most innocuous of remarks and ready to wage war over some of the stronger. One night, watching the evening news in the dorm's common room, a group of us saw nothing amusing about a local weather-caster's remark that the temperature was "either below freezing or else a Radcliffe girl is hanging on to the thermometer bulb." Enraged, we called the TV station with demands for a public apology. The meteorologist informed us that he'd already had seven other calls from older Radcliffe alums who'd found the remark funny.

"Where is the Promised Land?" I asked myself in 1977, two years out of college, having watched myself and most of my friends become mired in a massive traffic jam of confusion. I began to reflect on how much of my ambition for my own career had come simply as a response to the enormous social pressure sparked by the feminists and by my mother. The Women's Movement came about in an effort to give women a greater freedom of choice—but with the movement came a compulsion not to go into homemaking roles, a reverse of the traditional social pressure: a femin*ist* mystique. While the femin*ine* mystique had promoted to our mothers the rosy image of the eternally contented housewife, the femin*ist* mystique force-fed us a dose of liberation and promoted the ideal of the independent professional woman. It led us to believe that the marriage and motherhood offered by the old mystique were leftovers, the dregs of human existence.

Despite their antithetical doctrines, the two mystiques had one crucial element in common: both were extreme caricatures. One generation of women had discovered that housewifery was not automatically or always the solution to life's questions; I began to wonder whether career should automatically or always be the solution for ours. For a long time I did not dare to voice such an unfashionable, treasonable thought. Surreptitiously, almost ashamed of my own feelings, I began hunting for anything that would corroborate them. In my search, I spoke with a single childless woman working at a successful career who kept hoping someone would tell her to go home. I read a *New York Times* article in which a young woman executive confessed that she was no longer sure she wanted her career: she thought she might be happier at home, but felt compelled to stay with her job because it was her obligation as a woman of the 1970s not to make such a traditional move. *Money* magazine ran an article which supported my thesis. "Sadly, some women who were content to be housewives a few years ago today feel pressured by the Women's Movement to find important work outside the home." [12] It went on to point out that some women will take *any* kind of part-time work, even if they have no financial need—work which "makes housewife look like a dream job." [13] As a sign of liberation, one of the women featured in the article had just taken a job the feminist movement would condemn as the most oppressed—top-less go-go dancer in a nightclub.

With the advent of birth control, abortion, open sex, and the supposed right to work, young women of the 1970s aren't going to marry out of necessity. We are supposed to be free of the trap that caught our mothers. Perhaps we are. But in destroying one snare, we have fashioned another. In watching those who felt this reverse pressure, I began to see that some of us were increasingly divided against ourselves—unable to accept the old-fashioned ideals of marriage and motherhood and yet inadequately prepared to embrace the alternative.

Regardless of our individual shapes or sizes, this pressure staples, folds, and packages us into assembly-line boxes bearing the label "career woman." "I never thought of myself getting married, but I never thought of myself in a career either," one woman confided to me. "I really wasn't oriented toward either of them, and I found that if I began thinking about a career it scared me, and vice versa. I was sort of caught in the middle."

As I began to hear that others felt as I did, I grew more bold; talking with other women—friends and strangers alike—about my observations, I found I got more and more reaction. At dinner parties, cocktail parties, and business meetings, the subject elicited immediate response. Spurred on by my own doubts and feelings of being caught in the middle, I found I had developed an insatiable curiosity. I wanted to know how my own peer group, above and beyond the experiences of my immediate friends and acquaintances, was responding to the same sets of influences.

And so I set out to interview young women my own age, to write a book about the life choices they were making. Where were they? How had they got there? What were they feeling? How were they working out the daily dilemmas? I asked them about everything from their childhoods, to their parents' relationships, to their sex lives, to their careers. It was, inevitably, a search for myself, and for my own answers. By listening to and weighing the choices others had made, I was hoping to see my own choices more clearly.

I began this book to justify my own feelings about career ambivalence and hoped to find that nearly all young women felt the same way I did. It totally unnerved me when it became apparent that my conflict was only one of a vast spectrum experienced by women my own age; some had no career ambivalence at all.

But though I found many women in very different places than I, there was still one startling similarity between me and everyone I interviewed: virtually all of us were in the midst of, or had recently been through, a life crisis. Gradually, I began to see another pattern, and have used it as a handle with which to approach each interview in this book: in every life story the concept of "role model" was a crucial factor. Often the life crisis resulted from a conflict between the role model a woman had been raised on and the one which the feminist movement espoused; or, on the other hand, when the role model feminism offered was not compatible with a woman's current needs. This provoked an inevitable "identity crisis," as each individual tried to decide who and what she wanted to be. The only solution to being caught in the middle of two warring role models is to admit one's human limitations and choose accordingly. By looking at the expectations these women had for themselves, and the effect the Women's Movement had upon those expectations, I was able to see how each woman arrived at the choices that now shape her life.

Gradually, I relaxed with the knowledge that the book I wanted to write would never be a statistical study, where input and response would line up in a neat row. It would only define a problem and raise a forum—and try to offer a method for finding one's way out of the wilderness. With this realization, I let go of the leash I had fastened onto my ideas and simply allowed the interviews to run free. Eventually, I began to enjoy hearing the rich difference between one woman and the next. In each life story, I found a mirror for some of my own conflicts and problems.

Originally, I had planned to do one hundred interviews and then choose the best fifty, but I rapidly found that each interview was the best, with individual merit of its own, and it became almost impossible to pick between them. I stopped interviewing after number thirty, when it became apparent to me that I already had enough material for three books. It was from this group of thirty that the final fifteen were selected. Thus, the interviews in this book are not meant to be taken as vast generalizations on an entire generation of women, but rather as a kaleidoscope of viewpoint and insight which will reflect patterns we find in our own lives.

Over the course of a year, my friends and associates let me know whenever they ran into a young woman who was articulate and willing to talk deeply of her life; consequently, all the subjects were chosen by word of mouth. Born between 1945 and 1955, raised in the various strata of the white middle and upper classes in America, all are college educated. I selected this population because of my feeling that other groups have entirely different experiences governed by radically different factors: the poor do not have the luxury of choice and the black experience is one carved out of a background of racial oppression and limitation. At the time of the interview, each woman was living in Massachusetts or New York, but I did try to achieve a geographical spread by talking with women who grew up in cities and towns in many regions of the United States. I also sought a variety of career choices: here, housewives sit side by side with executives. Each interview was tape-recorded and ran from five to eight hours.

So that each woman could speak freely, I promised to change her name in the book; in addition, I took the liberty of altering some insignificant background detail to help preserve the privacy of those so willing to share. Despite this, all important data—such as place and date of birth, college choice, career choice, and so on—have been kept intact. Perhaps most important of all, none of the biographies in this book are composites—the integrity of each remains untouched. My own interpretation is clearly evident in both the presentation of the material and the conclusions drawn, but the facts of each life are just as I heard them.

While doing an interview for the book with a Radcliffe alumna in March of 1978, I was startled and amused to hear her vivid recollection of the article which had so upset me and my roommates three years before. "I remember early, hearing Katharine Hepburn saying, 'You can't have it all,' and [me] rejecting it," she said. "I remember thinking, 'I don't think that's true.' There is a point when adults try to say, 'You've got to be realistic, you can't have it all,' but I think we tend to say, 'Well, you're just saying that because you've already copped out.' There's a period when you have to believe it's all possible, I guess. And then there's a period when you have to learn that you have to make those choices. ... It seems like part of growing up is making your choices—from having the field and making those choices, rather than having them made for you."

We are unique, I thought to myself, because for the first time in history there are no longer any clear-cut social mores that dictate who we are supposed to be, no economic circumstances which force us to struggle toward specific goals. We no longer have definitive role models. We are, finally, all on our own, on the open sea of choice—caught between two worlds.

Part II

Like Mother, Like Daughter

We ended up being seventies models of the forties marriages of our parents.
—HALLIE PARRISH

My parents dropped out of college to elope at the impetuous age of nineteen. Years later, my grandparents were still harping on their children's ill-conceived choice, trying to impress one simple idea on my adolescent brain: an early marriage makes for a bad marriage.

The Women's Movement reinforced that idea for me. I assumed that every halfway aware woman would see the folly of committing herself to a man at such an early age. But as I proceeded with the interviews for this book, I found a whole group of young women who had been weaned on that same "feminine mystique" that Betty Friedan had damned so vehemently. Their backgrounds provided them with shining examples of the traditional wife and mother; no one had made any attempt to refute that image.

These women came from varied backgrounds, ranging from the conservative aristocracy to the provincial middle class. The single element they had in common—and it was in common with no other group—was their wholehearted acceptance of the notion that a happy woman was a happy housewife.

And so, to my surprise, I discovered a large "silent" group of women rarely publicized in the news media, women for whom marriage was the inevitable waterfall at the end of the river, even in the turbulent 1960s and 1970s.

The three in "Like Mother, Like Daughter" married early—either just after high school or while in college—and proceeded down the path their female ancestors had trod for centuries. Their stories, in fact, reminded me very much of

33

the lives of our mothers' generation: they too began to discover, eventually, that marriage was not amiracle drug
which transformed their lives or gave them purpose.

Instead, they grew restless, discontented. Finally, throwing
off one identity, they looked around frantically for another.
In the wings, they saw the feminists waiting for center stage,
doing a hard-sell bump and grind, advertising the "New
Woman." And so, like many middle-aged housewives in the
late 1960s and 1970s, they used this popular new role model
as a lever to help them break free: from marriage and housewifery to divorce and career. Divorce and career became as
compatible as soup and sandwich—you couldn't have one
without the other.

How far they actually took their careers, how well they
succeeded within their fields, differs from woman to woman.
Some have already found a deep fulfillment, while others
remain as discontented as before, career having been only a
stopgap measure in a period of need. Feminism provided
them with a convenient ideology, an escape hatch out of the
prison which had grown so intolerable. Given time, they may
find new needs which will not be so easily satisfied. But for
now, in each case, maintaining their identities as "career
women" is all-important. They feel it is the only identity they
truly own.

One

Hallie Parrish

He would make a perfect husband, Hallie decided. She intended to marry him. Tall, svelte, and good-looking, he had been her dinner partner for the evening. Chris Parrish was twenty-four, a graduate of the University of Pennsylvania, just about to begin business school at the University of Chicago after serving six months in the Army Reserve. His experience had given him an air of casual grace and savoir faire. He had a presence which drew people to him, a presence which made up for Hallie's lack of self-confidence and direction.

Breaking with the tradition in which she had been raised, Hallie took Chris as her first lover six months after they began dating. She was eighteen years old. By twenty, complying with the tradition in which she had been raised, she was engaged.

Curled up on the couch in front of a roaring fire, she was very tall and very slender, with auburn hair that curled softly around her fine-boned face. The first years of their marriage were even better than she had imagined, she told me. But by her twenty-sixth year, it had all grown a little stale. Boredom and a sense of vacuity marked her life more and more.

She felt she was stagnating. Worst of all, she was beginning to wonder about Chris: had they ever really been able to talk, to share things? He didn't like her emotionalism; she found his formerly admirable, cool exterior more and more isolating. "It was just a totally separate life," she told me, firelight shadowing the sadness in her eyes. "He had his life and did whatever he wanted to, and I had . . . whatever I wanted. It was just fine, and we basically just saw each other and had dinner and entertained people. And that was it."

This isolation was familiar to Hallie; she had seen and felt it all before. In fact, I decided, she had been weaned on it: she had unwittingly built a relationship modeled on her parents' miserable example. It was all quite ironic. "The only goal I set when I was little was 'I'm not going to have a marriage like my parents'.'" She looked at me. "Bong! There I was!"

Firstborn in 1949 to an affluent Episcopalian family of five, Hallie Loring grew up in an old stone house built in the mid-1920s in an elite suburb of Chicago. Her environment reflected her privileged outlook on life: the small community was filled with professional men and their families—the sort of place where life centers on the country club during the warm months.

Her childhood home was a place where everything looked fine on the surface, but was barren and silent down deep. Arthur Loring was a stockbroker totally absorbed with his clients. His eldest daughter did not interest him much. He expected nothing from her and asked for nothing in return. "He was very preoccupied with business and he spent a lot of time playing golf, playing bridge," Hallie remembers. With a father who offered her no vision of what her own future might hold, who never encouraged her to have ambitions, she looked to her mother for an indication of what life might be for an adult woman.

Emily Loring ran an efficient household with the help of a maid, a cook, and a nurse. She did not join the morning kaffeeklatsches or the noontime martini crowd at the club, but was busy instead as a fund-raising trustee on the Chicago Art Institute and Public Art Society boards. She was the perfect example of a philanthropic, concerned society lady. Like her husband, Emily did not lavish much attention on her daughters. Nevertheless, she was present often enough to exert some influence. In years to come, Hallie would follow her mother's example, seeking fulfillment on fund-raising boards—but for her it would not be enough.

Her parents seemed to deal no better with each other than

with the children. Their lives were independent, isolated, and whenever someone had to accommodate or compromise, it was always Emily. Watching her parents interact taught Hallie an early, important lesson: women are seen, but not heard—at least, not very much.

Her parents' aloof ways made communication difficult for Hallie. It was a difficulty which would persist for years to come, in all her relationships. "I didn't realize it at the time, but I realize it now," Hallie remembers. "I floated a lot. What happened to me is that I am a very private person. I don't talk about things."

These early experiences set up a pattern which would be repeated again and again throughout her life. Despite the fact that she had every advantage, as well as stable, if disinterested, parents, Hallie felt unloved. She continually wondered what she was doing wrong to alienate her parents so. In desperation, she became a "pleaser," modeling herself on Emily's accommodating behavior with Arthur. She was always the one to jump whenever anyone wanted anything, always the one to agree, always the one to bring the flowers to dinner. Early on, she found that being naughty elicited no more attention from her father than being good; she learned not to expect too much from anyone.

The paucity of parental input began to take its toll. As she grew older, she didn't have any specific goals beyond those tradition dictated. Her mother simply could not understand why any woman would need or want a career, and she let her daughters know her opinion on the subject. Volunteer work was enough for her, and she assumed it would be enough for them. Despite this, during these early years, Hallie did discover an interest which would eventually turn into a career in years to come: movies. "I can remember scenes from when I was very little. I can remember shots. I can remember cuts." She also discovered she liked going to museums, in keeping with the example set by her mother's work in the arts and by her grandmother, who was an art collector.

She longed for the demonstrative affection she saw at the home of her friends. This gradually grew into the desire for a traditional future, with a traditional family quite different from her own. "My positive feelings about families were with other people's families," she said sadly. "I do remember thinking that the family I was with wasn't my real one. Somewhere out there was my real family, which was warmer than the one—these almost strangers—that I was with."

Her friends became all-important, her only source of lasting affection. School was their meeting place, and so early on she looked forward to going each day. In addition, she discovered she had a talent for reading, math, and science, and this brought her encouragement and support from the teachers. Her favorite story was *Mrs. Pigglewiggle*—a tale where children commanded all the adult attention.

Shyness accompanied her right through childhood into adolescence. She continued to approach people tentatively, afraid of being disliked, wanting to please them—that well-established pattern. She tailored her behavior, her thought, her speech, even her appearance—wearing her auburn hair at a medium length, she removed its natural curl with tin-can-size rollers and lived in fear of rain and mist. Slender, with large blue eyes and a soon-to-be-graceful five-foot-seven frame, she towered uncomfortably over most of the boys in her classes. This too added to her shyness. Having had no brothers, she just didn't know how to handle boys. Nevertheless, they were important to her.

Right from the beginning of puberty, it was clear that from now on boys would be the goal in her never-ending search for affection and approval.

The situation at home was a mirror of her inner tension: if her parents wouldn't give her what she needed and wanted, she was determined to find it elsewhere. For the first time, Hallie began to fight with her mother, mostly about typically rebellious things—when to come home, how short her skirts could be, when she had to clean her room. Argument made Emily nervous; she was uncertain of what her daughter would do next. Once again, she just didn't have the time, or want to make the effort, to cope with her child—now a stubborn, defensive teen-ager. Hallie's animosity toward her father accelerated, too, as she began to feel ever angrier with his lack of interest in the family. She stopped blaming herself and began to wonder what was wrong with him.

In a house where fighting had been taboo, this uproar of emotion was simply too much; it was agreed by all that the time was opportune for boarding school. An elite academy for girls in Massachusetts became Hallie's new home during her sophomore year in high school. There she found a surrogate family built on her peers and advisers. In addition, she enjoyed the freedom her new environment offered. The students could go to Boston every weekend, and there were dances with the men's schools in the area. Curfews were liberal; you could smoke.

But it was more than that. Here she fitted in; here she was liked. Camaraderie ran high, and together the girls experimented with foul language and exchanged secondhand stories about sex. Talking a good game was requisite—but firsthand sexual knowledge was still too risqué, even in the 1960s.

Even in this new environment, her parents' earlier lack of caring rankled. Emily had never taken the time to explain sex to her daughter, and instead had "hurled a book" at Hallie. But Hallie was confused; she couldn't understand what came after the man and woman met and before the merging of sperm and egg. It was yet another issue that made her feel awkward and mixed up.

Naturally, true to her "pleasing" pattern, Hallie wanted most of all to be accepted. She yearned to be a popular girl. At home in Chicago, fitting in with her family had meant keeping a low profile; at home in school it meant being friendly, outgoing, nice and easy. She felt, too, that men looked for this kind of girl: "Intelligence was nice, but somebody funny and non-threatening was a lot more important." The women in her class who were aggressively intelligent often had problems being attractive to men and women alike—but, fortunately, aggressive intelligence was obviously not Hallie's cup of tea. Once again, her image of the quiet, forever flexible woman was reinforced.

She began dating in high school, though mostly in groups, through the traditional extracurricular organizations and dances; much of her early love life was conducted via the postal service and Ma Bell. Because Hallie was looking for companionship and approval, she found herself attracted to men with a good sense of humor, people who really liked to talk. Unlike most teen-agers, she found looks not terribly important. "I did not have relationships with people where you go out and hack around and have good times, blah blah blah and that's it," she told me. "I was attracted to people who were slightly shy, actually. And who liked being in one-to-one relationships."

Meaningful time spent with boys was an effective way of easing her perpetual sense of isolation. For Hallie, nothing was simply casual. She needed to have each encounter mean something; talking and sharing were of ultimate importance. Sadly, though, she didn't have enough self-confidence to reveal herself. In accordance with her belief that she was responsible for pleasing the world, she became a listener. "In retrospect," Hallie now realizes with disgust, "I wasn't saying shit about myself most of the time."

Even at this stage of her life, she was too frightened of peer disapproval to risk making independent decisions. An outgrowth of this was her strict adherence to the sexual bylaws: nothing from the waist down. Her community of peers generally disapproved of sleeping around, and the very real fear of pregnancy was another deterrent. But on the other hand, the avant-garde attitudes of the 1960s had begun to take root, even at the conservative academy, and Hallie accommodated to these new ideas too, straddling the fence along with everyone else. "Intellectually, I think if you asked us, 'Is it all right to sleep with somebody,' we'd say, 'Just fine'; if anybody did it, we were shocked."

In this area, her parents proved no more communicative than about anything else. Her father would never discuss premarital sex; her mother said she thought living together might be a good idea—theoretically—but for God's sake her daughter shouldn't tell her about it. Once again, they had turned aside her questions, fears, and needs.

Boarding school had given Hallie the sense of direction her parents had not. She knew her next goal was to get to college: it would take care of her life for another four years, years in which she wouldn't be required to make any earth-shaking decisions. She had continued to do well, especially in math and science; these subjects seemed like possibilities for the future. But in her junior year she was skipped a year ahead in math to an advanced course, and this success was too much to handle. Frightened by the challenge, she choked; by senior year calculus was out of the question, and she began to increase the odds against any chance of a future in the hard sciences. Without knowing it, she was tracking herself increasingly toward a destination similar to her mother's.

She applied to Boston University, Barnard, and the University of Pennsylvania, among others. She had good grades and high board scores. An urban coed college was important to her, and BU and Barnard were her top choices. She got in everywhere except the latter, where she was wait-listed. BU had an accelerated program which she had been impressed with when she was interviewed there, and so Hallie sent in her acceptance card. Penn, considered almost universally to be a superior institution, went by the board.

She entered Boston University in 1967, a member of the class of 1971. She fell in love with her program immediately—small, familylike, it attracted the brightest people from the liberal arts college. Hallie had anticipated easy A's, but found, to her surprise, that the program was tough, with five hundred pages of reading a week and a strict quota of requirements to be fulfilled before electives were allowed. No graduate students ever taught classes—only professors. The program forced her to think concretely about her future, something she did not want to do. Nevertheless, after finishing the first two years she did make a decision, declaring a major in film. She began to take photography and television courses exclusively.

Despite her interests in the visual arts, she could not repress a natural talent in the sciences. "I was the *star* in biology. I was greatly encouraged [by professors] to go on in [it]. But it wasn't a passion." Biology was not a field well populated by women, and Hallie did not think along revolutionary lines. She was still conservative, and naïvely believed that there was no correlation between one's major and one's future. She chose photography, a more creative, less competitive, less directed field. It would be easier to distract herself; it would require less planning for the future. Photography was an *interest,* not a career choice.

In her freshman year, she took another major step in modeling herself upon her mother's example: she went in for what she viewed as "philanthropic" work—by joining the Students for a Democratic Society. In the fall of 1967, SDS was not yet a hotbed of radicalism; it was thought of on campus as a liberal, community-oriented group, a group which ran projects like sponsoring hot lunches for school kids. "They were very much into civil rights at the time," says Hallie. "They were pretty much against the war. But not in terms of big demonstrations." No one was trashing anything—yet.

As before, Hallie established herself with a group of her peers immediately; this time she belonged to the intellectual crowd, a group who wore blue jeans, army fatigues, and secondhand clothes exclusively. The alteration in her environment made Bob Dylan's song "The Times They Are a-Changing" seem an understatement. For a basically conservative girl, the times were unnerving. Drugs, sex, politics— the world was topsy-turvy. "It was a free-for-all," Hallie remembers with a wry smile. It didn't really suit her nature, but she went with the flow, determined to fit in.

During her freshman year, drugs were a pretty new game: only grass and hash were readily available. But by sophomore year mescaline and heroin began to turn up. "Bizarre drugs, hundreds of drugs, pills, reds, ups, downs, greens, and blacks. Just unbelievable. Drug pushers would keep lists," she said, laughing in wonder. "They couldn't remember what they were." Then she grew solemn. "Sophomore and junior year, people were overdosing left and right. A few deaths in the community."

Hallie stuck with marijuana—typical, I thought, of her general middle-of-the-road position about most things. But she did make it known she would be glad to baby-sit for trippers, keeping them out of trouble while they were high. All around her was a whole generation of young people looking for any way at all to escape their lives. Psychedelic drug trips and acid rock helped some. But she could see that their loneliness persisted. Along with drugs came another panacea: sex, as easy now as turning on a faucet or putting the needle on a record. In a blinding search for intimacy of the heart, men and women who were strangers bartered with their bodies. But Hallie kept her distance; to her peers she looked like a liberal doing her own thing. In reality, she did not fit in with their world, but would not let anyone know it. She needed to feel a part of things, but her conservative grain continued to make her hold back.

In the ensuing years of Richard Nixon and Cambodia, rap sessions replaced schoolwork. Radically political professors forgot about classes and exams. During the Cambodia upheaval in Hallie's junior year, the university closed down altogether. She grew annoyed. While a generation set the world of its fathers on its ear, Hallie held herself aloof.

And hand in hand with the antiwar movement came the confusing Women's Movement. Liberation had become highly politicized, and very popular. "If you were antiwar, you were also a feminist, it was a package deal," remembers Hallie. While she was against the war, she was not nearly so emphatic about the other. She just didn't perceive herself as an oppressed minority. Hallie honestly believed she could do anything she wanted—*if* she wanted to do it. And so, although she read Friedan and listened to Steinem, she remembered little of it later.

Given her background, I was not surprised to hear that she

did not identify strongly with radical women or surround herself with them. Conservative at heart, she had dropped out of SDS as soon as it grew even slightly militant. But women's liberation was not something you could easily drop out of. Among Hallie's intellectual peers, there was intense pressure: "To say you were anti-feminism was like saying you were pro-war." And so she went along with it all silently. Her real feelings were symbolized when she resisted the standard trappings of liberation—continuing to shave her legs and wear a bra. Underneath, a search for intimacy—not independence or career—was the primary goal.

Moreover, she found that the women she knew who had difficulties in their dealings with men were those who talked most vociferously—and, to her, obnoxiously—about feminism. "They really said terrible things to women. Some of the most sexist comments I've heard said to women came from those women. It was not a fraternal kind of thing. It was not kind; it had none of the positive aspects that the civil rights movement had. It was really very oppressive."

But the situation was made even more disturbing because Hallie's female friends were not the only ones eschewing her unspoken, but still major, ambition—marriage. In the radical BU environment, few men were looking for a wife who would be a homemaker. Hallie felt they wanted a friend, a companion, a partner. "Basically, an independent woman who would be capable of leading her life while the man led his life. They could then come together on a certain joint life in the middle." Inevitably, it reminded her of a marriage she had long known: that of her parents.

Naturally, this threatened Hallie. She needed a man who would define her; she would accommodate to him, and he would return the gesture with love and approval. In the summer after freshman year, she once again fell back on her conservative upbringing and took part in the age-old tradition of "coming out." Flying back and forth to Chicago, she went to an unending whirl of dinner dances, supper dances, tea dances, luncheons, and balls. Hallie, the mild-mannered women's libber, was at heart a debutante.

At one of these parties during the winter of her sophomore year, she met Chris Parrish, whom she soon viewed as the solution to all her problems. They dated throughout that year and the next, while she slept with several other people at the same time. Sexually, she was foraging about, keeping pace with the liberated life-style—yet she was also in the process of making an emotional and legal commitment to Chris. The dichotomy symbolized once again her imprisonment between the old and the new.

Although Hallie's skill in biology could have provided her with a career in medicine, or with a Ph.D. that would have opened the doors to a research fellowship, she wasn't taken with either idea. Nor did law appeal. She toyed with the idea of working in visual arts or educational television, but anything hard core or specific seemed out of the question. Unconsciously, perhaps, Hallie began to think just the way her mother did about careers for women. "Men have to have a career. And I knew that had I been a man I would have been a doctor or a lawyer. But since I was female, I didn't have to have [one]." To avoid having to make a real decision about her future, she allowed her emotional commitment to take her out of school and off the battlefield of choice.

The first compromise she made was in leaving BU. Throughout the fall of her junior year, she commuted from Logan to O'Hare like clockwork each weekend to visit Chris. Then, in March, she called a halt; they must either make a commitment or stop seeing each other. It was a ploy with a carefully calculated effect, a ploy that worked perfectly. She moved to Chicago and planned to enroll at Northwestern.

But her planning was woefully inadequate, reflecting her true concerns. Northwestern couldn't take her until the winter semester. In September, she registered at the Columbia Film School in Chicago, casually planning to continue her work in photography and television. All of two weeks later, she and Chris were engaged. As with generations of women before, her halfhearted attempts at education and a career ended in November, when she and Chris got married.

Tradition had finally triumphed. Despite the haste, the

Parrishes' wedding hit all the Chicago society columns: 675 people strong, with a reception at her parents' posh country club, no expense was spared. Hallie's upbringing had groomed her for this life-style all along. And, too threatened to marry someone who might want her to be an independent woman—as the BU men did—she chose, as her mother had years before, a man steeped in the tradition of the non-working wife. "I moved right into step behind Chris," she admits. "I realize in retrospect that I lived through him. It worked like a charm for years, [I] loved it, was incredibly happy. Loved it, wonderful. Who are you? Mrs. Chris. What are you going to do? I'm gonna be a wife."

At the time, Hallie felt her marriage was modern, but now she sees it as a marriage modeled very exactly on her parents' example. Despite its slight trappings of liberation—her husband might occasionally help with the housework—the basic issues had not changed. The woman's identity was still defined by the man's—even if she did keep her own name.

Hallie forgot about school, not to return for eight years. She had moved from the protection and financial support of her parents into the intimate cocoon of marriage without ever having had to stand on her own two feet.

With marriage came money; conveniently enough, Hallie did not have to adopt the female roles of either career woman or housewife. Chris's family wealth enabled him not to work, either. Although he finished business school, he never took it particularly seriously, she says. "We played. We were kids, we were absolutely kids who had been given everything. This is me at age twenty-one. No problems in the Western world. . . . I was happy as a clam."

They spent weekends training horses at their country house on the family farm and weekdays entertaining in the city. Completing the image set by her mother, Hallie began earning her wings doing community work on the boards of museums, hospitals, and musical organizations. She was now a lady of leisure.

In 1971, the bubble began to burst: Chris finally decided to get a job. They moved to New York City, where he had been offered a position in a well-known investment banking firm. They settled happily into a luxurious apartment on the stylish East Side of Manhattan.

But Chris's working hours stranded Hallie. Her constant playmate no longer by her side, she tried to fill her time by keeping company with the decorator. She and Chris did the new apartment up royally, and Hallie played the gracious hostess, running a "hotel" for Chris's clients and any friends who came to visit the city. The precepts of women's liberation were very, very far away.

Slowly, her life seemed more and more routine. In 1972, in a halfhearted effort to return to school, she took a few courses in film at Hunter College. Committee work once again drew her attention, this time on the board of a child-care center. But what had been enough for her mother was not enough for her. She had been giving away her own single identity as fast as she could, even heaving women's liberation aside because she so desperately needed to be with someone. Now, with her partner tied up elsewhere, she was really back to square one. Marriage had not solved her problem of isolation; it had only postponed the inevitable. For a while, she had been able to take refuge in their communal life rather than face her own.

But avoiding herself finally caught up with Hallie. In 1976, a feeling of unreality overtook her; she looked back over the past six years and couldn't put her finger on where the time had gone or what she had accomplished. During my interview with her, she had been able to document every event with an exact timetable, but when it came to the years of her marriage, she was extremely muddy. Frowning, she tried to pinpoint events, but vagueness permeated everything.

Finally, she began to re-evaluate her life and found it wanting. Her father had died of a heart attack in 1975, a real shock. As I followed her narrative, it seemed that she first began to notice marital problems at this time, although she did not leave Chris until a year and a half later. I suggested that perhaps Arthur Loring's death had triggered something within her—surely the dates were too close to be coincidental? A tension filled the air. At first she denied any connection. Struggling with herself, she finally, reluctantly, agreed that the death might have brought her a sudden understanding of how quickly life comes and goes, how easy it is to "futz it all away." She had to begin dealing with her own life, and stop living through her husband. There was a new need in her life; she wanted to feel the danger of committing herself, of risking something important.

This was the girl who, only six years before, had been too scared to risk choosing a career. During college, she had sought the stability of having a husband and money. Now she began to remember all she had known and discarded then. She finally understood that her old 1940s ideals were wrong; that Friedan and her advocates were right. Her husband could not be the sole reason to live, laugh, and cry. She had to stop being a "pleaser." And so, using the ideology she had rejected years earlier, she jettisoned ages twenty through twenty-six, as well as her mother's role model, and decided to start over.

It wasn't easy, and she was scared; but the necessary identity crisis finally occurred. "If I wasn't going to be Mrs. Chris Parrish, who the hell was I?" she asked herself. Looking for mentors, she found them within the feminist rank and file. She took their examples to heart, and soon even formed a women's consciousness-raising group with her closest friends. Here she could constructively discuss her new feelings and ideas.

The next step was to go back to school. Although she had been taking courses haphazardly at Hunter, the separation from Chris was a catalyst which drove her to full-time attendance. Working hard, she received her degree in eighteen months, in May of 1977. Then she continued to take responsibility for herself by beginning to job-hunt. "Bleah," she remembers. "That was depressing. Advertising agencies weren't hiring at the time, and most film places were cutting back." Nevertheless, she did find a job that October, working at a video center which produced medical documentaries.

Starting at the bottom, she did anything she could get her

hands on. One year later, she had reached the position of assistant director. "I am involved in every step of the operation. Technically, I'm learning a lot. I do the camera work, I help with the lights, I help with the audio. When the program is being aired, I'm either doing the audio work or I'll be doing something called technical directing . . . I do everything from A to Z." But even while she is still somewhat of a go-fer, and though the pay is practically nonexistent, she loves the work. She is happy.

For the first time in years, Hallie is beginning to feel fulfilled. The sense of vagueness that accompanied aimless day-to-day living has ceased. She feels that during the last few years she has made the greatest personal growth of her life—learning how to cope with her need for intimacy. She is able to live alone, and enjoy it. She has come to grips with herself. Hallie never need be dependent again. "It's a security nobody can ever take away from you," she told me happily.

She has become more and more ardently feminist, and tends to evaluate much of her life in this light. Accordingly, she has begun to re-evaluate her relationships with men. In keeping with her new identity, she has begun to resent the pseudo-feminism she finds in her male peers. "The young man's image used to be, 'Here's my wife, here's my car, here's my house.' Now it becomes, 'Here's my *working* wife, and here's my car, here's my house.' It's the same old shit. . . . You're just playing with a different Monopoly board and different pieces." Male sexism is most apparent, she thinks, in the realm of childbearing. "I hear very few bitches from men when their women stop working to take care of the children."

On the other hand, Hallie is beginning to be aware of the reverse side of the coin. I was surprised to hear her speak with so much insight about career when hers is currently of such importance to her. Nevertheless, she has recently seen that working is not all fun and games. "Women got sold a bill of goods," she told me heatedly. "Men knew that working was shit from day one. Men aren't working because it's going to *fulfill* their lives and make them interesting people. No, men are working for money."

Despite her divorce and all her new ideas, Hallie has not become embittered on the subject of men. One of the by-products of living alone was that after a while she became able to seek male companionship without being threatened by merging identities. In late 1977, she started dating an old friend of her husband's, one of his classmates from the University of Pennsylvania. Hallie and Brian Hadley had known each other for five or six years, and soon their friendship blossomed. She found a warm, emotional man who could reciprocate her feelings. Their relationship is intimate, full of the everyday sharing that she missed so much with Chris.

Brian is someone she would like to have children with. She feels an acute biological pressure, having just turned thirty, knowing a family must come soon—just as her career in film production is beginning. Managing a career and children simultaneously requires both stamina and sacrifice; these are facts to which she is reconciled. By free-lancing in film, instead of trying for a secure position in a production company, she would have extra time for the children without giving up her career totally. She feels certain she will never return to her former way of life. As is true for many men, her work is her identity—and she will hold tight to that at all costs.

Fortunately, Brian is a free-lance architect with a lot of flexible time. He has committed himself to taking on a great deal of child care. In addition, they are financially able to pay for outside help. Her career may require her to change cities in the near future; I asked whether Brian would be amenable to this. Alternatively, if he needed to move, would her new career tolerate the jump? Moving would be catastrophic for him, she says, since all his work comes from clients built up over many years. Still—perhaps naïvely—she believes they would honestly consider the option and weigh the alternatives before accepting or rejecting anything.

But these plans seem inadequate to Hallie as she watches her friends all around become more and more panicked about how to handle children and career simultaneously. She knows her future is forecast in their lives. "A number of my friends are in their early thirties. These are career women, and they are in *terrible* shape: they've put in their time, they're just beginning to get really good promotions, and it's the last ditch for babies. It's a terrible decision. They lose either way."

Hallie Parrish has not really resolved any of these conflicts, and has the foresight to know it will not be easy. Nevertheless, she is not deterred. She is no longer a "pleaser," no longer a society committeewoman who does charity benefits; she is determined to maintain her singleness within her relationship with Brian, or with any other man. In other words, she has moved very far from where her mother stood. Despite all these changes, however, the traditional life-style is still very much a part of her. Ultimately, reaching out in such a radically new direction has enabled her to backtrack a little toward her more conventional side. Having clearly established that her life is not her mother's, she can now borrow a little from Emily, as with her plans to remarry—if not Brian, then someone else—and to create a family. But even these conventional desires are tempered by the strong stamp of her own personality. Unlike her mother's generation, she will only compromise her career interests, not abandon them.

A large part of Hallie, certainly, wants to have her cake and eat it too. Like many of us in the same situation, she acknowledges the need to make choices with a certain naïveté, without really admitting emotionally how difficult it will be. She has not lived it yet, and she wastes no time imagining it. Although she recognizes that soon she may find herself caught in the same vise as her friends, she does not want to deal with what that will mean to her life. When the inevitable decisions and sacrifices which are part and parcel of being an adult finally catch up with Hallie, her new strength—won with the aid of feminism and her own powers of self-evaluation—will be an invaluable asset. Halle Parrish lives one day at a time right now, but she has the ability and the tools to cope with the future if she chooses to do so.

Two

Julie Fowler

The only elements Hallie Parrish and Julie Fowler had in common were traditionally oriented mothers. Apart from this, their lives contrasted like night and day; while Hallie finally entered adulthood by the back door at twenty-five, Julie had no such choice. She was pushed over the precipice at the tender age of fourteen—when the doctor sent her father home to die of lung cancer. On that first night he was back from the hospital, from the depths of sleep Julie heard a thump in the hallway outside her door. Getting out of bed, she found her father crumpled on the floor, half his body flaccid, his face contorted. She dimly realized he had had a stroke.

As she told me the story, we sat cross-legged on the floor of her apartment, drinking Tab and talking. Despite the sunlight streaming in through the bay windows, despite the abundance of cheerful green plants and familiar handmade furniture, for a few minutes Julie was back in that dark, nightmarish hallway; the scene flashed before her once again, etched on her eyes. Currently a third-year student at Harvard Medical School, she was able to describe her father's illness in great detail.

"My mother went into hysterics," she remembered, pushing her long blond hair back from her face. "For obvious reasons. It was a little bit too much for her to bear." It was to be only the first in a long line of tests for Julie. Suddenly, she was responsible not only for herself but for her siblings and parents as well. "My sisters were starting to wake up and wonder what was going on. I remember methodically going through, closing their doors, and telling them to stay put. Going to the phone, calling for an ambulance, calling the doctor. I knew something was wrong, but I knew he was still alive. And that my mother was screaming her head off and running around . . . They went by ambulance, both of them."

She stayed behind to quiet her younger sisters; in the dark of night she tried to explain something she did not quite understand herself. Her mother came back a few days later, after a short hospitalization, but her father never left his hospital bed. After his death, Margaret Fowler had another nervous breakdown. Julie strapped responsibility for the family on her back.

After returning from the hospital again, Margaret went east to learn about the accounting business her husband had left her. All alone, Julie was in charge of Barbara, twelve; Karen, nine; and Judy, seven. Throughout the weeks of mourning, she had never allowed one tear to slide through her iron grip. Everyone was depending on her. Only when talking with the family priest had she been able finally to break down.

Coping with her father's death made Julie grow emotionally even stronger. Although she was unaware of it at the time, self-reliance and capability became her middle name. It would be many years before she discovered how independent and self-sufficient his death and the accompanying responsibility had required her to be. One day, these abilities would come to her aid in directing the flow of her life, but not before they caused her tremendous emotional turbulence. It would take a traditional marriage to show her how unconventional, how very different from her peers, she really was.

Julie grew up in a closely knit family which gave her variable emotional support right from the start. Born in 1949, the eldest daughter of Richard and Margaret Fowler, she began her life in Cleveland in a tiny apartment atop the bar her father ran. Her environment taught her not to expect anything too fine from life. Her parents' marriage, too, taught her what to look for in the future. Richard and Margaret were warm and affectionate at their best, but Richard's drinking presented a huge problem. The way Margaret handled it was an eloquent statement for the young children about the interactions between men and women.

Finances were tight, and Margaret continually complained that her husband drank their money away. But instead of dealing with him directly, she manipulated her four daughters into pleading with him to stop. "We would try all of our little tactics," Julie told me sadly, pushing up the sleeves of her brilliant-colored caftan. "It still wouldn't work."

Worse, the Fowler girls were asked to intervene in the arguments which were liquor's inevitable aftermath. Returning home from his bar, Richard often responded abusively to his wife's queries about how much he'd had to drink. Although the fights remained verbal, he made his physical superiority known, often throwing things around, breaking furniture and china. He always ended by promising Margaret that he wouldn't do it again, but these were alcoholic promises he could never keep.

Julie's mother appeared saintlike, the forgiving martyr, unwilling to speak up against her husband. A deeply religious woman, Margaret Fowler was a powerhouse who preferred not to make an issue of her strength. She always deferred to her husband and never presumed to win an argument. Julie identified with the womanly example her mother set, but she really had more fun with her father. He encouraged her to be independent; together they would sit in bars and talk about any topic she wanted to. Still, early on, she instinctively felt Margaret was right about most things. Nevertheless, the attitudes Richard had planted would, one day years later, spring to exuberant life.

When Julie was in the third grade, Richard moved the family to a small community in the "land of golden opportunity"—California. Although he had no job awaiting him, he soon bought a franchise in an accounting company and did reasonably well. The family stepped up into residential suburbia. Each small house which lined their street had exactly the same lot of land, three baths, and identical front doors. It all seemed quite luxurious compared to what they'd had before. Julie's goal was to live the rest of her life in precisely this sort of place.

Still, money was never really plentiful. Richard set himself high standards in his role as provider, standards he could never quite meet. His feelings of failure drove him to drink away what little money he saved in a vicious cycle of self-hate. But despite her husband's alcoholism and the ever-tightening family budget, Margaret's forceful personality and her deep Catholic faith made her determined that the children have a proper education. She wanted her daughters to be young ladies, well trained in the social graces. Thus, although Julie liked all aspects of her parochial school, and did well, she was pushed to concentrate on the more feminine subjects of English, art, and handwriting. Math went practically untouched.

Julie could see that if a man was the center of a woman's life, it would be important to have someone who was a successful benefactor. Margaret began educating the girls extracurricularly in every quality she felt they would need to snare a "proper" man. Disturbed with her husband's behavior, she was determined her daughters would have a better future than her own had been, and so gave them every advantage she had not had herself. Julie remembers it all with an incredulous smile. "While we didn't have much money, I had piano lessons, tap-dance lessons, formal dance lessons to the hilt.... We didn't have very nice clothes, we didn't eat well. It's all a question of priorities. We didn't have a car [but we did have] cooking, dancing, painting lessons. She was building four wives.... Your goal in life was to be a good wife and a good mother, [to] raise children in the Church."

Julie's future responsibilities were clear from an early age: as a good wife, she would keep her house running efficiently; raise her children to be loving, obedient, and God-fearing; and never raise her voice or her mind against her husband. It did not take long for Margaret's ideas of the complete woman to fly home and roost. Julie's interests reflected her traditional bent. Fascinated by romance, she read any love story she could find, even obvious "garbage." She began to idolize a baby-sitter, a senior in high school, who seemed the epitome of every girl's dream: inundated with boyfriends and, best of all, a cheerleader.

Margaret had taught her daughter to be a capable, efficient woman within her social sphere. Julie's enormous responsibilities after her father's death reinforced these early lessons. Her ability to thrive at age fourteen with her father dead and her mother thousands of miles away was testimony to the independence of her spirit—but, at the time, Julie did not recognize it as such. She saw only that mothering and being housewife for her young sisters came easily. She was good at it.

When she returned from the East, Margaret took over Richard's accounting business. To everyone's surprise, she was more successful at it than he had been. But Julie didn't think about the implications of this. She saw only that her mother was fulfilling an unpleasant, unnatural task, a task necessary for survival. The lesson: a woman does anything she must to help her family.

Margaret, working full time, was forced of necessity to treat Julie as an equal, an adult. She was carrying half the weight, after all. In fact, she had so much freedom that there was little to rebel against. The one major source of contention was religion, and even here Julie won out. It was the first move away from the traditional: at sixteen she refused to go to church and a big, tearful fight followed. Eventually, she and her mother called a grudging truce, backed off, and respected each other's opinions. Overall, it was a very unusual situation for a teen-age daughter and her mother.

Of course, once in a while, Julie let down her hair and allowed herself the luxury of being a teen-ager. Piling all her girl friends into the back of her mother's car, driving to San Francisco, she would try—mostly unsuccessfully—to get them into bars. Occasionally, she would go to a drive-in movie with a boy. Here Julie followed the strict mandates of her social group. "If I was out on a date," she remembers, "I was a perfect lady. I might kiss him, but I wouldn't let him touch me. And I certainly wouldn't cuss and drink and smoke [as with girl friends]."

Because there were no parochial high schools available for Julie, her mother sent her to public school in 1964. Her first year there, she found it hard to break in; cliques had already formed. In addition, flat as a board and five foot ten, she felt unattractive. At least, true to form, her mother had made certain she would not have to go into the dating years with braces on her teeth—that had been taken care of earlier. Deciding to win over everyone by sheer force of personality, she volunteered for everything, keeping a "nice" smile pasted on her face all the time—even when she didn't feel like it. Before long, she was a firmly entrenched member of the popular crowd.

Continuing down traditional paths, she maintained the arts as her favorite subjects. She took only required science, and did not enroll in math beyond the compulsory third year. She edited the newspaper and yearbook and hoped to be an English teacher or reporter. But although she did not want to admit it, it became increasingly clear that her natural talent was in math and science and that she honestly lacked ability in subjects such as journalism and English. When the time came, she resolutely ignored her SAT scores: high in sciences, very low in verbal skills.

Julie did well in her courses generally, but never took school seriously. Her carefree behavior in school contrasted sharply with her maternal, responsible approach to her sisters. Actually, however, these attitudes were just alternate sides of the same coin. At home, she received hard-core training for motherhood; in school, she actively pursued the future which society prescribed—being a popular girl whose main orientation was the opposite sex. "I never did a stitch of homework," she recalls. As long as she wasn't failing, or sounding dumb, "schoolwork never got in the way of anything." She much preferred dances and dates—or the football games, where she was a cheerleader.

Fitting in was a major concern to a girl whose whole

future rode on her popularity and social status. Accordingly, she conformed to the attitudes of her peers, just as she conformed to her mother's pressure to be a successful young lady. Like mother, like daughter, Julie and her friends borrowed their moral codes from their parents' books. They did not question the "save it for your husband" ethic. "You could kiss and you could hold hands, but there was no feely-touchy involved," she says.

She started dating at fifteen, the age deemed appropriate by both her mother and her peers. After all, she didn't want to be an old maid. Right from the start, she took dating as a serious business. Peter Curtis was, awesomely, a freshman in college; after their second date, they were pinned. Social accoutrements mattered more than his personality. "He had a car, so he was really nice," she said, laughing. "That was a big thing. We could go all kinds of places." After eight or nine months, this steady relationship broke off and she switched tacks, dating various young men almost every weekend for a year.

As she had been taught, Julie did not consider a career seriously at all. Though she took SATs like everyone else, she did not expect to go to college. And, as it happened, she never did bother to apply. Much more important, and definitely more final, she instead met the boy who would be her husband.

Paul Ranier was a former star quarterback. "It was perfect," she told me sarcastically. "A match made in heaven by Ann Landers." Bright, strong, good-looking, he started dating her in the spring of her sophomore year. At the University of San Francisco, Paul was preparing to go to a school of pharmacy. Right away, Julie knew he would be a good provider—a quality her mother had emphasized for years, a quality her father's example had underscored. The Fowlers knew his family; his father was a professor at the nearby junior college. He was six years older than Julie, and while this made him uncomfortable, he seemed more mature and stable to her because of it. Needless to say, Margaret Fowler was thrilled.

They dated conventionally for a year. Then, on Christmas Eve of 1967, he asked her to marry him. Naturally, it was a welcome idea, the fulfillment of every expectation Julie had ever had for herself. Ten years later, however, with the benefit of hindsight, she told me that she had married him because she "wasn't doing anything else."

Margaret's aspirations for her daughter were complete: in January 1968, Julie graduated a semester early from high school; in March, she walked down the church aisle in a conventional gown with a chapel train and veil, and with five attendants. The reception was at the country club.

Although Paul had pressured Julie for sex before their marriage, she had repeatedly refused, in accordance with her training. Now, for the first time since their arguments over religion, Julie discovered that her mother's teachings were not infallible: when I asked if she was glad she had saved her virginity, she was bitter. "No. He was rotten. He was absolutely horrible. It really was no experience. He would literally have an orgasm on my leg before ever entering me. He would do that time and time again. And then he was very good afterwards at just rolling over and going to sleep."

Ignoring this failure at intimacy as best she could when they returned from their honeymoon, Julie set up house, modeling herself on her parents' suburban example. They had planned for her to provide the major income during Paul's last year at college and while he was enrolled in pharmacy school. But naturally, considering her background, she had no marketable skills. "I had worked at a hamburger joint through most of high school, but I didn't want to slop hamburgers," she remembers. Consequently, in January, she had enrolled in a six-month training program for medical assistants, and so unknowingly took the first step which led her away from her mother's ideals and dreams.

It was the start of her real working career. She learned basic office techniques: taking X rays, keeping charts, typing, billing: Finishing her training in June 1968, the same month Paul graduated, she got a job in a surgery clinic.

Of course, in accordance with his upbringing, Paul did not

intend to have a working wife for long. He wanted someone to take care of the house and raise his children. When he married Julie, they had not discussed the issue of her employment; if they had, she would probably have agreed with Paul. But she did not anticipate how important working would become to her or how far she was from being ready to have a child right away, the way Paul wanted. Fortunately, there was no confrontation, because she failed to get pregnant. With no sex education, knowing nothing of birth control, she rode on luck and Paul's lack of sexual expertise. Then, later, when she began working, new information became accessible to her; she insisted on starting the pill.

She simply did not want to have a baby. Working was fun and more fulfilling. It made Julie feel independent, self-reliant, able to support not only herself but her husband as well. She did not want to be chained to a small child. For the first time, she began to realize the depth of her independence and her strength. Previously, she had thought these qualities could only be used within the home; now she knew otherwise.

Predictably, however, Paul did not view her job the same way. "His attitude was that I was working only because it was necessary now; and as soon as he was done, I was never going to work another day in my life. He was very adamant and very strong about that." Their radically different views began to create problems. "I would come home from a long day at work," Julie says, "and he would come home from school and expect me to cook his dinner, have everything perfect and on the table. I'd tell him, 'Go to hell, I'm tired. I'm just as tired as you are.' I started demanding equal time." Simply, she was not willing to abdicate responsibility for her life and let Paul run the show.

Suddenly, the minor differences between them began to seem major. He wanted someone "subservient," someone who would cater to his every whim. She was tired of being a maid. Concomitantly, she began to realize she simply did not need to depend on a man as her mother had taught. Another of Margaret's theories began to sink out of sight.

Julie now looks upon this period as a necessary evil, a time that entirely altered her way of thinking. "What marriage was supposed to be and the way it actually turned out were two entirely different things." But with the shock came a sense of vindication. She had always been self-sufficient, but her social training had not encouraged her to think of managing on her own.

During her time of discontent with her husband, feminism surfaced in her life. With her friends, and with the nurses in the San Francisco hospital where she worked, she began to read and think about women's expectations. These discussions, coupled with her own new feelings of independence and love of working, slowly stirred up questions about her marriage and herself. The Women's Movement provided her with her first role models of women who *chose* to be professionals. Julie started looking at her mother in a totally new light; with amazement, she realized that Margaret had actually improved the family business—without any help from a husband. Suddenly, this seemed as important as her achievements within the home.

Paul denigrated her new support system. He said it was stupid; in reality, he had a double standard. "It was, 'Women can be equal, but not my wife,' " Julie told me with a sigh.

In reality, Paul was threatened by her growing discontent and her increasing involvement with the movement. He was certain feminism was causing the problems in their marriage. In truth, it was. Julie was using women's lib to move toward independence—and away from Paul. The movement justified her belief that she was right and Paul was wrong, giving her the feeling that *she* "wasn't crazy." Her feelings of self-reliance were normal, she told him firmly.

Throwing aside the last vestiges of her background, she told Paul she wanted an annulment. In September 1968, she asked him to leave their apartment; he did. Her relief was tremendous. Compared to her feelings about their marriage, not even court seemed difficult. "The most traumatic thing, I think, was dividing up our albums," she said with a laugh. Paul contested the annulment for some time, continually asking her to let him come home. Julie did not relent; she knew it would never work.

Courageously, she began to build a new life. Still, being alone was hard, and she saw no harm in beginning an affair with a surgical resident from her hospital. The contrast between this casual relationship and her marriage proved that not everyone was like Paul. Her new lover "was superb, very understanding . . . really good for me. He would talk to me. . . . He contributed a kind of attitude [that] sex was fun. It was a fun thing to do; a nice thing to have between two people." But she made clear from the start that she would not be tied down. She was too young. There were many things to experience.

She poured her soul into her work, now obviously of critical importance. When she had learned everything she could about one medical field, she worked to get licensed in another. Finally, she made the big decision: college was essential.

In 1970, with priorities clear, she had no trouble picking up her worldly goods, leaving her surgical resident behind, and moving to San Mateo. There she enrolled in a community college where she felt she could swing excellent grades and a scholarship that would enable her to transfer. She was still a little unsure of her capabilities, but by working the night shift as a nurse's aide, she put herself through the two-year program.

Horizons expanding, she delved into new interests, no longer worried about what was appropriate for a young lady. A love for the outdoors flourished into camping trips and jogging. Science and medicine were now real interests. She sought out people who agreed with her liberated viewpoints and had no difficulty finding them. She began dating again, reinforcing her good experience with the surgical resident. Her sexual mores were radically changed. "I liked [sex]. Once I had decided that, if the timing was right and I liked the person, or if I felt good toward him, then it was never, 'Will he respect me in the morning?'" She continued to choose warm, sensitive men to whom she could really talk. In fact, after an initial rampage of sleeping with many different men, she also began to find the confidence to say no to some. It was an indication of her growing sense of self.

Going on peace marches, avidly reading the feminist canon, involving herself with encounter and women's groups, she forged a new life. As a sideline to her interests in feminism and medicine, the issue of women's health piqued her concern. When she discovered that her mother had taken the potentially carcinogenic synthetic estrogen diethylstilbestrol (DES) while pregnant with her, she started a seminar on the drug and its embryonic effects for those who did not have the medical know-how to research the topic for themselves.

She did well enough academically to qualify for a full scholarship to Berkeley, and transferred for her third year, part of the class of 1974. To continue being an independent woman who could make her own way in the world was her immediate goal. She found much security in striving toward this.

And so, despite her active love life, she did not allow any man to become seriously involved with her. Career was the first priority. During her Berkeley years, she had five different men on the string at once, all in different fields, all filling different needs. She told none that she loved him. "I would say, 'I'm very fond of you.'" She was tired of playing games, and so chose men who could deal with her liberated views on sex and career—men who, she says, all had professional sisters or mothers. It was part of a newly established and long-lasting pattern. "I seem to be attracted to men who are comfortable around women, and that usually means men who have grown up in a house with women there, and strong women."

As she grew older, she felt more secure with her own life and with feminism. Berkeley was a hive of discussion on all women's issues in the early 1970s; there she found overwhelming support for her fledgling career and met many people in the same situation—going back to school after a marriage.

On the other hand, as the movement became more strident, Julie refused to get boxed into petty discussions over bra-wearing, leg-shaving, and the like. The reality of her concrete career plans was far more important than the ethereal rhetoric of liberation could ever be. Still, she demonstrated for equal rights on campus, and was coming increasingly to the realization that soon she would be part of the male-dominated working community. Julie regarded equal rights for women as survival.

Finally, during her senior year, she decided to capitalize on her scientific leanings and enrolled in Berkeley's Ph.D. program in physiology. But after two of the five years, she began to feel claustrophobic with lab work. She liked being with people, not test tubes. She didn't need the yearly tension of grant applications, or the solitude. Suddenly, finally, medical school looked like the right choice.

Fearing that admissions committees would not take her record, with all its shifts, seriously enough—despite her summa cum laude from Berkeley—she applied to twenty-nine schools. She also worried that her age—twenty-seven—would count against her. But despite these fears, even Harvard, Yale, and Columbia accepted her. It was the greatest achievement of her life.

She chose Harvard; it had a reputation for being the best, and she felt she would be comfortable in Boston—a heady brew for the girl who had never even planned to go to college.

Unlike many of her new classmates, Julie really loves medical school. It is challenging, stimulating, and a privilege. Now in her second year, she has come a long way.

Her work in Harvard's clinics has been an eye-opener, however. There, she feels conspicuous in a way that disturbs her feminist sensibilities. "We'll be sitting in a group with three or four male students," she recounts, "and I'm the only woman. ... Invariably the instructor will sit there, look at me, talk to me the whole time, and never even look at the guys. That's starting to get on my nerves. I haven't quite decided how I'm going to deal with it, or what I'm going to say. See, that's very covert. You can't hang your hat on that. You can't scream and holler, 'Stop looking at me!' "

Margaret Fowler is proud of her daughter's career. She has gained new recognition that a woman needs to be self-sufficient—in case of emergency. She now sees, somewhat, that to limit a woman's role to the home can be stifling. Both professionals of a sort, she and Julie can share a great deal—more than ever.

Nevertheless, Julie says, Margaret is still a product of her environment. "She would be just as proud if I would get married and make babies." Her main expectations and goals for her daughter remain unchanged. In fact, she has been pressuring Julie to hurry up and find a man. "Mother has this concern," Julie told me with a hoot of laughter, "that I am getting up in my years, and I'd better grab any man I can before I lose my looks." Margaret still fears it's all downhill for a woman after age thirty.

Even without her mother's prompting, for the first time in ten years Julie feels safe enough about her own identity to allow herself to fall in love. This time, she has selected a man with a strength of character equal to her own. She's not afraid of being pushed around anymore. Tim Wright is a freshman at Harvard Medical School, only twenty-one years old, but his youth doesn't faze her. "As a result of meeting him," she confided to me, "my outlook on remarrying has changed.... I'm not saying that I necessarily see myself marrying him. What I see is that it is possible that one man could encompass all the things that I need, want, and look for. So many times the men I would date would be weaker than I. I'd get bored. I could manipulate them easily, although I wouldn't want to, it would kind of happen. I did not usually feel they were my equals."

A whole new world has opened up. She has found that a man can be as strong as she and still respect her. True to her pattern, she has picked a man with powerful women in his background—his mother is a concert pianist—a man who is consequently able to cope with her liberated ideas. "He sees me as his equal. . . . We meet head-on a lot," she ruminates. "I mean, we fight! We do. We have these lovely little verbal battles over these obscure little points. But it's great, they're real intellectual challenges." He is also extremely supportive of her work; because they are in the same field, he can sympathize with the sacrifices she must make.

They talk of marriage often, but, at present, simply to love and communicate is a big step for Julie. "Right now, [marriage] scares the shit out of me," she admits. She feels her desire to have children will be the major motivating factor. As she nears her thirtieth birthday, she does feel inevitable biological pressure. The desire for children bred into her years ago has resurfaced. Of course, she realizes—with trepidation—that children will be an enormous commitment, will require rebalancing her entire life. But she is confident of her career ambitions. "I will never be the stay-at-home mother. That's for sure. And that's something I will always stick to."

Speaking practically, she claims she would stay home with a baby for the first six months, but then feels she would have to have a live-in nurse. "If the male felt that it was important for one or both of the parents to be there—that is, not farming it out to somebody or having somebody come in—if the male felt strongly about that, my compromise would be, 'OK, that's fine, but the equal amount of time that I take away from my job to be at home you have to do [too].'

"How can you be a doctor and mother simultaneously?" I asked curiously. She felt the answer might be taking a part-time residency, a half-time program which would require twice as many years. In addition, she intends to use hired help.

She is a professional and that will always come first, she claims, despite her emotional commitments and the biological pressures. "It's a question of priorities at this point," she says. "Medical school is number one. I put Tim second. Actually, I put Tim third; I put me second."

But despite her sense of confidence, I could see that she realized the pitfalls inherent in her scheme. A part-time residency itself would be an enormous sacrifice, because it is rarely offered at the best hospitals, and it would require a diminished income for an extended period of time. In addition, Tim is not willing to take a part-time residency too, so that he could help out with the child care; he wants to go into academic medicine, and such a concession would endanger his standing. The bottom line, Julie realizes, is that he cannot and will not assume any of the burden. It is hers, and hers alone.

Further, living between cities and commuting doesn't make much sense if one residency is in San Francisco and the other in Boston.

As I talked with Julie, I was overcome by her sense of joy with herself and her life. I wondered what lay ahead for her in the future, what she wanted to get out of the next several years. She worries a lot about the time medicine requires, she told me. She is virtually unable to find the time to pursue anything else. While medicine is a fulfillment for her, it is also a limitation. She dreads turning into an egocentric, myopic, boring doctor like those she encounters so frequently in her hospital work.

The medical student I interviewed is not all that different from the young woman who took care of her family when her father died and her mother fell apart. Rejecting Margaret's teaching that a woman's world was solely comprised of hearth and home enabled Julie to eventually rediscover those talents integral to her personality all along. Independent, self-sufficient, Julie Fowler has attained a new security, and so is able to give of herself freely and openly. She now must deal with a whole different spectrum of problems than those for which she was trained. Having finally gotten far enough away from her old life-style, she can view it objectively and see that there are certain aspects she wants to rekindle—marriage and motherhood. Although she has not really faced it, in order to fulfill these desires as well as those of career, she will almost inevitably find herself forced to sacrifice something. It may well have to be part of what she has fought for so long: her number-one priority, career.

Three

Lisa Matthews

Nothing in her life had prepared Lisa Matthews for that rainy, dark morning. It was 5:30 A.M.; her husband still hadn't come home from the bar where he had gone to meet a friend early in the evening. Finally, she called and asked if Jack was there. He was not.

All alone, her mouth painfully swollen from dental surgery the day before, she could imagine only the worst. Unlike Julie Fowler, she had never developed the strong resources necessary to cope with a moment of real crisis—her mother's sheltered life having been her only example of adult womanhood. Nevertheless, she put a jacket over her bathrobe, covered her hair with a fall, stuffed her feet into clogs, and went out to find him. Instinctively she knew he was with the mistress he had "given up" three months earlier.

She drove to the other woman's apartment; Jack's car was parked in the back. The rain poured down. She banged and banged on the door.

Finally, Jack came out to see who it was. "What are you doing here?" he asked nervously.

"What the fuck do you think I'm doing here?" she remembers saying. Then she charged past him into the bedroom, bent on killing the girl. Jack pulled her back. "I just went hysterical, just screamed bloody murder. . . . I just screamed that this whore was fucking my husband, as loud as I could . . . went after her a few times, and never got very far. He was scared to death of me, he pulled me off her but then wouldn't get near me because I was screaming."

She demolished the apartment. She pulled pictures off the

walls. She shattered the ashtrays. In the middle of the debris, her fall lay like a dead rat.

Lisa refused to go home. Jack finally called the police. "I was afraid to leave," she told me with a catch in her voice. "I didn't know where to go. . . . I knew right then that I could not, just could not, stay married to this person. Ever. . . . At that moment, home wasn't home anymore."

Drinking coffee in Lisa's Cambridge, Massachusetts, apartment four years later, I couldn't believe that this slender, gentle-eyed secretary could have been so violent. We sat together on the floor of her bedroom. A violin stood in the corner, a handmade quilt lay folded on the bed. But the breakup of her marriage had been the disintegration of her whole existence. She had failed in the one area in which she had been educated to succeed. Her background had not taught her how to cope with a husband's betrayal; she had been a protected child and then a protected wife. Her discovery of Jack's infidelity plunged her into a harsh reality; running from it, she would make a radical departure from all she had ever known.

Thomas and Katherine Matthews were a Nebraskan couple who set a happy example for their three daughters, never fighting in front of them. Born in 1951, the baby of the family, Lisa spent her childhood looking forward to having this kind of secure home life when she grew old enough to marry.

She remembers her early years as a time surrounded by the warmth of family. The house they owned was small, with one bedroom, but it was on a nice quiet residential street with a big backyard. They lived comfortably and concluded that a person couldn't ask for much more out of life than they had already.

Five years after Lisa's birth, the Matthewses—like Julie Fowler's family—moved to "the Promised Land," California, with all its opportunities. They settled in a small town just outside of San Francisco. Thomas, a licensed pharmacist with a degree from Drake University, found a place as a manager in a large new drugstore. Katherine, although a housewife, was a working woman too, selling cosmetics and sundries. She worked side by side with Thomas, while single-handedly managing the household simultaneously. She set an example her daughter would follow for years to come.

The Matthews family, conservative, wholeheartedly believed in the precepts of the American dream. Katherine fitted perfectly into the mold of the housewife who worked only because a family of five could be hard to feed. Religion was another facet of their conservatism. Devout Presbyterians, not only did they attend services each week, but each family member belonged to a Masonic organization which supported the church: the Eastern Star for Katherine, and the Rainbow Girls for her daughters. Thomas was a proselytizer who kept hotel rooms well stocked with Gideon Bibles.

A quiet man, with little sense of humor or flexibility, Lisa's father was also a member of the John Birch Society. Early on, he began "protecting" his daughters from those who were ethnically or racially different. The housing he chose for his family reflected his conventional bent. In California's tract developments, every fifth house was built with the same floor plan. You always knew what your neighbor's home looked like, sight unseen—it was the same as yours.

Matthews projected his ideals onto his children, expecting them to lead conventional childhoods which would blossom into conventional adulthoods. His daughters would be modeled on his wife's example. There could be no opportunity for them to be different.

For Lisa, her father was a distant patriarch. Only during her tomboy years did they have anything at all in common, shooting bows and arrows together. But such camaraderie was short-lived. Katherine, an outgoing woman, was far easier to identify with. Though not a college graduate, she had a natural ingenuity which Lisa admired greatly. Her mother was a sensitive, ever-present, loving adult who tempered her husband's strict regime. It was a system of checks and balances; the family was a tight, reliable circle headed by the complementary figures of a warm, nurturing mother and a strict but dependable father. It would be the kind of marriage and family life she would seek later on.

In keeping with his nature, Tom Matthews gave his daughters few responsibilities. His attitude toward his wife was similar. He held the family purse strings closely to himself; the children were never deprived, but there were few extravagances. No one dared challenge his views on sex, politics, abortion. Such realms were exclusively male. If there was ever any difficulty in making his salary stretch, Lisa was never aware of it; to this day she cannot even estimate how much money he earns. Such overprotective behavior rendered Lisa extremely dependent, almost incapable of making decisions or trusting her own judgment.

Still, she looks back on childhood as a good time. She was strong-willed and rambunctious, and perhaps a bit spoiled. Unlike Julie Fowler, whose father's death forced her to become an adult at age fourteen, Lisa carried only limited responsibilities—helping out with the dishes after supper, cleaning the house Saturday mornings. The family of five was a strong unit. Her parents' marriage seemed rock hard.

Family ideals were even reflected by the Matthewses' favorite television shows. After supper, the whole clan would tune in "I Love Lucy" or "Father Knows Best." Thomas allowed them to watch only those shows which projected the stable, middle-class American. On every front, then, a code of traditional morality, expectations, and behavior sealed Lisa into her future.

Grammar school turned out to be another supportive environment. Generally, she did well throughout these years without trying very hard. Her parents never pushed her to strain herself academically; ultimately, their expectations for her were limited. School was mostly a place to be social, to make friends.

Boys were not a part of her world at this early stage. With no brothers, she had no opportunity to identify with or even experience the ambition bred into a young male. She remembers no future orientation at this time other than being a wife and mother, an aspiration that stayed with her through high school.

Lisa's family offered her a second example of what life could be for an adult woman, this time a negative one. Of the women in the family, only Thomas's sisters had gone to college. They were college-educated spinsters—a sequence presumed to be inevitable.

Thus, as a member of the class of 1969 at the local high school, Lisa wanted most to learn skills that would help her as a homemaker. She had studied violin in grammar school, but eventually gave it up because home economics class conflicted with orchestra. Expecting to have no real use for her studies after graduation, she did not push herself. If she worked at anything, it was in those areas considered socially acceptable and appropriate for a young woman. Career and college were anathema to her, as they were to most of her peers. She was an average young woman, nothing out of the ordinary—just as her father had so carefully molded her to be. "There was nothing abnormal at all about not wanting to go to college," she told me.

In her teens, despite her basic acceptance of her parents' mores and life-style, Lisa began to wonder increasingly about their marriage. They did not communicate very well, she decided, even though they never fought. They never went anywhere together. She slowly came to the conclusion that her mother had married not out of love but from fear: her first fiancé had died several years before they could marry, and at twenty-two she had been in danger of being considered her small town's old maid. When Thomas Matthews, with a college degree and good prospects, had walked into her life, she couldn't afford to refuse. Lisa, looking at her mother's example, determined she would never get herself into that trap. She would marry only for love.

Gradually, Lisa began to step out with her peer group, letting her friends set her moral codes the way her parents once had. Like many high schools, hers had rigid cliques; Lisa belonged to a small group of shy, conventional girls— not the popular, cute cheerleaders, but not the smart, ugly grinds either. There was strong pressure to conform, especially in dress. Knee-length skirts with sweaters in her freshman year became thigh-high dresses by the time she was a senior. Emblematic of her stance, she cursed easily with the rest of her crowd, but never let her parents hear one indiscretion.

Nevertheless, despite the profanity and hints of rebellion, the morals of her group were very much in keeping with their strict upbringing. As in so many other areas, her parents did not discuss sex with her, because they wanted to protect her from it. She and her friends knew very little about it, and their school offered no sex-education courses. Consequently, all their limited early experiences were fumbling, based on trial and error.

She was younger than most of her friends and, consequently, frustrated: she wanted to be successful in the only sphere she was allowed to operate in—dating. But Thomas didn't want his daughter taking up with just anybody. Though she actually did fight him a little bit, she obeyed him. "I was never wild," she says. For Lisa, every rebellion was a halfway measure designed to fail. She smoked cigarettes twice, but never became hooked, and was not much intrigued by alcohol or drugs.

Tom Matthews finally allowed his youngest daughter to go on a date when she reached sixteen. Quickly, she established a pattern of falling for men her parents could not be happy about. She liked irresponsible boys who hung out on the street corner with cigarette butts dangling from their lips, drinking beer. She now admits it was a reaction to her evolving image of her father. "I've always felt that [he] was a sexless type of person. To this day it's very hard for me to imagine my parents having sex." But even though she was rebelling against Thomas's sexually repressive personality, she was not able to throw off his teachings entirely. Most of her boyfriends pressured her to sleep with them, but she continued to refuse, determined to save that prize for her husband, as she had been taught. For the first time, and not the last, she was caught in the middle of two worlds. "I never slept with anyone else except the guy I married," she now says, sighing. "There was always so much guilt . . . and you were scared to death that somebody was going to catch you or you'd get pregnant."

At a dance in 1968, she met Jack Sampson. "I was physically attracted to him," she remembers. "He fitted into that macho type, a little on the wild side . . . smoked, drank beer." He had even experimented with drugs. Soon they were going steady.

It was their senior year in high school; in June, unless he changed his mind and went to college, Jack was due to lose his student deferment. Knowing he would be drafted, he joined the Marines. He proposed to Lisa just before leaving for Vietnam in August of 1969.

She accepted.

If it hadn't been for Vietnam, Lisa told me, she would have gotten married then and there. She had no itch to travel, to see or experience new things. College couldn't have excited her less. Her idea of contentment was settling down early, avoiding the specter of being an old maid. There was nothing she wanted more than Jack.

Katherine and Thomas interceded, however. They felt she was vulnerable, too young. Of course, they had encouraged her to gear her life in precisely this direction. She was confused; why were they changing their tune? The real story was that Thomas felt Jack was beneath Lisa. The pharmacist did not enjoy mixing with a boy who wanted to be a carpenter. And so, switching tacks, he encouraged her to go to college, secretly hoping she would forget about her fiancé. Eventually, Lisa allowed them to persuade her to enroll at the local junior college—but only because there was little else to do while waiting for Jack to come home.

It was a small step; she lived at home, and the curriculum was anything but taxing. Starting the two-year program in September of 1969, just after Jack left for Vietnam, she majored in early childhood education and began to think, for the first time, of getting a job as her mother had done— perhaps in teaching. She explored the idea by working at a day-care center for nursery and pre-kindergarten children. She also started helping out in a local private school. En- gaged to a soldier, with days filled with work and evenings with classes, she had little time for socializing. If nothing else, it was a good stopgap measure.

In February of her first college year, Jack was able to take a short leave in Hawaii, and asked Lisa to come out and meet him there. Needless to say, her parents were aghast. Lisa's mother finally volunteered her services as chaperon. After some discussion, Jack's mother agreed to make the trip also. The three women stayed in one room, with the door barricaded and the two mothers as bodyguards. Jack stayed on an entirely separate floor as a precaution.

Lisa had always intended to preserve her virginity for her husband. But now a new factor entered her consideration. On his first day in 'Nam, Jack's tank had hit a mine, and he had narrowly missed being blown away. "[It] was a heavy trip," she explains. "People from [my town] were dying like flies over there . . . the guy who used to sit next to me in math class died. Everything lost its perspective. I mean, what [was] my virginity compared to someone's life?" It was a realiza- tion she came to all on her own, something from which her father could not protect her. And so, one night after going out for dinner alone, they sneaked back into Jack's bedroom and made love.

In the summer of 1970, Jack returned from Asia for good and enrolled at the same junior college. Lisa's parents con- tinued to encourage her not to marry until he was out of college. But he didn't much care for school. After one year, he decided to drop out to work in his father's carpentry business.

That same June, Lisa received her Associate of Arts degree and toyed with the idea of continuing into a full four-year program, but she decided against it quickly. Underneath, she simply did not feel that it would be wise for her to have more education than Jack. Her college-educated spinster aunts had demonstrated the dangers amply. But instead of admitting to this, she used a convenient excuse: the nearest appropriate college was Sonoma State—an hour's commute away. She would never have asked Jack to move.

As Lisa was making this important decision, she simultaneously lowered her sights in another way. At her junior college, she had aimed for a job in special education. But on graduating in 1971, she found the field overstocked. One job teaching autistic children had five hundred applicants. Discouraged, she took a job as cashier in a local supermarket. At first, she assumed this "mindless" work was temporary; then she began to enjoy it. It was employment similar to that her mother had done at the pharmacy. Best of all, having money of her own to spend was wonderful.

Later in 1971, a few small schools in neighboring towns called to inquire if she was still looking for a teaching job. She told them no. Checking groceries at the supermarket had become a way of life. Anyway, she and Jack were at last going to be married.

She finally walked down the aisle in January 1972. She was almost twenty-one, and, like her mother thirty-one years before, felt in danger of becoming labeled an "old maid." The newlyweds were soon living a rich life, keeping up with the tempo set by the other young couples they knew. Jack's growing income was quite tidy when supplemented with Lisa's substantial supermarket earnings. They rented for a year, and in 1973 bought a house, a car, a truck, a vintage model A Ford, and a boatload of furniture, including the indispensable color TV, firmly establishing themselves as a couple that fitted beautifully into the provincial society surrounding them. And since neither Jack nor Lisa wanted children right away, they could afford to spend their money on luxuries that even her parents couldn't afford. She had done them one better.

From that pinnacle, in a life produced and packaged by the social traditions around her, she never even dreamed of the ultimate divorce. Her parents had always protected her from real stress. And so, when her marriage began to suffer problems, she was simply at a loss. Her husband was domineering, uncommunicative, a stereotypical chauvinist. Arguments became frequent. Jack fell into the nasty habit of walking out of the house and not coming back for several days; afraid to stay alone, Lisa would run home to her parents. The fights were petty, she now says. "I got up every morning at six o'clock and made him breakfast. . . . If I broke the yolk on the egg he wouldn't eat it." In short, her husband recognized her terror at being left, and constantly manipulated her fear. "He would just get mad and say he was going to divorce me. He'd stay overnight at a friend's house. I'd be very upset. The next time we had a fight, he'd stay away two nights."

In November 1973, after a fight, Jack left for a whole week. At first, she panicked as usual. Then, for the first time, she began to be rational. "Oh, fuck this," she said to herself. "He always comes back." That week she didn't go home, didn't even tell her parents he had gone. Instead, she went about her own routine and actually came to like it some. It was the first time she had ever been able to tolerate living alone.

Finally, Jack called. In the grand tradition of the forgiving wife, Lisa welcomed him back. Making up, they decided to go out for dinner. In the car, driving to the restaurant, she asked innocently where he had spent the week. "At Diane's," he said nonchalantly. At first, she didn't react. "It was not in my background even to imagine he'd gone out with somebody else," she recalls. But it didn't take her long to realize he wasn't talking about a platonic relationship.

Stunned, she silently ate her dinner while Jack described the affair in gory detail. Intellectually, Lisa had always regarded adultery as immediate cause for divorce. But she had no emotional mechanism with which to deal with this betrayal. "Jack wanted me to call her to ask what she did sexually that he liked!" she told me, incredulous. It was the ultimate irony: the prize she had been taught to save as the bedrock of her marriage was unwanted. Her inexperience was a liability, not an asset.

Over the next few months, Lisa desperately tried to repair the damage. She couldn't fail here; it was the only life she knew. She changed her working hours to be at home whenever Jack was free. She let him boss her around, let him blackmail her with the threat that Diane was waiting for him with open arms if Lisa gave any backsass. She threw herself into it completely, desperate to win back control over the mainstay of her life.

But eventually she had to face the facts. He was seeing Diane again, despite her efforts. Often when Lisa answered the phone, the other party hung up. Finally, defeated, she began to follow Jack when he left the house. She was a nervous wreck.

In March 1974, complete disaster struck. On that rainy morning that she would never forget, she found them together and tried to tear Diane's apartment apart. The police came and took her to a local crisis center, where she calmed down slightly. She didn't want to face her parents with long discussions of what had happened, how she had failed in the one thing they'd raised her for. Instead, she called her mother and asked her to pack a suitcase and take her to the airport. She ran away as far as she could from the awful shambles of her marriage and all her dreams. She ran all the way to her sister's apartment in Boston.

There, in a city that natives like to call "the Hub," Lisa discovered a new continent of experience. Her sister was running a grant program for the Massachusetts Council on the Arts and had her own staff. She was wrapped up in a world Lisa had never dreamed of. Her friends were doctors, lawyers, professional people. It was Lisa's first introduction to the Women's Movement, and the timing was perfect: with her dreams and self-image shattered, she desperately needed a new life plan. The feminists had one to offer her—and it was one which conveniently required no men.

She spent that first summer waiting on tables in Martha's Vineyard. It was a strange, disconnected time. At twenty-two, she had little real education, and most of her contemporaries were about to enter graduate school. She was an ex-wife in a world of singles. By summer's end, however, she had made a rapid adjustment. She put on twenty pounds, made friends, went on partying and drinking binges. And she filed for divorce. Moving further from her upbringing, she experimented sexually, having several affairs. Swinging with the tune of the times, she now didn't need an emotional commitment to enjoy a physical relationship.

Back in Boston, she got a full-time clerical job, feeling acutely her lack of a B.A. in a city teeming with overeducated intellectuals. It was clear that here a college degree was a social passport. In September 1974, she enrolled in Boston State College's night program, paying her way by working during the day. Beginning as a business major, she soon switched to English, which seemed the easiest and fastest way to complete her remaining degree requirements. It was that precious piece of parchment—not the knowledge—that she thought important. She needed to fit in, much as she had fitted in during high school, and she couldn't do it without the proper accoutrements. Being able to say she was a student gave her a certain panache.

Tired during night classes, she used No-Doz frequently. Studying was out of the question, but the program was not particularly demanding. She sneaked by with B's and C's.

Receiving her B.A. in June 1977, she took a secretarial job at the Harvard School of Public Health, a job which she hoped would give her a sense of a field she might like. Describing her work to me six months later, she played down its clerical aspects, embarrassed just as she once had been by her lack of a bachelor's degree. She now feels that secretarial work is demeaning. She has latched on to a new type of role model—the feminist career woman—and has fallen short of that ideal in her own eyes.

Nevertheless, she has done little to change things around. Recently, she even asked the personnel director for a job-title change from "secretary" to "staff assistant." But the new title has not changed her duties or her pay scale. Defensively, she told me she is staying at Harvard to learn more about the field of public health. I thought to myself that going to graduate school would be more informative than typing memos.

Clearly, her real problem is an acute lack of organized direction. For Lisa Matthews, having a career is like keeping up with the Joneses. It is the necessary admission ticket for a young woman who wants to participate in today's social circus. Without it, a girl is considered old-fashioned and dull. But Lisa is constantly looking for excuses, unable to admit she's a secretary. As she admitted to me early in the interview, she would gladly return to working at a supermarket cash register, because she enjoys this sort of mindless work. But that would be as much a failure in her new role as her marriage was in her old.

Since coming to Boston, Lisa has dated a number of different men somewhat aimlessly, but has not allowed herself to become serious over any. She actively discourages those to whom she feels attracted, because they threaten her. Leather-jacket types no longer catch her eye; the intellectual, verbal man with a graduate degree fits her current self-image.

Her attitudes toward marriage have changed radically. She now views it, understandably, as a trap, a sublimation of the woman's identity, and sees little room in her life for a long-standing relationship. But while she revels in comparing horror stories with other divorcées, and gives much lip service to the concept of independence, her ideas are couched in the language of stability. "I find it hard to think of saying, 'This is *ours,*' because I want things that are *mine* so that they . . . will always be there."

She rejects another former value—having children—with little conscious ambivalence. Nearing thirty, she deliberately blocks out the idea that soon it will be too late to change her mind. She claims to have no maternal instincts—an interesting comment, I thought, from a girl with her upbringing, a girl who had once wanted a job in early childhood education. She now claims that women who are interested in marriage and children are neurotically driven. "It's all around me," she says. "They're grabbing whatever is around, even if it's not very good."

Even her living situation is emblematic of her need to escape any reminder of the past. Sharing an apartment with four medical students, she has taken on the bohemian Cambridge life-style that was so popular in the 1960s, a life-style she missed by marrying so early and coming from such an insular community.

In the process of rejecting old values, she has come to rely greatly upon feminism. It has given ideological credence to her new way of life, a perfect solution for a woman running from the despised identity she had abandoned in California, the identity her mother had worn so gracefully. She refuses to cook or clean house, and rarely does laundry. She no longer wears a bra, and has let hair grow under her arms. In short, she has abandoned anything that could possibly remind her of being a housewife.

Lisa Matthews worries as much about society's expectations as she did in high school when dating the captain of the football team. Now, she feels, her peer group expects her to be a career woman, and so she tries to succeed within this sphere, too. Feminism came to her when she was vulnerable, lacking identity. She seized it blindly. While marriage may not have been the answer in the past, a demanding career is probably not the answer for her future. She lacks real career commitment, being just a little too content with supermarket checkout lines and office typewriters to make the necessary sacrifices.

She has made a quantum leap in creating a new life for herself in Boston. Perhaps, with time, she will discover exactly which aspects of liberation really suit her—as Julie Fowler did—and discard the rest. Like many of us, Lisa Matthews may eventually find herself a lot closer to home than she now anticipates.

Part III

The Waiting Game

I don't think I thought about a career. That's why I'm going through a lot of problems now. My thinking process is a little late. I'm latent. But I don't think I'm to blame. I think it's the times. . . . It was always instilled in us, "Don't worry, it'll happen. . . . Why should you worry about the future—some rich man who is intelligent will come along, marry you, keep you just the way you were brought up."

—ANDREA SHAPIRO

The women who played the "waiting game" grew up assuming they'd never have to take care of themselves. From dolls to Nancy Drew to college, they never worried about the future, or even how they would support themselves, much less about that foreign idea "career." As with the women in "Like Mother, Like Daughter," they believed with all their innocent hearts that life would be for them as it had been for their mothers. And so they too sat back and waited for a white knight to come and sweep them off their feet, like Cinderella, to a castle in the clouds.

They waited.

And waited.

Times had changed. The four women in this section grew up to find that marriage was not the inevitable waterfall at the end of the river. Before they could take that step, the Women's Movement charged onto the social scene, radically altering the rules of the game. In college-educated America, the definition of a woman's success shifted perceptibly from the social to the professional—from an engagement ring to a career. Confused, these women weren't sure whom to listen to or which example to follow. They were caught tightly between the homemaking futures they had always envisioned and the new social expectations which appeared on the rising wave of feminism.

Further complicating the crisis, they found that fewer and fewer men were attracted to their traditional goals and ideals. When no man appeared immediately on the horizon, these women did not return to their parents' homes to wait out the interlude. Instead, with resignation, they went to work to wait out the interlude. This did not seem contradictory in terms of their goals, because some of their mothers had worked, and still managed to keep their family the first priority; instead they classified working as an inconvenience. They looked at their jobs as necessary solutions to a temporary situation, last resorts until they found their final niche in someone else's arms. They never really thought of them as careers, because in their hearts they could not believe it would be too long before a man rescued them from their own independence. But the waiting game had just begun. Often the few months they had envisioned turned into years, and their jobs seemed a poor consolation prize.

The Women's Movement had changed their world in an unplanned, unpleasant way. Instead of giving them more choices, it had limited those choices in which they were most interested. Not surprisingly, few of these women found themselves able to champion a cause that had brought them only confusion and disappointment. Most continued to resist the career pressure brought to bear on women their age, and did eventually find the homemaking roles they had sought so determinedly.

Nevertheless, they are substantially different from the housewives whose lament Betty Friedan sings in *The Feminine Mystique*. For this group, an identity crisis occurred not over *being* a housewife, but over *not being* a housewife. After spending some time alone, forging their own way, earning a living, these women decided that marriage and a traditional life-style was really what they did want after all. So far, they appear to be very content. Of course, only time will tell. Nevertheless, I do find their eventual choice of homemaking extremely powerful, because, forced to try on the feminists' "better way," they ultimately decided it was not a suit cut to fit their lives.

Four

Katherine Townsend

The diamond sparkled under the soft light, its clean, sharp facets shooting up a brilliant rainbow of refraction. A traditional engagement ring for a traditional southern girl. It was the fulfillment, at least on the surface, of every expectation she had ever had. But, slowly, as I heard the history of the ring, I began to realize just how far Katherine Townsend had stretched to make her childhood dreams come true.

Blond and blue-eyed, she was born in Raleigh, North Carolina, in 1954 to Robert and Ann Townsend, native southern Episcopalians. Her brother, Mark, followed two years later, and for a short time, at least, they were a closely knit family, a family that depended wholly on Rob's income as a life-insurance salesman. But in 1957 life for Ann, Katy, and Mark changed drastically. Rob, with an alcohol problem and a heart condition, dropped dead of a fatal coronary.

Although his widow received some veteran's benefits, they could not begin to cover the costs of raising two growing children. Years before, Ann had given up work to care for her young ones. Now she went back to a secretarial job—but only after finding a capable, maternal black woman to care for Mark and Katy during the day. She was determined that they would not want for love or attention. The kids played with Bessie's children after school, and a great love grew between the two families—within the locally appropriate racial boundaries.

To Katy and Mark, Bessie was like a familiar, endearing relative, an extra mother for those hours Ann was not at home. They lived in a little house in the center of a small North Carolina town. In the warmth of the neighborhood Katy saw her future: outdoor barbecues, croquet on Sunday afternoons, honeysuckle on the trellises, and a passel of children. It all had an aura of security—the kind that had seemed lost forever when her father died. Gradually, the children became used to having their mother all to themselves. Aside from Bessie, she was their sole means of emotional support and approbation, and to her young daughter, she seemed an ideal woman. Sweet, sensitive, she appreciated her children's emotions and tried to draw them out about how they felt. She did not discipline them severely, but gave them a reasonable amount of responsibility. Most important, she never allowed her busy life to encroach on her time with them in the evenings. Anyway, it was clear from the start that she was working only for Katy and Mark.

In spite of Bessie's help, however, Ann was having a tough time. A traditional southern girl, she had not been raised to lead a solitary life, or to be solely responsible for the support of her children. She wanted very much to remarry. And so, in 1961, Ann's boss became Katy's new father.

Duncan Stapleton was a divorcé, a middle-aged man who had just lost custody of his four children to his ex-wife. Adopting Katy and Mark gave him a new and instant family. A conservative southerner, he placed a high premium on traditional values such as family; later, he and Ann had two children of their own, the last when she was forty-five years old.

The Townsends were given their new father's name and instructed to call him "Daddy"—much to Katherine's resentment. But with time he would come to be her father; Robert, who had died when she was so young, slipped from her memory easily. And so she looked to Duncan for all her early lessons on men. Well-off because of his construction business, he had built his own big house, surrounded by a great deal of land, at the edge of town. They all moved in after the marriage. It was a step up from the small house in the center of town, and carried with it a powerful message.

Duncan was an able provider; security was truly at hand. Ann could even give up working.

He was a generous man, a man who made sure the children had everything they could possibly want: bicycles, clothes, trips to the state fair, ponies. He pampered Katy's rambunctious urges, her itch to go and do things.

But Duncan exacted a high price for these gifts—absolute obedience to his conservative edicts. Worse, Katy began to hate him for taking her mother away. The Stapletons took frequent extended vacations, often for a month at a time, leaving the children in care of their nanny. He imposed a dictatorial attitude on the entire household, Katy recalls. "We called him 'Daddy' and kissed him every morning, said 'yessir,' and never talked back, never expressed our feelings. What Daddy said went." Clearly, the man of the house had the power to run the show his way.

But acceptance of this came hard to Katy. Her spunky personality was irrepressible, and she was inclined to sass him back. If he tried to spank her, Ann would intervene, leaving Katy with only a feeling of confusion. "I just didn't understand ... why Mother kept telling me I couldn't say anything, and that I had to be nice—and that Daddy *really* loved me. I knew it was all a pile of shit." Only one thing *was* clear: Ann had betrayed her for this man. "I couldn't believe in Mother anymore," she told me, in despair at the memory. The intimate Townsend family was gone, a loss not easy to recapture. In years to come, Katy would seek the warm, easygoing love she missed so much.

Despite it all, Katy was able to recognize her stepfather's laudable qualities. Even a man who was a strict disciplinarian could be fair. She began to view reticence as a male trait—men could care for you silently while giving no indication of their feelings whatsoever. "He's the type of person who *wishes* he could come out and say, 'I love you,' could remember to call you on your birthday. He just doesn't have the touch with little things." Duncan was a smart, commonsensical man, a traditionalist who gave her sound, though unwelcome, advice. Above all, she respected him.

Another authoritarian influence reinforced the Stapleton view of home: the Episcopal church. An ideal Christian woman was gentle, charitable, ever flexible, while the ideal husband was a solid citizen who confidently sheltered his flock.

Each Sunday, Katy and Mark were dispatched to religion classes. She came to revere the hushed mood in the church during services, the sun flooding in through the stained glass. And she also appreciated the active social life the church offered, as it provided her with playmates of similar, safe backgrounds. There were ball teams, pancake dinners, bazaars, bake sales. All were run for charity by women who volunteered their services. Everywhere Katy looked she found traditional role models; not once did she meet a career woman.

The TV shows they watched also depicted warm family life: "Leave It to Beaver" and "Dick Van Dyke" were Katy's favorites. Her reading followed true to traditional form—*Nancy Drew, The Secret Garden, Strawberry Girl.* In these entertainments, she tried to recapture the warmth she felt missing from her new life with Duncan.

In school, English was, appropriately, her favorite subject, and she enjoyed writing poetry. Art and geography similarly held her interest. Math and science, on the other hand, were strictly boys' subjects. More important, school was a good place to socialize, and Katy was anything but shy. She developed an early fondness for boys, because they were fun to play with—kickball, rollbat, and jump rope—as her brother had always been. In a brief rebellion, she took up the role of tomboy. Nevertheless, she still dreamed of being a cheerleader, and settling down with a husband and family when she grew older. When her younger brother and sister joined the family, she changed diapers and baby-sat frequently; it all came naturally. She had no other thoughts for the future.

Minor skirmishes with Duncan became a major adolescent rebellion as she entered puberty. They argued continually over petty issues like staying late after school, or how short her skirts could be. Still, never once did she question more major things—such as his attitude toward her future.

The perfect escape from her stepfather's restrictions occurred to her during ninth grade: boarding school. A parochial, all-woman's institution in Richmond, Virginia, was not too far from home—but far enough. Its reputation for the conventional satisfied her parents, and to her delight Duncan allowed Katy to join the class of 1972 for her sophomore year. Freedom at last. She promptly gained twenty-five pounds, cut her hair, and, predictably, grew a crop of pimples. At Christmas, one look at her eldest daughter made Ann Stapleton cry.

Basically, school was fun, a place to socialize and develop those skills which would later help her pursue traditional goals—skills which had nothing to do with her studies. Katy found she enjoyed being with a group of girls who organized everything and told her where to go, what to do. It was a hangover from her relationship with Duncan; she found it easier to tag along than to lead. She belonged to a "pack" of preppie girls who ordered their clothes from the catalogues of L. L. Bean—a Maine camping store whose rustic shirts and rough boots were rapidly becoming chic. The pressure to conform was extreme: Katy and her friends wore the same necklaces—three initials hanging from a chain—with earrings to match; cardigan sweaters with covered buttons; hair short and curled. "No matter how bad the style looked on you, you wore it," she recalls.

They related to one another on a purely superficial level, spending their free time on traditional diversions like fraternity parties at neighboring boys' prep schools. But even in the South some new 1960s attitudes were beginning to encroach in measured steps. Pot had largely replaced alcohol. The school offered a course in sex education. Some of Katy's friends had even turned their backs on the tradition of keeping chaste until marriage; and, suddenly, not being a virgin was something to be proud of.

In addition, the young men Katy and her peers dated increasingly expected more than a good-night peck on the cheek. A girl needed to offer something the boys couldn't find just anywhere. "We thought that [to be popular] you had to be loose—just to go out and want to get laid," she says.

But she didn't want that for herself. To defend against the peer pressure, in the ninth grade Katy latched on to one particular boy, with whom she kept safely in touch by letter. To her relief, they saw each other infrequently during the next three years. Finally, to preserve this relationship that was so important to her image, she slept with him, reluctantly, in the twelfth grade.

A few of her classmates married after high school; most went on to college. Katy herself had no real goals—except, perhaps, finding a man. Floating along, she never worried about money—Duncan sent her an allowance of one hundred dollars a month. Nor did she worry about how the upheavals of the 1960s were changing the climate she would have to live in as an adult woman. She never really kept up with current events anyway. The term "women's liberation" had not penetrated her world.

Thus, when Duncan and Ann wanted her to go to college— it would make her better rounded—and began exerting great pressure, Katy resisted, "sick" of school. They prevailed anyway. She considered working, but rejected it quickly. Afraid of being trapped into living at home again with Duncan, she applied to Hollins College, early decision. Though her boards and her grades were mediocre and her attitude apathetic, she got in.

As she neared high school graduation, the desperation to find a husband began to build. She was almost eighteen, fearful of getting caught short. Her mother's example of unmarried life had made it perfectly clear that a mate was essential—even Duncan was steady and better than nothing. Therefore, she was already in a serious frame of mind when she met Lance Masters during the summer before college. A year younger than she, Lance was a native southerner attending a Virginia prep school, a young man born and bred to the same traditions as she. They began seeing each other on weekends during Katy's first year at college. As she had been trained to do, Katy kept the relationship on a featherweight level. She was entertaining, catering to Lance's every whim. They had little intellectual exchange and relied mostly on car races, beach parties, and smoking dope for amusement. She categorized it, six years later, as a "nice casual relationship." But it grew steadily over the next five years, and, listening to her describe its ups and downs, I could see something she could no longer face—it had been anything but "casual." At least, not for her. Lance was her future, her white knight, her admission ticket to the arena of matrimony.

Hollins College was a painless and easy transfer from high school. It had a gorgeous campus set high in the mountains of Roanoke, Virginia. One thousand women attended this sall traditional school; the graduate speech clinic had all of twenty-five men. As usual, Katy belonged to a conservative set. She and her "pack" were always clean, neat, and pretty, and lived all together in a dorm. By contrast, the students they thought of as "women's libbers"—weirdos—lived on a hill set apart from the quad. These were the first women she had ever met who were more interested in career than in men. "There were rumors that they were all lesbians," she revealed to me in a confidential tone. Shockingly, they dressed in peasant shirts and dirty dungarees, with long, greasy hair hanging down their backs. "They were a disgrace to the sex!" she remembers thinking.

These "queer" girls imported older women for a series of career workshops, a series which brought the "women's lib element" to campus. The Hollins girls were exhorted to "come out of the domesticized, servile . . . attitude that our mothers always had." At first, threatened, she didn't want to hear what they had to say; finally, she did go to one workshop, but made jokes about it. It never occurred to her to read feminist literature.

These "strange" young women were interested in their

studies and careers; Katy was not. She and her group were concerned only with partying, drinking, and being social. "We were sort of closed-minded," she remembers. "Into going out and getting married—getting a husband and never getting out of the South at all." Watching nationally visible feminists on TV, she thought their demands were too strident, "and they all looked like men." Feminists seemed to hate men, in fact, and this repelled her.

Predictably, she devoted her full time and energy to the opposite sex. Even in the non-liberated dorms, sneaking boys in and out of rooms was great sport. Over the summer after freshman year, she broke tradition by living with Lance while he took physics at Harvard Summer School. It was a compromise even a conservative girl had to make in those sexually open times. Besides, she thought of him as a serious future prospect, and he did satisfy her requirements for a socially appropriate beau. But they communicated very little about important things. As her mother had with Duncan, she acquiesced whenever they disagreed, bending over backward not to alienate him.

In the fall, she returned to Hollins for an aimless, druggy semester, and her parents decided something had to be done. In January of 1974, they put Katy on a plane bound for Paris. Each of the thirty-five girls in her year-abroad program lived with a different French family. She switched her major to French, and took courses in French conversation and art. In spare time, she and her friends traveled on Eurail passes.

The year abroad gave Katy a certain perspective. Living once again in a real home, she fell away from her brief flirtation with drugs. Returning to the United States, she found a new resolve: to enjoy her studies at home as much as she had in France. Now philosophy courses, film courses, history courses filled her schedule. She began to pull good grades, and made the honor roll for the first time. "I was a new person when I got back from Paris," she remembers.

It was clear: the time had come for her to settle down and

get serious. As usual, Duncan had been right. But what was there for her to get serious about? She was enjoying her studies more, but still saw little use for them after graduation. And Lance, a junior at Harvard, was not exhibiting the signs she wanted. He made no move to finalize the relationship. In fact, he seemed, if anything, to pay less and less attention to her. Promising to come for weekends and then standing her up, he disappointed her again and again. Slowly, Katy began to grow panicked. It was senior year— where was her engagement ring? What would she do at graduation if Lance didn't come through on bended knee?

Beginning to fear she had invested in him too heavily, she started dating someone else. It worked like a charm. Running to her side, Lance confessed his jealousy and begged her to take him back. She did—even without a proposal.

A compromise was reached. She would move to Boston after graduating and get a job there, while he finished his senior year at Harvard. Duncan objected—hoping she would take a secretarial job near home—but this time Katy prevailed. Although she had not left college with the expected diamond solitaire, she was sure that by the end of his senior year Lance would be willing to commit himself.

But she arrived in Cambridge to discover just how much Lance had changed up north. His goals and interests had altered radically, as he had fallen in with an extremely preppie crowd—complete with Brooks Brothers shirts, and heavy on the starch. Once a "good ol' boy" with limited resources, he now used all his spare money to pay social-climbing club dues. Most of his free time—incredibly—was spent on the back of a polo pony, instead of with Katy.

This would all have been fine with her had not Lance's attitude toward her undergone changes too. She had found her own apartment at the beginning of the school year and a job as a secretary. Now she worked behind a typewriter as her mother had years before. Even finding this meager job was "a very humbling experience."

But it didn't suit Lance's new self-image that the girl on his arm had no higher aspirations than secretary or housewife. Surrounded by career-oriented Radcliffe classmates, he pushed Katy to try for more. "He didn't appreciate that ... what I wanted out of life was to have a family." Lance's attitude was a symptom of the changing times, but Katy could not recognize it as such. Confused, she only felt the pressure brought to bear on her, pressure for which she was unprepared. She had never dreamed that to be socially successful she might have to be more than pretty, winsome, and charming. Other people had always defined her identity. Now Lance wanted her to play a role in which she felt totally inadequate. It was a crisis with which she simply couldn't cope.

At the time of my interview with her in June of 1978, Katy had a new job as "staff assistant" in the Harvard Office of Executive Programs in Health and Policy Management. Her weekly paycheck amounted to a take-home of $120. Unlike Lisa Matthews, she freely told me that her job requires much typing and phone answering. But she likes it anyway. She hoped that in the fall a reorganization of the department would bring her more responsibility and better pay; however, this did not impress me as a major concern. Although she had occasionally considered getting a graduate degree in education and doing art therapy with retarded children, she was rather lackadaisical and unmotivated about it. It simply is not what she wants most.

Slowly, she has begun to resent those friends at work who pressure her, as Lance did, to move up the employment ladder. After getting over her initial intimidation, she has finally begun to think seriously about who she is and what her personal ambitions really are. In the final analysis, she has decided she is much more similar to her old conservative classmates at Hollins than to these newly independent women at work. As she described these old friends to me, she seemed to be really talking about herself. "They want to be back in that period when a girl graduated from college and there were plenty of men around who wanted wives. [They wanted] to get married, and settle down, and raise a family, and not have to be burdened with the thought that they have to go out and find a job to prove themselves—especially when they have no skills. . . . Then they have to go and learn to type and get stuck in shit jobs."

As Lance put increasing pressure on her for career, she began to realize that a breakoff was inevitable. He simply didn't want the kind of future she did. Finally, in October of 1977, after more neglect on his part, she wrote him a self-protective "dear John" letter. At this point, he begged her to marry him, but she had had enough. Almost unconsciously, she became more and more convinced that all she wanted in life was family, with enough freedom to pursue her extracurricular interests. She didn't know how she was going to make it happen, but she certainly was determined.

In December of 1977, she met Michael Rosenthal, now her fiancé. It took them little time to get close. Michael currently works in a lab at Harvard. They spend a lot of time together. He is often busy at night, and sometimes she goes with him to the lab to watch him work. I could see from her description that Katy had finally found a man to share her goals. They planned to be married in June of 1979.

Then she dramatically told me the story of her engagement ring. It was a story that symbolized just how far from her background she has gone on her search for such a man. The ring came from Poland, the only family treasure to survive World War II and Michael's parents' endurance tests in concentration camps.

Katy knows little about Judaism, and clearly does not perceive the strong, often unspoken sense of identification which is part and parcel of being a Jew. Nor does she perceive the xenophobia. She was surprised by the Rosenthals' shared sense of heritage as they watched the TV series *Holocaust*. Although they never speak of the war, she told me that evening she could have touched its immense weight behind the wall that divides past and present. Once, on college vacation, she had visited Dachau and Treblinka, but its impact did not come home. That night, she saw only too clearly: what was only fiction to her is part of the Rosenthals', and Michael's, history.

While these aspects of Judaism set Michael and his parents apart from Katy, they also provoke a reaction to which she strongly relates. After watching their world shatter into nullity, the Rosenthals, like many other Jews, find family uniquely precious. Although Michael was born after his parents left the camps, they have passed on to him this urgent sense of preserving continuity through the home.

Michael is basically atheistic; he and Katy have no strict specific religious beliefs which come into conflict. They plan to be married in a secular service and raise their children in a non-religious home—but one replete with the warmth of family tradition. Of utmost importance are their joint expectations: Michael wants his wife to raise their children and care for the home. Naturally, Katy agrees. She has gone far afield to find a husband, farther than she would have dreamed of going had she been born twenty years before. But now she is content. "I have no qualms about my husband being the breadwinner, or having higher degrees than I do," she says happily. "I'd much rather enjoy art, reading, and nature outside, and take my kids for a stroll, than sit in an office."

She is increasingly in touch with her own down-home drives. "I'm thinking maybe it's not [my] calling to rise up the ladder and improve [myself]. It's been the most frustrating thing to me because everyone says, 'What are you going to do with yourself?' and I say I don't know.... I feel pressured when [I feel] people are going to judge me."

Katy loves working with her hands and has become quite adept at the precise, fluid strokes required for elegant calligraphy. She believes, and not unreasonably, that this is a hobby which will mix well with child raising. She is determined not to fall dormant or idle.

Because she has accepted not having a real career, because

she is happy with that decision and is finally beginning to deal with the peer pressure, Katy now has the self-assurance to admit a carefully tempered brand of feminism into her life. In the past few years, her mother's marriage to Duncan has taught her a powerful lesson. As a child, Katy watched Ann's whole world revolve around her husband; what he said was law, without question. Recently, Ann has begun standing up to him in small ways, making her presence known. Katherine, with her spunky spirit, has supported her mother in this. Now she feels it is important to keep commitment to a man in perspective. "I'm not going to go through what my mother went through. I'm not going to lose contact with the world when I start raising my children and just devote my life to them and to my husband, thinking of him as a god. He's a companion, the father of my kids, someone to grow with. Someone to talk to. And when he comes home at night, I want to be able to tell him more than how many diapers I changed."

Her position, she feels, is one of compromise with the present. But, getting down to brass tacks, her life and future expectations are patterned closely on her mother's example, although she is glad to be out of the South, where men still dominate their women totally. "My stepbrothers have wives who are already staying home with the kids while their husbands go out and play basketball," she said with disgust. On the other hand, her relief over not being a career woman is enormous. Finally everything seems in balance. Katy Townsend will gladly be a housewife—just so long as she is the housewife with a difference.

Five

Karin Blake

What was still a dream of the future for Katy Townsend was everyday reality for Karin Blake. Karin was the first bona fide housewife and mother I interviewed. The idea of meeting this traditional woman piqued my curiosity: would she be one of the "walking dead," or might she actually have dared to be happy?

She lived in a large, rambling farmhouse in Wayland, Massachusetts, with a wide front porch and acres of open land. Privacy. Lots of room to play. As I drove up the driveway in my VW Rabbit in mid-March 1978, I was stopped by a three-foot blond policeman who directed traffic from a knee-high puddle. With three muddy fingers, he authoritatively pointed out where I should park.

We gravely discussed the depth of his small ocean, then I walked up to the screen door, found it open, and let myself into a busy kitchen. Seated at the long wooden trestle table was another small boy, younger than the first, but just as cloaked in peanut butter as his brother had been with mud.

Karin Blake poked her head around the edge of the refrigerator door and asked me to sit down. Coffee appeared. The peanut-butter orgy on the other side of the table continued, and I feared for the life of my tape recorder. As we began talking, I watched her youngest get that childhood staple into eyes, hair, nose, and ears.

The circumstances of the interview were by far the most chaperoned I had encountered to date. I wondered how I could ask Karin when she lost her virginity with a big-eared child staring at me. But despite the lack of real privacy—even during nap time the boys proved irrepressible—this was simply not a place you could feel uncomfortable. Here there was clutter and noise and the humid scent of wet snowsuits drying on the radiator. It was a picture of grandma's kitchen in the Welch's grape jelly commerical—but it was real.

I couldn't help but compare the atmosphere to the solitude and calm, undisturbed waters of the bachelorette apartments I had been through. And, although Karin's home was filled with interruption and therefore frustration—on my part at least—it was undeniably like being back in the womb.

Finally she sat down with me, the midmorning shadows in the kitchen accenting the bones in her face. With the children tugging at the long sweater vest she wore over her dungarees, we began to talk about her childhood. Gradually, I came to understand that she had created such a home because it had been a part of her from the very day she was born.

In 1949, Karin became the second child in a traditional Episcopalian family that lived in a small provincial town outside an industrial city in western Massachusetts. Kathleen and Richard Byrnes had married early and promptly begun on their brood of four. They were average suburban people in an average suburban neighborhood. Bringing up the four kids was quite a struggle, since the family relied solely on what Richard could bring home as a fledgling insurance salesman. Kathleen ran the household full time. Thus, male and female roles were clearly defined from the start as breadwinner and homemaker.

Typically, too, they sometimes bickered about money—the only real sore spot in a solid marriage. Even so, they tried to shelter the children from this source of tension, hoping family warmth would act as a stabilizer. It did, on the whole. "They really busted ass for their kids," Karin remembers fondly. The arguments taught her an early and important lesson: even in hard times, the Byrnes clan stayed together. It was one thing you could count on.

Despite the hustle and bustle of everyday living, both Karin's parents spent a great deal of time with the children. Richard, an only child, now reveled in his great troop of playmates; Kathleen knitted endlessly, mitten after mitten, sweater after sweater.

Basically, Richard Byrnes was a traditionalist who put his children above all else. Conservative to the core, he set an early example of honesty and hard work for everyone to emulate. One year, when the IRS audited his tax return, an agent made a deep impression on Karin when she overheard him say he'd "never seen income taxes that were so straight." Richard's opinion carried great weight in the household, and inevitably he expected to be obeyed. Like Lisa Matthews's dad, he tried early on to wall his daughters off from the hostile outside world. The message was clear: women were weaker and needed to be protected.

Self-confident, articulate, Karin's father could debate any issue dispassionately. In contrast, Kathleen would often get so involved in a discussion that she would run rings around herself. She shied away from arguments with their inevitable defeats. And so, as role models, Karin's parents followed a stereotyped pattern—an emotional woman whose word carried little weight, backed up by a strong, rational man who ruled his roost with conviction. The Byrnes family had government by absolute monarchy. A wife was a royal courtesan who maneuvered for the favors of the king—but a courtesan to whom the children turned for nurturing in times of crisis.

Several times during Karin's childhood, Richard uprooted the family to follow employment opportunities. Karin hated these moves. They forced her into the position of being a new girl in school every few years. Gradually, she developed an insecure feeling of unpopularity—a feeling she would spend many years trying to overcome. At an early age, she realized that belonging to an established group was very important.

To add to her feelings of being an outsider, the subject she did best in—math—was not deemed particularly appropriate for a young girl. Quickly she learned to feel uneasy about her prowess in a man's field, and set about to minimize it. After all, even her father thought it inappropriate for her—in contrast to his clear interest in Karin's brothers' math grades. "Pretty is as pretty does," would be his only comment to his daughters.

Naturally, Karin's future orientation had already begun to move in the direction to which her father pointed. She didn't think in terms of schooling or career; mostly, she wanted to grow up to "be nice," a happy housewife like her mother. Career, her father said, was a poor substitute for motherhood.

Not until adolescence was her self-image fortified with a little more self-esteem. The Byrneses were getting more prosperous, and in te seventh grade she made a final switch—to a posh private school in an elite Boston suburb. Her sense of academic limitation would never leave, but from then until graduation in 1967 she finally began to make permanent friends and achieve some status with her peers. In 1964, on the rise, Richard moved the family to Brookline, a nearby town. The new house was a formal brick residence with buzzers and servants' quarters—formalities that the Byrneses never used, needless to say. Nevertheless, it would give them an air of social elegance; it would lead Karin to expect more from her own future. With the new prosperity, her parents' marriage looked more and more secure. Old tensions dissipated. It was a good example for a girl entering womanhood.

Karin was now an adolescent. At an age when most of her friends were beginning to question their parents' authority, she was more and more her father's daughter. Almost without realizing it, she paid less and less attention to her studies, despite natural gifts. She hated the rigid academic environment; instructors classified her as a bright "under-achiever." Already she had tracked herself into a future where her academic standing would not carry great weight.

In sharp contrast, she became overwhelmingly interested in a predictable new hobby—boys. Having reached her full five-foot-seven height early, she was taller than some of them, but that didn't stop her. She loved dancing school, discovering a new forte—being blond, blue-eyed, and attractive. As an added bonus, girls were attracted to her, too. Soon she was one of the most popular in her class.

While most of Karin's classmates didn't date at all, she was often busy with boys from local private schools, or even with ones in college. This pleased Richard immensely; in fact, if she turned down a date, he would grow immediately concerned. By junior year, she even had a steady—a freshman from Harvard. It was not coincidence that she chose a young man from her father's alma mater. For the next several years, she would continually be attracted to men who closely resembled her dad—traditional, Ivy League, strong, and very moral. In fact, she would not finally settle down until she had found someone as strong as Richard Byrnes, someone who resisted putting her on a pedestal.

Her nature conservative, Karin fully intended to be a virgin when she married. She had no doubts. Her peers in the all-female academy agreed. "That school produced more virgins," she chortled. "Men were almost people you had children by because you had to. It was the middle of the Dark Ages there." Sex was not an issue on her dates with her steady. Martin Bauer did not press for more than a goodnight kiss, even after two years: he wanted to marry an untouched woman.

Karin's father had squelched her early pride in her math ability. Now, with his daughter a teen-ager, Richard Byrnes made certain no extracurricular interests would mistakenly turn into ambitions. One year, after she had worked in a summer playhouse for several months, she came back to Brookline full of ideas about being an actress. Richard was unimpressed and let her know it in no uncertain terms. Then he set about to protect his daughter from herself, thinking he knew best: he hired a professional acting teacher from New York to come and listen to Karin audition. On cue, the woman confirmed his belief that Karin had "no talent."

Her other jobs, far less fanciful, were also typically female. Mostly, she baby-sat. It was a preview of the future she expected. "Careers for women didn't start until I was in college," she recalls. "You were a secretary or got married, and it was obviously better to get married."

Still, she always planned to go to college—because she hoped to find a husband there. Being well educated was important—even her mother had gone to Vassar. Moreover, her academy pressured its students to shoot for elite Seven Sister schools. Karin was particularly interested in the University of Pennsylvania, and really wanted to go somewhere coed. But Richard, still firmly at the helm, said no. He also wanted her within easy reach: she couldn't apply to schools more than one hundred miles from home.

Ultimately, working within her father's restrictions, she applied to Smith, Connecticut, and Bradford, hoping for the former. Even with extraordinarily high board scores and a sound overall record, no one encouraged her to stretch beyond those colleges. Most discouraging was her interview at Smith, where she was told that her interest in mathematics was unfortunate, since as a women's institution, Smith was not interested in math majors. Even in 1967, then, her early lessons on subjects appropriate for women were being reinforced.

Connecticut, on the other hand, welcomed her skill, and it seemed a good second choice when Smith rejected her. At her high school, "Conn" was considered an "almost Seven Sister," she recalls, "for people who didn't get into Smith." The rejection was probably not that bitter a pill, I reflected, considering her traditional ambitions.

Connecticut was a small all-women's suitcase school when she entered it in September 1967. She lived in a dorm on the pretty rural campus, and majored in math. Despite the isolated nature of the college, Karin hoped to broaden her horizons—to meet new people and ideas, to expose herself to an outside world she'd never seen, and to meet a man. But to her distress, she soon found that Conn was as cloistered as high school had been. Before long, she hated it. The school was academically unchallenging. Even advanced calculus was so easy she slept through it and still got an A. Gradually, lack of interest began to take its toll. Rebelling, she refused to participate in zoology's dissection sessions, and so drew an F for the semester. But it really didn't seem to matter. Zoology was irrelevant to her future as a housewife.

Still, the issue of her future was in many ways the root of her dissatisfaction with Conn. She had met no boys she really liked or who had really liked her. No one measured up to the standards her father's example had set years ago. Besides, engagement rings were rarer and rarer among her older friends at Conn. Each year, more graduating seniors set forth toward careers, and Karin wanted nothing to do with it. By sophomore year, she began to look for a way out. She told her dean that she wanted to transfer to Penn—a coed school. The dean vehemently attempted to convince her that such a choice would be a mistake; later, in fact, Karin would feel that this woman sabotaged her transfer. Whatever the real reason, she didn't get in—a result greeted by a loud chorus of "I told you so's" from her father.

Had she truly been interested in transferring, I felt, she would have made several applications, not banked on just one. Or she might have fought harder against the dean's objections. Blaming someone else for her failure was just an excuse to cover her decision to drop out entirely that fall, never to return to college. In fact, she left school for specific, though unconscious, reasons. Her goal was to raise a family; college was supposed to have been a place to twiddle her thumbs while waiting for the appropriate fiancé. But Connecticut had proved a poor meeting ground for future marriage partners. Surely she could find useful work in an area where the prospects were better.

Karin had expected to spend four years treading water in college, away from home. Now, out of school and living with her parents—whom she partly blamed for her predicament— she started pounding the pavement, looking for any job that

would pay her own rent. Resentful, she turned down a position Richard got for her and took instead a lowly job in a
student information booth at the Harvard Business School.

The work was boring and "stupid"; the men around her
were neither. She was thrilled.

Then a bit of luck came her way. The secretary to the
director of admissions took a temporary leave of absence,
and the director found her so adept that he eventually asked
her to remain permanently. When he was promoted to dean
of students, she went along as his assistant. Now a typewriter
was no longer the center of her desk. She started to compose
his letters and weaseled her way into faculty meetings—
where only corporation appointees were allowed—to take the
minutes. "I handled everything," she told me, voice tinged
with pleasure, "from sewing on his buttons to sending his
wife roses on their anniversary. . . . I was organized enough
to do everything for him."

She finally felt appreciated. Here, efficiency and organization counted. The job was exactly what her parents had
raised her to do. She was her boss's alter ego, in some ways
practically his wife.

She worked at the Business School from 1969 to 1972,
years when the Women's Movement was, in some ways, in its
most vocal, most visible stages. The Equal Rights Amendment, stalled in committee for forty-seven years, was finally
brought before the House of Representatives. President
Richard Nixon's Secretary of Labor announced the first affir-
mative action quotas for women in federal contracts. Major
corporations who were accused of discriminating against
women—such as AT&T and Corning Glass—were forced to
sign consent decrees with the federal government.

But Karin's experience with feminism was minimal, even
though she worked for a university whose students were
politically quite radical. The lack of interest was no accident.
The basic premises of the Women's Movement were a threat
to a girl whose goals revolved around being an efficient
organizer in either the business world or a home. Deliber-

ately holding herself aloof, she made excuses for her non-participation. "I worked with people who were between five and thirty-five years older than I was, and women's lib was kind of a joke to them." She felt Harvard treated its women employees fabulously; yet when I asked about her salary, she evaded the question by telling me that "everyone" at Harvard was "underpaid."

I had received similar answers from Lisa Matthews and Katy Townsend about their jobs. It was an excuse I found again and again among women without specific career aspirations. They were happy with what they had. They didn't care to fight for rights; a nine-to-five job was far more than they had ever really expected. More and more, it struck me that they did not even perceive that real discrimination against women existed. Even Karin did not see this, although she worked for a bastion of "male supremacy" which was under student attack for the painfully few women numbered among its ranks of tenured professors. When Gloria Steinem came to speak at Harvard during Karin's years there, she went with some friends. "Nobody listened to anything she said," Karin told me, to my amazement. Then she made the most telling comment of all. "But, boy, was she sexy-looking."

Despite her deliberate distance from feminism and all it represented, it continued to affect her life. No matter how she might rationalize, it was obvious that secretarial work and homemaking were becoming unfashionable. Moreover, most of her friends, who had remained in college until graduation, were headed for new and different careers—real careers. With her traditional goals, Karin was in limbo.

Naturally, she still kept her eyes peeled for anything that looked like a potential husband. In the fall of 1969, she began dating David Blake, a twenty-seven-year-old Vietnam veteran, just back from duty overseas. A Harvard graduate—of course—he was applying to the Business School. For the first time in her life, she came up against a man who was a constant challenge. He was more like Richard than any of the others had been—he didn't let her get away with anything. And he could not have appeared at a more opportune time: she was twenty and starting to worry.

In the fall of 1970, he entered Harvard Business School. Sometime during that year, she told me very reticently, she finally made that quantum leap into womanhood—relinquishing her virginity. By fall of 1971, when she was twenty-two, they were engaged and living together—but secretly. Back in 1969, the undergraduate dorms at Karin's beloved Harvard had gone coed, and even seventeen-year-olds could spend the night together openly. Still, a full two years later, the conservative Karin Byrnes drove mornings to the B-School with her twenty-nine-year-old fiancé hiding on the car floor.

In June 1972, after David graduated, they married; she was almost as young as her mother had been upon marrying Richard. Soon they moved to Washington, D.C., where a job under Elliot Richardson at HEW awaited him. Karin took temporary work as a production assistant to the NBC news team planning the coverage of Nixon's second inauguration. Her work was interesting, often taking her into the White House, but she loathed the people on the team. "At NBC all they discussed was sex and cars," she told me. "They didn't give a hot damn when [back in 1968] Bobby Kennedy was shot—but only if NBC was on television with it first." NBC paid her double her Harvard salary, but they felt entitled to treat her twice as badly, she claims. Clearly, she cared little for the obvious career advancement.

Meanwhile, her marriage was shaping up traditionally. She took care of the home, expecting little help. At first, David complained that she was not as intellectually oriented as he, telling her she "didn't read enough." After a while, however, he came to accept it. Nevertheless, pressured by their acquaintances to keep in fashion, she did decide to continue working for a while. Children would have to wait. Now that she was securely married, she could afford to flirt a little with feminism.

In January 1973, her NBC job ended. Just as she was starting to look for another, she discovered she was pregnant. Considering her public decision to put on a liberated face, the news was hardly welcome. As was also fashionable in the early 1970s, she began to consider an abortion.

But David really wanted the baby. Each night after he came home from work, they would discuss it at length—with the proviso that the final choice would be hers alone. For many weeks, she remained ambivalent. Then, at a ceramics course she was taking, another woman actually offered to buy the prospective child. Suddenly, something snapped. Her deep-seated traditionalism surfaced and she began to accept the idea that she would not return to work until after the child was born. Richard, of course, predicted that she would never return to work at all, and this, curiously, incensed her. For a long time, she persisted in the notion that her time off was only a maternity leave.

Finally, half a year later, she grudgingly had to concede that she enjoyed being a mother—much as her own mother obviously had. It was an emotional admission of the conventional woman she always was and probably will always be.

The realization began with the uplifting experience of delivering by natural childbirth; she felt new confidence in herself as a woman. "It makes you say, 'I gave birth to this kid and I can raise him better than anyone else.' " Then, staying home with the baby brought a special kind of fulfillment.

Following up on that first good experience, she had her second son—the peanut-butter maniac—in March of 1976. Since then, she has lived at home and never looked back. She firmly believes that her instincts as a mother far exceed those of any nanny she could hire. This attitude was reinforced one day while the family played baseball in a nearby field. Her youngest son wandered into the road while his mother's attention was turned elsewhere. Instinctively, Karin felt danger before she had even turned around. Running with the wind at her back, she was able to vault a four-foot fence and get to him ahead of her husband, plucking the child off the highway to safety.

Karin was almost the only woman I interviewed who could freely admit how important it was for her to be a mother. To deny this code, to go against the way she was raised, would have been to go against an integral part of her being. A chic job was just less essential. In addition, she likes the leisure of being a housewife. She has relished taking photography courses, pottery, and weaving. Her time at home is a luxury.

Still, she does plan to return to work once her children are of school age—just as Betty Friedan herself did. In fact, this is currently a major goal. "I think the hardest thing about having kids is the fact that you come last," she told me. "Your husband squeaks in as second place, and your kids are first. . . . I would like to . . . have a job of my own and do something for myself." She can cope with her current altruism because she views her life as open-ended. Eventually, she will be pleased to take any job that interests her, even "going back to typing" or working as a volunteer. She is not motivated by real ambition. "I wouldn't take the best job in the world with people that I hated." She would enjoy getting into politics or health administration, and sometimes dreams wishfully of writing articles part time for *Gourmet* magazine.

If anything, Karin feels the Women's Movement has made her life more difficult; it is hardly chic to be a wife and mother. She never believed she was oppressed as a woman; still, she acknowledges that feminism and the changing times have enabled her to win a small measure of freedom. When she and her husband go away and sleep in single beds, she insists, to her mother's horror, that David make his own. She can now make small distinctions between Kathleen's life and her own—despite their inherent similarities. "Women's lib," she says, "has made for more turmoil between David and me. I decide what are my priorities . . . I have the right to decide what's important to me, not what was important for my mother." This small step toward feminism reminded me of the limited freedoms Katy Townsend revels in.

She believes that the Equal Rights Amendment should be passed, but had one revealing reservation about it. "I'm not sure that women should have pregnancy leaves," she told me. "You've got to decide whether you want to have a kid . . . or whether you want to have a job." She firmly believes that kids raised by women who try to do both wind up being badly adjusted.

As I left Karin that windswept afternoon, one scene in particular stuck in my mind—a startling commentary on her life and that of her peers, and on how her family has become an integral part of her identity. In 1977, she returned to her high school for her class's tenth reunion, to discover something that would have amazed anyone had it happened in a previous generation: at the ripe age of twenty-eight, a class of forty-six women had produced exactly four mothers. And there was an even more curious aspect to that already strange afternoon; while Kathleen Byrnes had raised her daughter along ultra-conventional lines, for Karin—as for most young women today, caught between past and present—convention is no longer what it used to be. "I went to my reunion thinking I could hardly wait to ask the actress what she was doing—or the teacher, or the writer. . . . Instead, I was surrounded by people who wanted to know what it was like to have kids!" Karin shook her head incredulously, joyously. "All of a sudden *I* was the different one."

Six

Sarah Suskind

Karin Blake and Sarah Diamond both sought security, intimacy, and family warmth from an early age, but there all similarity ceased. Karin's insecurity began with her early school experience, and when she felt unhappy, she instinctively retreated to the shelter of home. For Sarah, even family left much to be desired, creating mostly persistent feelings of isolation. Rachel and Seth Diamond often stayed out late, leaving her alone with only the maid; Sarah frequently awoke from nightmares, crying for her parents in the early hours of the morning. Although they continually reassured her that they were only out for an evening, she lived with the irrational fear that they would never come home.

One night when she was twelve years old, she woke up crying; going to their bedroom, she found it empty. Her older sister was away at college; once again she was alone with the hired help. Finally, at 5 A.M., her uncle called. Rachel and Seth had been driving home on the expressway. They had collided with a truck; her mother had a broken nose, fractured ribs, and a concussion. Dimly, over the fear echoing through her head, Sarah heard her uncle say that her parents would be all right.

The incident, although a single occurrence, was emblematic. Sarah had felt alone most of her life, and she'd always hated it. Born in 1949 to parents already in their forties, preceded by a sister seven years her senior and followed by no one, she felt like an only, lonely child. This sense of remoteness persisted throughout adolescence, even though a remarkable resemblance to Marilyn Monroe kept boys crowded on her doorstep. Not until she married, in 1977, when she was twenty-eight years old, did she finally feel secure. Only then could she look back to see the wasted, unhappy years spent in pursuit of a professional orientation; for a decade, her mother and her own peer group had silently pressured Sarah to adopt something that never really suited her. Only a new intimate partnership could finally provide the close connections, the warmth, the feeling of belonging she had wanted desperately as a child.

Born and raised in Manhattan, Sarah Diamond Suskind lives there still, in a Fifth Avenue apartment with high ceilings, parquet floors, elaborate furniture, carpets, and drapes. We sat cross-legged on her king-size bed, informally, with coffee and the tape recorder between us. It was July 1977, before I had even contracted for this book. Sarah was the second person I interviewed, a striking woman with carefully coiffed blond hair, a voluptuous figure, and brilliant green eyes framed by thick lashes. Open, able to talk of her past very freely, she was less nervous than I and put me immediately at ease.

She had come from an environment many would envy: a rich family that spared little expense; even during the depression her father had made ends meet. But by the early 1950s, when Sarah was a toddler, the large business he owned kept him extremely busy. She missed him terribly. She looked up to him with a certain degree of awe; fair-minded and just, a giver of security, he was a distant but powerful example.

Her mother was a different story. With a master's degree under her belt and working for a Ph.D., Rachel Brown had given up a teaching career, reluctantly, to marry Seth Diamond and have children. She had been a very independent woman by 1930s standards; still, to her younger child, action spoke louder than words, and by the 1950s Rachel was mostly a housewife and mother.

In years to come, Rachel would transmit her stunted career ambitions to her youngest daughter, urging her to make something of herself. But, in reality, this was the last thing Sarah wanted to hear. The pressure from her mother would raise a central question that spun, Russian-roulette style, through her life: should she do as her mother said, or as her mother had done?

Very ambitious for their daughter from the start, the Diamonds enrolled Sarah in one of New York's most socially prominent and academically competitive schools for girls—an intellectual pressure cooker. In the thirteen years she went there, Sarah felt she never had a social life. On weekends, the students worked, nothing else. Besides, there was always the unspoken pressure from her mother, a pressure to achieve. As a result, peer involvement was limited; Sarah spent most of her time at home, alone. In this driven environment, her destiny was charted clearly even in the early years. "I don't think I ever wanted to get married," she told me. "I would [try to decide] whether I wanted to be a lawyer or a doctor."

Nevertheless, in all that time alone, she couldn't help but dream a little. She truly adored a very traditional girls' pastime: playing with baby dolls. Underneath, despite the professional ethic her mother drilled into her, Sarah sought connections, intimacies. Her favorite book was indicative of her real fantasies: *The Little Princess,* where an orphan revels in the love and warmth of a new parent.

Sports also gave her great pleasure; they were one small way she could draw closer to her mother and father, both of whom were very athletic. Even here, however, she was pushed to develop major skills in those activities that allowed her to excel on her own: ballet, figure skating, tennis, waterskiing. Nothing was informal or non-competitive.

Even in her small private school, too, Sarah continued to feel like an isolated outsider. The families who sent their daughters there were mostly New York old money—rich, Wasp, and somewhat anti-Semitic. Often Sarah was excluded from parties and dances. The Diamonds, although Jewish, were not particularly religious. Thus, Sarah's heritage closed some avenues without opening others. Her ethnicity was almost a total loss.

Her parents' advanced age did more than simply distance

them from her—it also set her apart from her peers. Ashamed of them, she often looked up to adults who were younger and more emotionally accessible—counselors at camp, her older sister's college friends. It was terribly important that they be young, pretty, and popular. Unconsciously looking for a different role model from the one Rachel provided, Sarah made Elizabeth Taylor an early heroine. On the other hand, Perry Mason, the hard-fighting but wise lawyer, was her hero. Even then, her idols revealed the essential conflict: the star attorney—patterned after her successful father but conveniently fulfilling her mother's desire for a career-oriented daughter—or the sex goddess—adored, worshiped, ageless, and never alone.

Little changed for her as she moved into high school years. She was still unhappy. Her favorite subject was history: it allowed her to escape into other worlds, other cultures. She continued to excel in nearly every class, doing as her parents expected and hoping to please them. By now, she had finally found some measure of camaraderie. She belonged to a small intellectual clique concerned with "ideas." They believed themselves the original bohemians; internal examination and self-discovery were the prerequisites for membership. "Our focus was, 'Is there a God?' or 'What happens when you die?' " she now says, laughing.

Meanwhile, she and all her high school classmates were slowly being funneled toward college. It was not something they even bothered to talk about, but something they simply accepted. "College, after the ninth grade, was the goal, the be-all and the end-all of everything you did." Despite this orientation, Sarah really had no plan for her future. She continued to hope she would never be in a position where she would need a career. But she couldn't admit it—publicly, or to herself.

Still, with a solid B-plus average, she applied to several good women's colleges. Competitive on the one hand, ambivalent on the other, she felt ashamed compared to her friends who were "Radcliffe material." Although her grades were quite good, a real lack of motivation kept her from applying to the top schools. Besides, what could be more threatening for a marriage-oriented girl than the highly competitive, professionally preparatory Seven Sisters? Instead, she stuck with institutions which were not so oriented toward careers for women—Wheaton, Sweet Briar, Mills.

An incisive commentary, Sarah felt, on high-powered women was one of her best friends from school. A brilliant girl with 800s on her SATs, president of student government during senior year, Sally Parker was second in the class at graduation. But shortly thereafter she suffered a nervous breakdown and ended up in a mental institution. Sarah saw a direct correlation between her friend's insanity and her brilliant mind. Risking such isolation for the glory of intellectual excellence was a gamble Sarah simply would not take. "Look where it all got her," she told me bitterly, pain surfacing in her eyes. Sally never even had a chance to establish herself in a relationship with a man, and so the disaster of her friend's broken life was the epitome of Sarah's fear—alone, behind locked doors, she had no one but the voices in her head.

In reality, then, she had little in common with her high-powered classmates. She was far more conservative politically and intellectually than she could ever let on. Most of all, she was silently—unconsciously—searching for a man. But even with her stunning looks, for a girl who went to an all-female school that wasn't an easy problem to solve. She didn't really go out with a boy until the end of eleventh grade.

For quite a while, she played the field, but then, in her eighteenth year, someone new walked into the limelight. A sharp young man from a poor family, Curt Robertson didn't intend to be poor for very long. He possessed real drive, the kind Sarah could only dream of mustering for herself. Unlike other boys of his age, he had a certain veneer, a self-confident sense of himself. Smooth, good-looking, "he could charm a snake out of a hole," she recalls. Sarah hitched her wagon to his star. Still aimless, although pushed constantly by her mother, she bent over backwards with the unconscious hope that his direction might rub off on her; or, that he would somehow take care of her.

Sarah's parents had never educated her about sex; now Curt undertook the task with pleasure—although she did not finally relinquish her virginity until age twenty. At last, however, she had something of herself to give, something someone else wanted. It was the intimacy she had always craved.

The relationship lasted from 1966, her last year of high school, until 1971, her college graduation. In many ways, it was the perfect compromise for her. While her mother and peers propelled her toward a career, she could fall back safely on the security a steady boyfriend provided. Of course, in that respect, a wedding ring would have been better—but Sarah was not desperate about that yet. Her mother hadn't married until thirty-one; a woman had to be pretty far along before she became an old maid.

Graduation from high school was a major event, and in Sarah's mind the future stretched out to an invisible horizon. In the fall of 1967, she entered the small all-girls Mills College in Oakland, California. She chose a school so far from home unconsciously, and yet deliberately. Her college years, she hoped, would be a break from the past, a break from her mother's demands, a break from the restrictions high school had imposed upon her. But it was not to be. At Mills, the gap widened between her hidden traditional ambitions and the more modern ones she had to wear as a public façade. The burgeoning Women's Movement aggravated her confusion over the future. It gathered force just in time to sweep her peers into the mainstream of its current and to render Sarah's unspoken goals an embarrassment. It became increasingly clear that educated women simply did not squander their talents on marriage and motherhood.

And so she drove her traditional urges even further underground. As feminism fought to open doors for women throughout the country, it simultaneously closed the one door Sarah had been trying to avoid but toward which she felt inexorably drawn. Because feminism inevitably threatened what she most wanted, she unconsciously held herself aloof, in a neutral, uncommitted stance, only participating enough not to appear different from everyone else. The idea of being a woman to whom career represented the most important facet of life would have terrified Sarah if she had allowed herself to consider the ramifications.

Quickly, she became more and more confused. Her world began to revolve around drugs and her work slowed to a grinding and final halt. Friends became far more important than anything she could learn in a classroom, and she fell in with a rowdy crowd, made up chiefly of foreigners. Her new life-style served a more useful purpose than mere escape: smoking dope wasn't all that different from drinking beer at a fraternity bash—both ensured a good social life and no academic standing. She also swung right into the social activism that swept the campuses in the late 1960s. Berkeley, only a few hours away, set the pace, and students in neighboring institutions did a war dance in time to the drums. The black movement appealed to Sarah; never before a political joiner, she now became a ringleader. She was determined to really belong—particularly in anything which could successfully distract her from her own future and the work required to make it happen. When black students at Mills took over the president's office, Sarah made sure she was in the forefront— a white Jewish American princess from New York City, pounding his desk and making radical demands.

Although the Women's Movement was also a big campus issue, Sarah did not choose to become involved. To fight for black issues—that would never affect her personally—was not threatening. Nevertheless, to keep up her image, she took a few courses in women's rights, did the standard feminist reading, and subscribed to *Ms.* magazine. She began using the slogans of the day as tools to defend against the "sexists" she encountered. In public, she said the independent career woman—someone who lived alone and never needed a man—was her ideal. Still, inexplicably, unconsciously, she curbed her natural aggressive tendencies in an effort not to drive men off.

In fact, her plans for the future were no more definite than they had been, and all this pressure for a career was becoming more and more uncomfortable to deal with. Still, when asked whether she was a women's libber, she always answered yes. Truly confused about whom to be, she felt frozen in between.

The men who came to the Mills campus professed to favor women's rights. She doubted it. Most young males, in her experience, believed that "a woman's place is in the bed." The men she dated wanted a good-looking woman who would threaten them neither with intelligence nor with ideas about traditional commitment. A girl had to straddle the fence in order to be popular. And, naturally, when it came to sex, all the men were big on liberation. "Either they were all for you being liberal about sex, just as long as you were only liberal with them, or there were some men who—if you weren't in a really heavy relationship—were for you being liberal with all men because then you'd be liberal with them." She continued to fly back and forth to spend weekends with Curt at Brown, but when, in her absence, he began to date other women and to sleep around as well, she followed suit. She still chose men who would dominate her, always as smart as or smarter than herself. She needed a strong man whose direction would make up for her dearth.

By senior year, Curt had receded into the background and she felt their relationship was deteriorating. It had become increasingly clear that he was not going to make a commitment to her. By college graduation, she put an end to the "charade."

When Sarah entered Mills, she had had no expectations of emerging with a career plan. "I was just going to go," she explains. "I had no hopes to fulfill. I never put myself in a position to be disillusioned, because I never started out with any particular idea in mind." But if she was safe from disappointment, she was not safe from the endless questions of her parents and peers about what she would do with herself afterwards. She hated those questions, hated having to say she didn't know. She thought perhaps she'd be a professor of French literature, but made no preparations, planned nothing which would help her follow through. In fact, by nearly flunking out, she almost ensured that she would do nothing at all. She simply did not believe that she *could* be a successful career woman, and, in truth, she had finally begun to realize she did not *want* to be one.

Even at this point of internal crisis, Sarah did not allow herself to think consciously of marriage; she ignored the question of how she would support herself. In 1971, graduation dawned with the crashing realization that she did not have even a single plan for the rest of her life.

Returning to New York, she took a little history part time toward a graduate degree. That lasted six months. Then she went to work selling at a department store. Desperately, she tried to find a niche for herself; meanwhile, her mother was pushing, pushing for the big career-oriented move. In response, she took the entrance examination for law school, but the results were discouraging. A school of social work was the next avenue of approach, but this too drifted away. Finally, she settled down with a job in her father's company. She could no longer fool anyone, not even herself, into thinking she was actively seeking a career.

The guilt was boundless. She had betrayed her mother's dreams, she had betrayed the new social codes set by her peers. But her own needs conflicted with what others expected, and so, in an attempt to work out her life, she went into psychotherapy. Gradually, over several wandering years, she began to relax about who she really was and what she really wanted. Little by little, she let go of the façade she had clutched for so many years. Living alone in her own apartment, she learned to tolerate her isolation. Slowly, a new side of Sarah began to emerge, began to surface—the traditional, modeled on what her mother had done, not what she had said. Slowly, she grew more comfortable with her new identity and pushed guilt over a lost career to the back burner.

In 1973, she found that which she had sought for so long:

Alan Suskind, a thirty-one-year-old vice-president in her father's company. He had but a single defect—a wedding ring.
Over the next several years, Alan and Sarah grew closer and
closer as friends. Finally, they stopped denying the inevitable
and became lovers. He left his wife and children in 1976, and
after his divorce a year later, they married.

They have built their home around traditional mores:
Alan is the breadwinner while Sarah keeps the house. He
does not push her toward a career, and she has relaxed in her
role as well-to-do homemaker: "Whatever makes me happy
makes him happy." Despite their conventional orientation,
however, she feels that Alan respects her as an intellectual
equal.

Like Karin Blake, Sarah Suskind was one of the few
women I interviewed who are not plagued by fear of job
shifts, children interfering with their work, or balancing a
schedule with their husbands. Those are simply problems
beyond the realm of her experience. And she likes it that
way. Curious to discover what Sarah views as her role in life,
I asked her to describe what she now does. Although for
several hours before this question she had looked at me
directly, she now shifted her gaze, avoided my eyes, and
stared at the tape recorder. "Well, I'm married. . . . I have
stepchildren every weekend. I myself am redecorating my
apartment. I've never had these responsibilities before, so at
this point they take up my time. . . . I'm really trying to make
as good a marriage as I possibly can, because this, I realize,
will be the focus of my life. . . . I know that and I feel glad
about it. I don't feel guilt or anything else."

She nervously lit a cigarette. Obviously, the guilt she had
stored away on that back burner still simmered. Having been
educated to do more than this, she was now committing the
ultimate sin of living through her husband. I pressed her to
confront her real feelings. "I'm not threatened by women's
lib as much anymore," she reluctantly admits, "although I
am threatened by it to a certain extent sometimes." When
someone asks her what she does, she gets embarrassed. She

feels she has to apologize for not having a career. Even worse, her mother has no sympathy for the issues which now occupy her time, like stepchildren who sometimes create problems; she feels Rachel gives her no credit and no support in her current role as wife and homemaker.

Nevertheless, she is content for the first time. Despite being raised by a mother who encouraged her not to emulate the example she set, despite the fact that traditional marriage was the one future the majority of her peers spurned, in the long run Sarah Suskind chose to defy them all. This time she made a choice solely for herself.

Seven

Andrea Shapiro

Andrea Shapiro's life was a mess. Somewhere along the line, something or someone had derailed her—but she couldn't put her finger on exactly what. It just seemed as though life had been promised to her as beef Wellington and had been served up as ground round. Like the other women in "The Waiting Game," after college she found that achieving her goal took longer than she had ever dreamed—far too long. She grew impatient. Still, she waited. Finally, unlike Katy Townsend, Karin Blake, or Sarah Suskind, she was forced to forge a career for herself. The alternative just never seemed to appear on her doorstep.

We were sitting in her small mid-Manhattan studio apartment in January of 1978. The setting gave me the framework of her story almost before I had turned on the tape recorder. Although most of the career women I had met lived in spare, undecorated surroundings, Andy had taken the time to create the aura of home. She had filled the large window at one end of the room with plants and covered the coffee table and bookshelves with seashells picked up at the beach. It was a warm, inviting place.

Curled up on her sofa with a mug of coffee, I tried to assess her covertly. She was small of build, not even five foot one, with dark curly hair worn short and soft. Her eyes were a lively hazel, and she talked with them almost as much as with her hands and mouth.

Midway through the interview, it became clear that Andy was trapped between feminism on one hand and her traditional upbringing on the other. Caught in the middle, she has found neither a husband nor a career about which she can be particularly enthusiastic. Her life is in sharp, severe crisis. As she spoke, despair crept into her soft-timbred voice. "I don't think I thought about a career. That's why I'm going through a lot of problems now. My thinking process is a little late. I'm latent. But I don't think I'm to blame. I think it's the times.... It was always instilled in us, 'Don't worry, it'll happen.... Why should you worry about the future? Some rich man who is intelligent will come along, marry you, keep you just the way you were brought up.' "

Andy was born in 1949, the eldest daughter in a traditional Jewish family of three girls. Her parents, Louis and Ruth Shapiro, set their children an unusual example in one respect, though—they had not married until their mid-thirties. But in most other ways they were quite conventional. From a wealthy family, Ruth had been carefully educated at Radcliffe College; despite this, after the children were born, she played the standard role of running her home and doing community work. Meanwhile, Louis supported the family by his medical practice and by successful speculation in the stock market. Even when quite small, Andrea understood that there were two goals in life: a diploma from an impressive college, and a man with money.

They lived comfortably in an affluent New York suburb, in a spacious, rambling Colonial. The neighborhood was wealthy, with wide expanses of lawn between each dwelling. But her father's opulence did not make up for more basic needs. Andy keenly felt the "coldness" of her childhood. On her street, one did not know one's neighbors, and the big, expensive house seemed to put distance between family members—each child in her separate room.

Worse still was the distance between her parents. The Shapiros' marriage was nothing she wanted to re-create in her own future. She dreamed of intimacy, warmth, partnership; here there seemed only the violence of her father's temper and her mother's self-abnegation. Lou Shapiro filled their lives with his impatience and anger; an oppressive patriarch, he ruled the roost with an iron hand, yelling and screaming, working himself into a fury. But, on the other hand, he could sometimes be magnanimous and kind. Accordingly, the girls learned to walk on eggs, trying to anticipate his variable moods. Docility became a way of life, and Andy looked up to him with admiration and fear.

Setting the tempo for her daughters, Ruth Shapiro bent under her husband's irrational rule with silent submission. Early on, she taught them an important lesson: the way to deal with an irrational man was to manipulate him subtly, and so she established her position without saying a word. When the family dinner table became a battlefield, as it often did, with Lou screaming and finally storming away, Ruth sat quietly, gritting her teeth. "She would not allow one tear to shed until he had gotten up," Andy recalls. "Then she'd burst out hysterically." Soon the middle sister developed anorexia nervosa—a disorder in which the person finds it psychologically impossible to eat—while the two other girls tended to be overweight.

In contrast to Lou's tyranny was Ruth's essential warmth. Consequently, she became a martyr in Andy's eyes—a warm, caring woman, a mother to be emulated.

When she entered grammar school, Andy began her search for the intimacy she didn't find at home. By the fourth grade, she was already concentrating on boys, not on her studies, in an active pursuit of a traditional goal: popularity. Happily, she pretended to struggle and resist when boys showed they cared by giving her a "pink belly"; she always graciously accepted a push on the swings. The message from her mother had come through loud and clear: men were troublesome, but a necessary evil. A woman needed a strong provider. Naturally, she also assumed she would eventually be a mother. Despite their problems, Louis and Ruth reinforced the idea that bearing children was "a tremendous fulfillment, a tremendous joy." Even her favorite TV show— Donna Reed—traded in the currency of family.

In junior high, she was still focusing all her attention on

the opposite sex: dancing school, bar mitzvahs—all were places she could be social with boys. But by high school, having discovered that her looks were not exactly earthshaking, she began using intelligence and good grades to establish herself within her peer group. Naturally, she concentrated her attention on the arts—a family pastime and one especially appropriate for a girl. But despite her efforts, Andy still felt like an outsider and this was devastating to a girl who badly needed the reassurance of social status. She was dissatisfied and self-conscious about her chunky build, and the constant embarrassment gradually wore her down. Finally, in the summer before her junior year, she transferred to an all-girls private school in Pennsylvania. It was less exciting, but less threatening. She repeated a year, finally graduating with the class of 1967.

The situation at home did not improve during her high school years, even after she left for boarding school. She did little teen-age rebelling—home was unstable enough already. When she came to visit on an occasional weekend, her father's neurotic behavior and unreasonable tantrums upset her. But, undaunted, she continued to hope for a better future for herself. Instead of letting her parents' poor marriage deter her, she became more determined than ever to find a suitable mate.

At school, she gradually began to lean on the comfort of friends instead of on her family. They were dependable and much less complicated. But she never felt entirely at home there. When her friends took off in forbidden cars, she was too afraid to go—early on she had learned the terrible price exacted when one defied authority. Jewish in a Christian school, she felt afloat in a no-man's-land. She refused to go to school chapel, and yet felt acutely her own lack of rigorous religious training. The whole thing was very disorienting, the muddy waters threatening. She needed to feel that her identity was spelled out, that her future was certain.

The same insecurities permeated her early love life because sex was a sticky subject for her. Sexual mores were changing rapidly in the mid-1960s, and she was confused about what was and was not permissible, caught fast between the conservative way she had been raised and the increasing permissiveness around her.

At first, she clung to her innocence, refusing anything more obvious than the inevitable cloaked erection that accompanied the newly popular "bear-hug" dance. But by eleventh grade, the pressure increased, and her conventions wavered under the threat of possible desertion and unpopularity. Although she stoutly refused to sleep with boys during high school, determined to save her virginity for her husband, she compromised by mastering the art of oral sex as an appeasement.

It was 1967, and she was about to graduate. America was in the midst of revolutionary changes—but Andy didn't really notice. She did not read a daily newspaper. She ignored current events. The early beginnings of the Women's Movement did not touch her, although she does remember hearing something, dimly, about *The Feminine Mystique.*

Meanwhile, college was the most immediate consideration: it was the key to finding the right sort of man. Andy did not view it as a route to a career because after all, she was not career-oriented but "interest-oriented." Nursing was her only thought about what to be, and it was a fleeting one at that; her mother had served with the Red Cross during the war. Still, in the eleventh grade, she did discover an interest which would eventually lead her to the art history job which she held when we met. It seemed to fit her image: her maternal grandfather was a famous collector, and the Shapiro home was covered wall to wall with valuable prints and oils.

She was an intelligent girl with high boards, but her C-plus average reflected her social—not academic—orientation. Still, she was dismayed when her college adviser suggested that the best colleges would not be impressed with her applications. It was a huge blow to her pride not even to apply to her mother's alma mater—Radcliffe. Worse, most of her classmates, it seemed, were headed for Ivy League and Seven Sister schools, while Andy wound up settling for Syracuse. Once again, she felt left out. She consoled herself with the thought that the college of her choice would at least be a good party school.

Syracuse was a huge mill-like university in upstate New York. She quickly joined a sorority to get that ever-elusive feeling of intimacy. As her mother had, she selected art history as a major, because it was enjoyable, non-threatening, something acceptable to her family. Burned once by poor grades, she worked hard: now, for the first time, straight A's filled her term report.

Nevertheless, Andy still spent a lot of time socializing, the sorority providing a natural outlet. "I was accepted into a very elite group," she recalls. Despite her new ethic of hard work and good grades, her even newer popularity became the real mainstay in her life. Now, to be a part of the "in" crowd, you simply had to smoke dope, and she had no real desire to buck that kind of peer pressure. The teen-age rebellion she had so carefully avoided finally erupted now that she was out from under her parents' watchful eye. By the end of her sophomore year, 1969, and throughout her junior year, she found herself involved more and more with all kinds of drugs and with the people who used them. She began "dealing," helping the junkies contact the pushers—not to make money but to keep friends.

She did, however, resist the increasing pressure to engage in sex with the boys she dated. Having a good social life was no longer simple—in fact, its complications underscored that her traditional aspirations were rapidly becoming untenable. Throughout her first two years, she managed to stave off the advances pressed upon her. No one had ever talked to her about sex, and her friends never discussed it. Finally, though, she sensed that no one would be impressed with her virginity anymore, and she grew ashamed of being so old-fashioned. In Paris, abroad for her junior year at the Sorbonne, she met Bill Cohen, a student on exchange from Cornell. Two Americans in a foreign land, they soon became good friends. During the year in Europe, he began to pressure her for a more intimate relationship. Doggedly, she put him off. But at last she felt she couldn't afford to be out of the sexual mainstream any longer.

Back in the United States, she finally gave in to him on the floor of a friend's apartment. After all the years of resisting, she was crushed to find that sex really brought them no closer, aroused no new emotions. "It was nothing," she remembers.

But the aftermath of losing her virginity was far more turbulent than the act itself. Returning to Syracuse later that fall, she began experiencing a mild discomfort—nausea and occasional vomiting. In very short order, discomfort turned to pain—violent abdominal pain. Dimly, somewhere in the back of her mind, it occurred to her that she might be pregnant. They had used no protection, had not even discussed it. "I was stupid enough to think that he was in charge," she said. By now, Andy was a traditional girl in one hell of a traditional predicament.

Finally, she called home, and after a short conversation her father asked if she was pregnant. "It was the first time sex had ever been brought up, and here I was, twenty-one years old," she said bitterly. Her mother flew up and brought her home. Hospitalized, then opened up in the operating room, she was found to have an ectopic pregnancy—a fertilized egg was growing inside her fallopian tube instead of in the uterus, where it belonged. To prevent it from rupturing, they removed the tube and the pregnancy was terminated.

To complete her crashing flight into the modern world, she recovered from the surgery to discover that Bill had fled—putting as much distance as possible between them. What had happened to those old-fashioned ideals of commitment, to the young man who married the pregnant girl friend? She told herself to start facing reality; this wasn't the 1940s.

The entire experience proved painful enough to keep her away from sex for quite a while. Returning to school later that year, she began to date a law student with whom she often spent the night. Straddling the fence, she would never make love with him, having decided to spend the year celibate.

Now, even more than before, she concentrated on studying in an attempt to block out the trauma. She was accepted into a graduate seminar, where she soon became the teacher's pet. Simultaneously, her work gained a sharper focus: career. "I felt very bright, I felt very knowledgeable. I was bilingual." With her attention newly directed to the future, she began to view her adviser, an art historian, as a "guiding light," a new role model. Margaret Barnes was a professional, invulnerable to men, an independent woman who gave Andy enormous support and encouraged her to apply to graduate schools. With no prospects for a husband immediately apparent, she began to realize she would either have to get a job after graduation or continue her education. Gradually, she began to consider a career in fine arts—only temporary, of course, but something to occupy her time.

Naturally, these new feelings were tentative. Mirroring her ambivalence was her lack of concrete planning. She took no part-time work in her projected area of expertise; not until the summer after college graduation in 1971 did she take a job at the Metropolitan Museum in New York. She still didn't quite believe that there would be no husband attached to the apron string of her diploma.

Accepted by the Institute of Fine Arts in New York, which she understood had the top program in the country, she intended to spend two years getting a master's degree. In 1967, entering college, she'd thought she would meet a man who would "take care" of her. Now, four years later, her plans were delayed, but her aspirations were the same. She now had a solution for what to do with the next two years; surely by then she would have met her mate. Responding to peer pressure, she publicly called this period of treading water "the beginning of my career."

In some ways, she tried to fit herself into the new feminist image, modeling herself more on Margaret Barnes and less on her mother. She worked hard in graduate school, but her program required much more work and a lot more brain power than she had ever anticipated. This was no easy alternative, no quick stopgap measure. She would have to invest all her time, energy, and emotion if she wanted to survive. But she saw no real option. So, putting her back into study, she stuck it out.

After receiving the hard-won master's, Andy moved from one art job to the next within the field over a six-year period. Each began with excitement and ended in boredom as Andy continued to try pursuing a career she really didn't want. Finally, she deliberately went on unemployment and designed stained glass to fill up her unoccupied hours. Then she tried volunteer work. Nothing was really satisfactory. Her growing feeling of discontent would not be easily wished away—except, perhaps, by a wedding band.

And that was hard to come by. The summer after her college graduation, Andy had met a man who saw her through the next five years with all its job shifts. Allan Stein was a graduate student at Brooklyn Law. Her five years with him were theclosest she had ever come to finding the family she dreamed of as a child. "I found him to be a wonderful partner—not sexually, but in terms of companionship. Very supportive. We cooked together, we'd always go away for weekends, we'd go visiting our parents. He fit right into my family, which was very important to me." He was a traditional Jewish man—strong, more than her equal intellectually, but infinitely less childish than her father.

This time, Andy took no chances: she went on the pill. Although many New Yorkers found it stylish to live together, Allan was not ready to make that type of commitment. He graduated from law school, moved into his own apartment, and began a legal practice in real estate. Then, in the fall of 1975, he finally moved in with her, although he still kept his own place and stayed there occasionally. Andy saw this as a preliminary step to the altar.

Allan expected Andy to be traditionally acquiescent, in terms of career, if they married. His job was a profession with a capital "P." They agreed to move to another city, regardless of her job, if he had an advantageous offer. His priorities were clear, and she willingly accepted them. She had let him into her life and relied on him. "I could never imagine what it would be like to break up," she says.

But time slipped by. Increasingly unhappy with her work, Andy began agitating for commitment. When it wasn't forthcoming, she let him know her displeasure subtly—as her mother used to do with her father. Her discontent with life in general gradually seeped into their interactions. She began to cheat on him, bitch at him, make his life miserable. After several months, her sabotage finally worked—all too effectively. He walked out, for good.

Crushed, she tried to renew an interest in career. It was not easy this time. Still, there was nothing else to do.

In 1977, she was hired to compile a reference book that would list all the works catalogued by over one hundred American art institutions. When I interviewed her a year later, she felt once again dissatisfied. The men she knows accord her field little respect in an era when women doctors and lawyers are especially in vogue. "In retrospect," she said with a wry smile, "I should never have chosen art history as a career. It's not practical. . . . It is a wonderful thing to be interested in, it's a wonderful hobby to have, but not a career." After six years in the field, she makes only $12,000 yearly. Her younger sister, twelve months out of business school, already makes $21,000 in investment banking. She focuses her bitterness on others: no one, not even her college adviser, warned her that the field was so limiting.

If Andy had had an eye on the future way back in 1971, she would have foreseen this problem. And with a wealthy family still behind her, she could easily go back to school or switch tracks even at this late date—if she could find the motivation. But she has never quite been willing to take her career seriously. Only when she stops counting on the marriage that may never come and begins to invest fully in her work can she hope for her situation to improve.

Since her split with Allan, depression has overtaken her. She knows that no man finds a morose woman appealing. In an attempt to break this vicious circle, she has begun therapy with a psychiatrist. Feeling more and more alone, she told me that no man wants to "keep" her. A single woman in New York City, she is reduced to meeting people in bars— which she does not frequent—or hoping friends will introduce her. She also feels her career choice has limited the men she comes into contact with. It is difficult to work up any enthusiasm for someone who makes his living at something she dislikes. "I want a professional person," she complains.

As she nears her twenty-ninth birthday, Andy Shapiro cannot ignore the situation any longer: her fears of being an old maid are growing stronger daily. In sharp contrast to her earlier reaction, she now philosophizes, in defense, that her mother didn't marry until thirty-one. Nevertheless, she feels increasingly like a third wheel in a world of twosomes.

Worse yet, she recognizes that she has at most another decade of safe fertility remaining. She says this is one bridge she will cross when she comes to it, but is worried. She wants children, but, like her mother, also hopes to maintain her outside interests or perhaps do some part-time work. She plans simply to readjust what she is doing—like a hobby—so that it fits in with everyone else's needs. "I'm too active a person to ever sit at home, have babies. I still feel that way. I will always, even if I'm making stained glass and selling it to Bendel's, I will always be doing something."

Interestingly, even though Andy's career and marriage plans are in disarray, she still does not identify with the Women's Movement. The past year has been the most painful in her life; right now, all she cares about is getting things back on the track. She wants to be content with herself, to find an inner peace, to find someone with whom she can share. She has learned to be self-sufficient, but finds no real happiness living alone. She has read no books on feminism; she would not, she claims, know Betty Friedan or Gloria Steinem if she shook their hands. She has never felt oppressed or restricted as a woman, and sees no link between herself and "those radical women." If anything, feminism has complicated her life, because not so long ago, her traditional ambitions would have been in fashion. Now she is boxed in, forced to choose an alternative she hates. She resents having independence "forced" on her. Bitterly, she lays the blame at the door of "modern times."

Andrea once expected her life to flow down a riverbed worn smooth by generations of mothers and daughters just as Ruth Shapiro's had. But after college graduation, she found herself in the middle of unexpected and uncharted rapids; she could not understand what force had brought her there. She now recognizes that "times have changed," that she no longer fits in—but she does not yet hold the key of adaptation and flexibility. Andrea Shapiro lives between two worlds.

Part IV

Mavericks

My father would always say, "It's good to be the black sheep. Don't just follow the crowd. ... Be yourself, stand for what you are. It's better to be different."

—ELAINE MAGDAAL

The women in this section have always been mavericks, a little bit different from those around them. As children, they chose to identify mainly with a professionally oriented person—whether their mother or their father. From an early age, these women *expected* to have careers. And they did have them—but with an unforeseen hitch.

We might call them America's first generation of born-and-bred career women; all devoted their full energies to that end. Unlike the women in the previous two sections, they never worried or thought about marriage or motherhood very much, but assumed that one day it would appear on their doorstep. Being part of a couple simply wasn't a primary goal. Career and a personal life did not seem to be irreconcilable alternatives. After all, their parental role models seemed to be setting good examples of how both could be incorporated and managed.

As they grew older, the burgeoning Women's Movement began to enter their lives. Surprisingly, their general reaction was one of indifference: they had known such expanded expectations their whole lives. Why, after all, would they need a movement to support a career drive which was as natural to them as motherhood was to other women? Moreover, some felt that the feminist position was too harsh; the movement's unstated assumption that one would choose career over family, if it came to the crunch, was threatening to women who desperately needed to believe they could have both.

Still, with the Women's Movement subconsciously reinforcing their expectations, they rarely stopped to consider how their professionalism might affect their personal lives, or vice versa. They pushed aside such ominous thoughts, and refused to see or believe that they might be required to compromise one for the other—or, even worse, to choose between the two.

Until now.

The twelve women I interviewed who fell into this pattern (five of whom are presented here) were in the midst of a crisis, or had just resolved one—a crisis which centered on the new realization that eventually they would have to choose. Suddenly, nothing was very clear anymore. They saw for the first time that their fathers, while setting strong professional examples, never had to cope with the additional responsibilities and chores of motherhood. They saw that their working mothers made many sacrifices within the sphere of their careers to provide their children with the necessary time and nurturing. And, to their surprise, these women suddenly found that motherhood was an appealing and important aspect of womanhood for them—important enough at least to be considered seriously.

All of it came as a revelation: they were completely unprepared for what the Women's Movement brushed aside as "unnecessary choices"—choices they now find not only necessary but unavoidable.

Eight

Rebecca Madison

Rebecca Madison grew up in pioneer country. Her people: proud, independent, with a frontier heritage. Her land: rolling prairie, windswept, without mountain or tree to break the gaze of the eye straight to the horizon. Only the Rawhide Buttes raised their heads above the grassline.

Her voice was dreamy. Full of remembering, she was a million miles away from her Cambridge, Massachusetts, bedroom, where the tape recorder lay between us on a queen-size bed. Her pioneer identity began in a small Wyoming town, population 1,800. Each August after World War II, the townspeople gathered to celebrate "The Pageant of the Rawhide"—an outdoor spectacle retelling the legend of how the nearby buttes were named. Her family would dress in period clothing and ride in a horse-drawn covered wagon, portraying an early band of settlers on their way west. Each year, starving in the prairie, a young man would promise to shoot the first heathen he saw if only the Lord would help the group.

But his target did not turn out to be a vicious brave; instead, it was a lovely young Indian maiden. The young man kept his promise anyway. Her tribe swarmed over the prairie, encircling the wagon train. The youth gave himself up. Moving to the foot of the buttes southwest of where the town now stands, his captors skinned him alive.

A dramatic tale, it captured the essence of the Old West in which Becky Madison wanted to live. It was the embodiment of her dreams—but dreams that a twentieth-century girl could only playact. Still, she immersed herself in fantasy.

The Laura Ingalls Wilder series was her childhood Bible; she modeled herself on the tough, courageous women of the West. And when, in her early teens, she discovered there was no western frontier to conquer, she journeyed east to find a career. There she would learn that conquering a career was more complicated, for a woman, than setting up a frontier hearth had been a century before.

Born in 1952, the eldest daughter of three, Rebecca grew up in a small, comfortable house on Main Street, surrounded on all sides by cottonwood trees. John and Sarah Madison didn't have a lot of money, but they had enough. A closely knit Episcopalian family, the Madisons placed much emphasis on tradition. Christmas. Easter. Evenings, they often sat all together in front of a roaring fire, playing games and watching television.

Becky's very early childhood was filled with warmth, laughter, and pride. "They were the best parents, in the best town, in the best state, in the best country in the world," she recalls. John Madison was editor in chief of the *Herald.* An enthusiastic man whose work kept him politically up to date with the world, he encouraged his children to expand their minds. Right from the start, intelligent dinner-table discussion was integral to family unity. He was a man to be admired, respected. Becky emulated him from an early age.

Sarah was somewhat less impressive. Becky thought of her mostly as a mother, although she occasionally did serve as a substitute teacher. Drawn to the greater excitement of editing a newspaper, Becky looked to her father for the role model she did not find in Sarah.

But not everything was in such apple-pie order at the warm Madison home. Her parents' violent arguing sometimes woke Rebecca from a sound sleep. It terrified her; she wanted to cry out and tell them to stop it. The tidal wave hit in her fifth year. For no reason she could understand, her parents divorced. Safety, security—all spiraled down the drain. Devastated, Sarah uprooted her children, moving to

Laramie, where she resumed teaching. It didn't take long for Becky to decide that while family might be a source of security, marriage held no such promise. It clearly didn't pay to depend on a man.

Unfortunately, Rebecca blamed herself. She felt her father would not have divorced her mother had she been a good, lovable little girl. Gradually, she retreated into a self-protective shell, willing to trust only herself, afraid of her power over others. She had great difficulty adjusting to the Laramie public schools when the time came to enter first grade.

Two years later, the seesaw tilted back to Rebecca's hometown: Sarah and John remarried. The incident merely confirmed Rebecca's belief that marriage was unstable, uncertain. She returned to school in the middle of second grade. She felt like an outsider. And now, at home, she couldn't count on stability. The bottom had fallen out once; it might do so again.

Gradually, loss became the one thing she dreaded most. In the end, she could really only trust herself. And so Becky Madison established herself as a dominant, aggressive child, a figure of authority in games with her peers. She was the teacher; her younger sisters were the pupils. She was the mother; they were the children.

But her strong personality did not limit itself to traditional women's roles. John Madison had always hoped for a boy; now he was pleased to see Becky's dynamic nature and went out of his way to encourage it. With his solid backing, she thought of career from an early age. "I wanted to be a doctor," she told me with a big grin, "and my father thought it was great." Believing in the uncertainty of marriage, she planned an independent future where only Rebecca could let Rebecca down. She devoured any book that offered a professional woman as its heroine—especially a biography of the first American woman doctor, Elizabeth Blackwell, or other pioneer women. By contrast, Nancy Drew, with her careful feminine exploits, bored her. She wanted to read of strength, endurance, and courage. Joan of Arc appealed in particular:

isolated, martyred, and deified. "I wanted to be famous," she confided. "Not movie-star famous: I wanted to be a crusader. I'd read a lot about nineteenth-century reformers." She laughed. "I would lie in bed at night when I was feeling frustrated ... and friendless, ... and I would envision what my biographer would say."

In school, she had no particular area of difficulty, but no teacher pushed her to her potential. Additionally, in keeping with her uneasiness about being emotionally demonstrative, she had trouble making friends. Aloof, she placed herself above her peers. To Rebecca, little girls' chatter seemed inane even when she was a little girl.

Because she envisioned a dramatic, solitary career, boys held little appeal, either. She assumed that at some hazy point in the future she might marry and have children, but thought of it little, knowing she would never depend on it as her mother had.

By junior high school, Rebecca was gearing up, spending most of her time on schoolwork. Soon she ranked near the top in her small school, a position she held until her high school graduation. Even though math was clearly a field of "male" expertise, she excelled in it, enjoying the logic and comforting order. She studied it eagerly for four full years, including trigonometry.

But, inevitably, as Rebecca entered adolescence, her view of the world began to change. Even a successful career woman needed helping hands, and so popularity among her peers became newly important. Ambitious by nature, she now wanted to be the most popular girl in her class, just as she had once wanted to be the smartest. A quick study, she began taking lessons from the successful girls around her. Painfully shy, plump, glasses overshadowing her face, she feared the cards were stacked against her from the start. "I didn't have any of the graces," she recalls. Still, like Andrea Shapiro, Rebecca plunged doggedly into contract-making extracurricular activities. She cheered at basketball games; she gave slumber parties. Finally, she became accepted—not for her appearance or her clothing but for her brains. It was barely enough. Hanging by her thumbnails to the periphery of the "in" crowd, she ached to be the center of attention. "The best, only the best," she told me.

Despite her unfeminine approach to the future, Rebecca belonged to a group which mirrored the conservative nature of the town, a conservatism she would eventually move east to escape. In her high school yearbook, there was one row after another of clean-scrubbed, wholesome faces. With a laugh, Rebecca claimed that *American Graffiti*—an early 1960s period movie—could have been filmed in her Wyoming hometown of the *late* 1960s. "Dragging main"—not demonstrating—was a favorite pastime for upperclassmen. Marriage, not career, was the expectation of Becky's female peers.

In short, she was very different from her friends, and no amount of popularity could bridge that gap. Her early identification with her father set her apart. During these years of exploration and growth, John continued to share and encourage her dreams.

Then something happened that would set father and daughter at odds for a long time, something that would sorely tempt her to reject all his teachings: for the second time in nine years, he asked his wife for a divorce. Becky was fifteen. "From that moment on, I was angry," she said. "Blamed him. I felt that he was very cold and that he was hurting my mother. . . . It was like the whole world was gone." Her parents never explained why they were separating; Becky only knew that she and her sisters stayed with their father while Sarah moved to Denver and resumed teaching.

Only years later did she hear the real story: her mother, having an affair with one of Becky's favorite woman teachers, had been careless and was discovered in flagrante delicto by her husband.

Bent on revenge, Rebecca did not cut off her nose to spite her face, did not disappoint her father by sabotaging her future. Instead, she unconsciously retaliated as her mother had done—with sex.

Before the second divorce, in keeping with her serious adult nature, she had done no adolescent rebelling with liquor or boys. She'd never even been kissed; and membership in the Masonic Job's Daughters reinforced traditional concepts of purity and chastity. Still, when she took a sex test published by Ann Landers, she was extremely threatened to find her low rating scored as what she felt was "queer or something." Even in a town where marriage was the only available contraception, it seemed her friends knew much more than she did. Typically, she decided to compete with them—and simultaneously defy her father.

"Twerp Week" arrived shortly after her miserable result on the Ann Landers test during her sophomore year in high school. This week the girls got to ask the boys out. Afraid to approach the captain of the football team—her real crush— she settled for second best. Mark Tryon was a sensitive young man and a talented singer, but he was clearly no match for Becky's intellect. She easily dominated him. Going steady, like most other young people in school, they wrote long love letters, joined the speech team, and were generally inseparable.

Kissing soon became a longing for something more. One night, staying overnight in another town for a speech meet, they made love. Rid of her virginity, she now qualified as a modern woman. In addition, surprisingly, she was carried away by the romance of it all: in a town where gossip was as prevalent as prime steer, she had secretly done the forbidden. It made her feel unusual.

They used no contraception—remarkable for a girl who prided herself on her maturity. She was still angry with her father about the divorce; the extraordinary risk of unprotected intercourse was a subconscious way of asking to get caught, or trying to hurt him. Throughout the summer and all during her junior year, she sneaked Mark into her bedroom, right over her sleeping father's head.

Finally, in July of 1971, she missed her period. She told her mother; Sarah told John. He washed his hands of the entire affair. His aloofness, naturally, made her even more angry. Mark offered to marry her, but that was the furthest thing from Rebecca's mind. Her mother arranged an abortion in Mexico City.

After terminating the pregnancy, Becky broke off with Mark, and returned to Wyoming for senior year. She began to see a psychiatrist. Having made her rebellion explicitly clear to her now distant father, she put that aside and invested all her energy in planning for her career.

Becky's grades were straight A's; her boards were excellent. Priorities were crystal clear: though she loved home, nothing was going to stop her from going to the Best College. Besides, with a journalist for a father, Rebecca had long been interested in the world outside the small town. "I read my father's *Time* magazine cover to cover every week. I read the newspaper and watched television.... I was very much shaken by the Democratic convention in 1968.... And yet, it felt like it was happening in a world completely apart from my own."

She applied to Radcliffe, Yale, and Stanford. For wanting to leave the state, her classmates thought her an oddball, a snob. Even John Madison wanted her to go to the University of Wyoming: like Becky's peers, he felt she was traveling an unnecessary distance for an education she could receive right at home. Finally recognizing the signals she had been giving him, he also wanted to keep an eye on her.

It had little effect. Rebecca was adamant.

A precise career choice remained up in the air. Tentative thoughts about being a journalist occurred to her; she even considered psychiatry. But she wasn't going to make up her mind yet. Then she latched on to the novel idea of being a female airline pilot.

During high school, even in her self-contained rural world, Rebecca did have a first contact with the Women's Movement. Her mother read *The Feminine Mystique* and then gave it to her. In speech class, Rebecca led a debate on "A Woman's Place." And—naturally—she was a vocal supporter of the "right" to abortion. Meanwhile, her peers jeered about the "crazy" liberated women. Once again, Becky was set apart from her friends. Shortly after her graduation, she read *Sexual Politics,* finding it absorbing. Feminism reinforced her desire for career, and she embraced it with one exception: she was disturbed by attacks on Henry Miller and Norman Mailer, whose writings she found extremely erotic. She wondered what was the matter with her that she could enjoy the work of chauvinists.

"It's like the story of the ugly duckling—I had been in the wrong pond," Rebecca told me happily. She entered Radcliffe College in 1970, and felt she had come home. The six-hundred-page Harvard course catalogue made her mouth water. Competitiveness aroused, she wanted to learn everything there was to know. Shopping around, she would eventually explore many different subjects before settling down in the field of American History. Predictably, her urge to understand the pioneer mind reared its head.

To Becky's surprise, the courses at Harvard were not as difficult as she had anticipated, because she had underestimated her substantial intellectual capabilities. Fitting in with the other women students, generally feminists, she finally did not have to fight for acceptance. For the first time in her life, she could now bare her heart openly, and she made several really close friends. Confidences, experiences, ideas—everything burst from her in a stored-up torrent.

But college life was not so simple as excelling in courses or discovering confidantes. At home, boys had admired her for her brashness; at Harvard, the males' large egos were threatened. She felt angry, bitter, antagonistic—and insecure: it wasn't her fault that "Cliffies" had a reputation for intellectual superiority. She resented the Harvard men who treated her like a chum during the week and then disappeared to court girls from less threatening schools on weekends. And yet—despite herself—she wanted them to like her. If she couldn't fit in here, then where could she go?

As a result, her sexual self-image fluctuated violently. Freshman year, she didn't have a real date until after Christmas. Career wasn't quite enough: she was lonely, needy, a small-town girl away from her family for the first time. She needed some warmth. There followed, over the next several years, a whole succession of relationships doomed to failure—doomed because she made men feel inadequate. Briefly, she envied more traditional women who didn't have such complicated problems.

By the time junior year rolled around, Rebecca was trying to concentrate more on career and less on men. She reaffirmed her belief that ambition was too important to be shelved in favor of relationships. As long as she had to rely on someone else for happiness, she would always be insecure. Enormous effort now went into her studies; straight A's were the reward.

But such concentration raised a new set of concerns. As college graduation loomed large on the horizon, she knew soon she would have to make a specific career choice; she felt lost, aimless. American history seemed like a dead end. She lacked specific skills—skills her friends in biology and chemistry had picked up from their majors. In short, she suddenly felt terribly insecure. And so, on St. Patrick's Day in 1973, she turned to Henry Freeman, a man she met at a drunken Harvard party. Though also a junior, he was two years older—having taken time off. He seemed mature, wise. His laid-back artistic temperament downplayed the need for any kind of decision—a philosophizing that was just what Rebecca wanted to hear. "He was the typical alienated, confused young man," she recalls. "Really hated Harvard; trying to get into humanistic education. Lots of high ideals."

She put off career planning and continued to enjoy her studies. High grades won her a grant to do the preliminary work on her honors thesis. Here she would be a pioneer: she had chosen—predictably, I thought—to study the life of an early feminist—Charlotte Perkins Gilman—whose papers had just been obtained by Radcliffe's Schlesinger Library. They were uncharted territory. No intense biographical work had yet been done on this contemporary of Susan B. Anthony.

For the summer, she and Henry sublet an apartment together—and were miserable. With no job, he moped around all vacation long, but nevertheless refused to help her with the cooking or cleaning. She began to find his lackadaisical attitudes disturbing. In addition, studying Gilman made her increasingly uncomfortable with what Henry meant to her. She felt guilty about her desire to be with a man.

Feelings of ambivalence carried right along into the thick of senior year. Her self-image as a feminist, as an independent woman, seemed to hang in the balance. Always before, she had insisted on paying for herself on dates; now, when Henry respected this dictum and no longer offered to pick up the tab, she felt neglected and hurt—even though she knew better. Being in love came to be more and more of an identity crisis. Increasingly, cut off from home, she was having new and unanticipated urges for marriage and motherhood. "I had a strong desire to re-create the childhood family that I'd known. . . . It would really threaten my [desire] for fame and fortune and what I was going to do with my life. I would start to feel really torn inside."

Rebecca is the young woman I described in Part I who told me she too remembered a nauseated reaction to Katharine Hepburn's statement that women—even in the 1970s—would have to make choices. The specter of career choice became more and more acute during her senior year as she began thrashing around for viable ideas, like many of her friends—male and female. John Madison, her old mentor, kept reassuring her that all doors were open to her. The Office for Graduate Career Planning encouraged her to go into big business. She even went to New York for an interview with Chemical Bank, but she just couldn't see herself in a gray flannel suit. She started to panic, and felt incapable of making a decision. Despair set in, as it had briefly the year before. "Before [senior year] I had said, 'Well, I'm in college to learn and to have a good time.' But then nothing came to me. Senior year ... I kept having this nightmare about the day after graduation. I'd be sitting on the sidewalk outside of the dorm with all my little boxes around me—with no place to go."

She had come to Radcliffe full of ambition and drive, filled with hopes and dreams. In the midst of her crisis, she asked herself why she hadn't found a specific direction. Ultimately, the blame was laid at someone else's doorstep: Harvard's. "I felt the only thing I'd been trained to do was to be a scholar," she recalls. "And I didn't want to be one."

Finally, she resigned herself to going out and finding *some* job—no matter what it might be. It didn't take very long: by July 1974, a month after her graduation, she began work at the Harvard Bureau of Study Counsel. She described it to me as "liaison work"—mostly making appointments and greeting people. Not once would she categorize the job for what it truly was: secretarial. Although she told herself she had taken the job to find out more about counseling, she learned little. Two whole years went by before her boredom became acute.

But 1976 brought changes. That winter, deciding to try her hand at psychiatric social work, Becky applied to Simmons College—an all-women's school in Boston. But her father refused to put up her tuition money, and Simmons had no loans available. Of course, had she wanted to go badly enough, she would have found a way; instead, she let uncertainty overcome ambition.

Next she tried the *Atlantic,* working as an assistant to the managing editor. She hated that, too. In utter desperation, she finally paid a visit to the Radcliffe alumnae career service. She could not understand what had happened to her life. Where was that ambitious young woman who had come east to seek fame and fortune? she asked herself. The career service had a better question: What was she most proud of?

The answer was easy: her senior honors thesis on Charlotte Perkins Gilman. The satisfaction of knowing a subject so thoroughly had run very deep.

Slowly, she began to consider getting a graduate degree in history. The cynical Henry had been a major part of her scorn of academics. Now, three years after college, he was working in a pizza parlor and living off a large trust fund. Rebecca wasn't particularly impressed anymore.

And so, ignoring Henry's sarcasm, she sought out her old Harvard history tutor. Over lunch one day in March 1977, this middle-aged assistant professor encouraged her to apply to the finest programs available—Harvard, Yale, Michigan, Berkeley, John Hopkins, and Columbia.

Since college graduation, Rebecca and Henry had been living together. But things were increasingly rocky. In limbo about her career, Becky had constantly looked to him for the security she seemed unable to provide for herself. A nasty cycle had developed over time: as soon as she would begin to depend on him, he would retreat. She quickly learned that he was attracted to her only when she acted brassy and self-confident. For a long time, she let herself stay in his shadow. But by the time she made applications to graduate school, she was also ready to make a decision about him. The lunch with her history tutor provided the perfect impetus: the very instant that Peter Woods mentioned—casually—that he was recently separated from his wife, Becky's interest flared. Peter was thirty-eight, attractive, an assistant Harvard professor. Best of all, he stimulated her intellectually, something Henry had not done for some time.

Although Peter seemed far out of her league, to her great joy he called a few weeks later to invite her to a dinner party. Gradually, things began to unfold. This man simultaneously encouraged the intellectual and the sexual parts of her. It was a new totality of self, one that radically altered the way Rebecca thought of Rebecca. "On every level, it was the most marvelous thing," she told me, hugging her knees to her chest. As she spoke, her cheeks flushed, her eyes danced.

"I couldn't believe it. I felt like I was living in a fairy tale." In June, they spent several idyllic weeks on Martha's Vineyard. Finally she had everything she wanted. She had settled on a career choice. The man of her dreams was sitting right beside her, inspiring her.

Peter was seeing other women, but Rebecca did not allow herself to think about that. The setup was complete. Several months later, one of those invisible adversaries triumphed—and Becky was alone, shattered once again by her greatest enemy: loss. But Peter had given her much of value. His support of her plans for a Ph.D. in history remained long after his love was gone. Fully aware even then of the astronomically tight market for history professors, Rebecca was—and still is—convinced that she will be one of the few to make it. Perhaps she is naïve, perhaps not. In any case, Peter helped her to believe in herself again. The night I called to set up an interview with her, an acceptance from Harvard had just arrived.

Now, a year after she was dropped by her professor, Rebecca no longer actively seeks a man to fill the empty spaces in her life. Once she allowed men to sidetrack her from her original purpose because of a certain facile belief that career would be uncomplicated. When under stress, she fell back on the security men could provide. Inevitably, however, she has turned to herself again. Now, more and more, she feels certain she will never again compromise her career for a relationship—or for motherhood. "It's not realistic to expect that I'm going to have a career *and* a husband *and* children," she now says. "At this point, the thing I'm most sure I don't want to give up is a career." She paused. "I'm really coming to the idea that I can't have it all."

She points out that she won't even be finished with graduate school until thirty-one—and having a baby right after that would undoubtedly sabotage any chance of succeeding in the competitive academic world. All in all, she acknowledges that children are simply not that great a priority for her.

Instead, she finds a different life-style viable—having several monogamous relationships and remaining single. In many ways, she says, the greatest challenge before her now is not to fantasize about having it all—a career, husband, and kids. "Thinking about getting married," she believes, "involved realizing what other thing I value that I might lose."

All in all, Rebecca Madison is willing to remain single or childless as long as her career proves stimulating. I had to remind myself—forcefully—that this sort of gamble is one we all, as women, must probably make one way or another. Karin Blake and Katy Townsend gamble that raising children will be stimulating enough to give up working; Julie Fowler gambles that medicine alone will satisfy her.

Ultimately, like most of us, Rebecca Madison has come back to the dreams of her youth—for her, the dreams of a career that are rooted in early admiration for and emulation of her father. And yet, even in those first days of ambition, even when she still lived in Wyoming, she never understood that inevitably she would have to sacrifice something to get what she wanted. The past eighteen months—in which she lived, at last, by herself—have been the key to her firm decision to be a career woman. Strong and independent, she has come to grips with the idea of being alone.

Thus, she has embarked on the long road toward professional success—well girded, she believes, for the journey ahead. Today, at twenty-five, her choices seem clear, and perhaps they are. But giving up future options—like marriage and family—may be a good deal easier now than it will be later on. The choices she makes today inevitably shape the rest of her adulthood. In many ways, Becky Madison has only accepted their consequences with her mind—not with her heart.

Nine

Judith Habib

It was late April, the soft time of early spring in Massachusetts, when the weeping willow begins to green and the
forsythia bears a faint tinge of yellow on its branches. I was
somewhat excited as I approached my appointment with
Judith Habib: she was an international marketing specialist
and I was already intrigued. Pulling into the parking lot, I
surveyed her building: monotonous modern brick with small
fenced-in terraces—a typical low-rise suburban development.
Inside, the narrow corridors were already somewhat dingy
and smelt of someone else's dinner.

Looking for the right door, I imagined the decor of her
apartment: tastefully but sparsely furnished from the pages
of a Bloomingdale's catalogue. I couldn't have been more
wrong. As I walked into Judy's apartment, I was walking into
another era—pre–World War I Europe, perhaps. Everywhere
I looked were great bunches of flowers—gladiolus, carnation,
iris, lily, rose—each scent overpowering the last. An oil painting framed in gilt hung above an old-fashioned sofa with
lace doilies on its arms. A grand piano, its dark veneer
burnished to a sleek shine, engulfed half the living room. In
one corner stood a china cabinet, where Judith's carefully
arranged crystal was arrayed beside exquisite hand-painted
ornaments of Venetian glass. Everything was made of deep
mahogany, wood with years of careful age behind it.

It all seemed so incongruous: the decor, remarkable for
any young woman's apartment, seemed especially unusual
for a woman who worked in a high-powered, male-dominated field. Before long, however, I began to feel that the

155

apartment was symbolic—symbolic of the inconsistencies and conflicts in her life. She was dynamic, she had a career that would win a stamp of approval from any feminist. And yet, only a few days before I interviewed her, she had married a very conservative man. Here, in the middle of glass and chrome suburbia, she had carved living quarters straight out of the Old World. I wondered what kind of background, what sort of childhood role models could have produced such a strange mixture of life-styles.

With neat dark hair curled around her shoulders, and her impeccable skirt and blouse, she spoke in precise, business-like terms and radiated an image of control. Clearly, this woman wasn't going to hand me anything personal on a silver platter. My work was cut out for me.

Born in 1952, in New York City, Judith was the first native American in a Jewish Italian-Yugoslavian family that escaped Europe in the years preceding World War II. The Bernellos were traditional Old World people with a strong brand-new patriotism: America had offered them a vibrant sense of life when all else was bleak, and they were grateful. Still, although they had crossed the ocean, they had brought with them traditions rooted in the world they had left behind—traditions that rubbed off on their daughter. Anthony Bernello, originally from Trieste, came to the United States just in time to be drafted and sent back overseas. Eventually, he became Eisenhower's Italian voice, broadcast just ahead of the liberating American armies as they crossed Europe. Anna Zito, Judith's mother, had been forced to flee into the Yugoslavian woods at the age of fifteen. For ten terrifying days, she had fought to survive in the wild, finally reaching the Italian border, from where she managed to come to the United States. She married Anthony in 1947. Together, they settled in Manhattan's predominantly Jewish Washington Heights, and Tony began his business career in a Brooklyn macaroni factory.

Judy was born in 1952, a treasured only child, a child who

looked up to her dynamic mother from the start. Anna worked full time as an office manager, while simultaneously making sure her household ran on greased wheels. A nurse was hired to care for Judith during the working day; a housekeeper took care of the cleaning. Even after a hard day, Anna was an energetic Superwoman—sewing, knitting, loving, nurturing. To Judy, she seemed successful at everything she touched. Despite Anna's activities, the youngest Bernello never felt neglected: her mother's first priority—family—was always crystal clear.

Tony and Anna may have been raised in small towns, in rather disadvantaged circumstances, but they were cultured people: she was an accomplished pianist, he was a collector of antiques. They were determined to improve not only their own lives but also the future they offered their daughter. Although Anna worked full time in an era when most women were happy housewives, the family was basically a traditional one. She might earn a hefty paycheck and run her office like a clipper ship, but Tony was the boss at home. When arguments erupted, as they did rarely, they followed a consistent pattern—one that confused Judy. Tony's Italian temper would get the best of him; meanwhile, his wife's cooler head invariably made better sense. Anna won the battle, but in the long run she always lost the war: Tony's superiority was the bedrock of family stability, a stability on which Judy's life would center.

The Bernellos also had an Old World concept of extended family—something that even in the 1950s had practically vanished from the middle-class American life-style. Anna's aging mother lived with them in Washington Heights; the nursing care she required would have seemed like an impossible burden to many. Judy helped her mother by emptying bedpans and holding her grandmother's hand while they exchanged stories. Early on, she acquired an adult seriousness which won her the nickname "the Little Old Lady" from her parents. She was forced to face death at a relatively early age, when Elena finally died at seventy-four. "I was brought up with a very realistic attitude," she recalls, "and not hidden from the negative aspects of life."

As a child, Judy already had professional goals. Anna's example gave the impression that a woman could do just about anything well—and all at once, too. While she assumed that one day she would marry and build a family, she didn't worry about it. Everything would come, given time. With no son to take under his wing, Tony gave his ambitious daughter much positive academic reinforcement. Judith's immigrant parents expected a great deal from her and she was most anxious to please them.

She carried her dreams along with her to grammar school, where early success made anything seem possible. At the top of her class from the start, she was skipped ahead in the middle of second grade; tests administered in the sixth grade placed her on a national par with high school seniors.

By adolescence, still firmly under her parents' rule, she felt no great need to be rebellious. The Bernellos were proud of her; she was a good child, an ambitious child, and they gave her all the freedom she could want. In 1963, the family moved from their rapidly deteriorating neighborhood to one of New York's more fashionable suburbs, and Judy entered a private all-girls high school. "It was for the cream of the crop," she recalls. Her parents had gotten their education part time, working their way through Columbia and Hunter—and they wanted the best for their daughter.

Tony's expectations were especially high, and she did not let him down. Three afternoons a week, after finishing the day at school, she took intensive lessons in music theory, choral singing, orchestra. Between her two sources of education, she often did homework until well past midnight. Her interests—atypical for a teen-ager—remained within the home; some of her most poignant memories from these years are the evenings she played cello to her mother's skillful piano.

Family financial arrangements symbolized her complete dependence on her parents. The Bernellos did not allow

Judy to manage her own money—giving her a sum of money to start a checking account was out of the question. Only when she was eighteen did they arrange for her to draw directly from their own account—and this was for emergencies only. Instead of working, she spent summers traveling with her family—or, later, by herself.

Between junior and senior years in high school, she attended the Albert Schweitzer College in Switzerland. It was her first move toward independence, the first time she had ever been on her own. But even this experience was insular and familylike. Like the other students at this elite school, she lived in a commodious and friendly dormitory with a rigidly controlled set of rules. French and German lessons filled her days and soon she was multilingual, like her parents. All in all, she felt perfectly at home.

At high school, Judy rarely participated in peer group activities, holding herself aloof from any and all cliques. She was different from everyone else, but it didn't bother her. Senior year, when her class voted almost unanimously to ban a dress code which proscribed pants for girls, she was the only dissenter. "I just thought that aesthetically it was much nicer not to see everyone wearing dirty jeans," she remembers. And, after the rule was changed, she still refused to wear them.

Her sexual mores also stemmed entirely from her parents. Anthony often lectured her on the value of being pure until marriage, and Anna concurred. Judy never dreamed of rebelling. "I was a goody-goody," she now says. She felt her sexually liberated peers fell into a stereotype of alienated youth who did poorly in school and spent most of their time smoking cigarettes. She was uninterested.

Despite all this, however, she did begin dating. Here too she felt close to home. Anna was feminine and attractive—a working woman and a mother. While Judy was hardly overwhelmed with excitement when thinking about men, she did find a nice Jewish boy from Long Island who became quite attached to her in the tenth grade. While professing to be uninterested, she nevertheless allowed him to escort her at various times during the next three years. She protected herself, I could easily see, by feeling intellectually superior to him. The situation lacked any sexual attraction and so couldn't have been safer.

Naturally, Judy was gearing up fiercely for college—the ultimate goal since she had been in grammar school. As she surveyed university catalogues, her parents once again took up a managerial role: they "asked" that she stay within a "reasonable" distance from home so that she could live with them for one or perhaps two years. Not surprisingly, she readily agreed: completely dependent on the parent-child symbiosis, she felt much too threatened to move far away. And so, with SATs of 650 in English and 750 in math, Judith seriously considered only Barnard and City College.

Thus, unlike most of her peers, Judy would find that college brought little change to her daily routine, "an easy extension of high school." Entering Barnard in September 1969, she expected nothing more than a good liberal arts education; her career plans had not yet focused on anything concrete. Still, as she had planned years before, she majored in math and was confident that this talent would eventually provide her with direction.

She was quite happy as a freshman, but gradually felt a little cut off. In order to be the well-rounded woman her mother was, she would have to improve her social life. Making a conscious effort to meet more men, she cross-registered for courses at Columbia and dropped her extracurricular music to leave time for dating. Career was of primary importance, after all, but a girl couldn't ignore the opposite sex completely. Judy assumed she would be married by age thirty; beyond that, she didn't worry much about commitment.

Nevertheless, her first relationships were doomed to failure. In the liberal Columbia environment, her traditional values were an anomaly. Still resisting the ubiquitous blue jeans, she stubbornly rejected the promiscuity around her, and won few friends.

Columbia was erupting all during Judy's first years there, the campus literally seething with political strife. Nevertheless, she managed to hold herself aloof from the furor. In fact, the more radical things got, the more traditional she felt. In particular, she drew back from the new issue of women's liberation. She agreed that women ought to be treated equally with men, and paid equally, but she couldn't relate to the general theme of oppression. She wasn't "hungry"; why should she "beg"? Just because women had plenty of opportunities in the 1960s—new opportunities—didn't mean she was indebted or obligated to fight for the cause. She utterly rejected the concept of reverse discrimination. "People expect things served to them on a silver platter because they're women. . . . I don't believe in having to work twice as hard as a guy to get to the same place, but I don't believe in doing nothing for it, either."

Feminism threatened her. The movement placed a woman's responsibility to herself above responsibility to a family. The whole idea of choice went against her mother's example. Anna had fulfilled herself *without* having to neglect her child. Why couldn't Judy do the same?

Between freshman and sophomore years, Judith—predictably—went to summer school. One night, she returned to her Dartmouth College room to find an emergency message. Frightened, she called the phone number given. Instead of a familiar voice, she got only a recording that announced the line was "not in service." Fear seized her. Suddenly something about the number looked familiar, and she realized it was the same as her cousins' except for one digit. Quickly she dialed again.

The news was a shock: her parents were in critical condition following an automobile accident. In a daze, she managed to find the dean of the summer school, and taking pity, the man drove all night long to deliver his numb charge to the hospital in New Jersey. Judy hazily watched the stripes of the road slide past, wondering if Anna and Tony were still alive.

Finally, at 4 A.M., she arrived: a look at her silent gathered relatives told her everything. The next day, she returned to the apartment to make funeral arrangements, and started to cope. While others around her wept, she remained detached and philosophical. "I was very grateful that they went together, that one didn't have to live without the other." Looking around, she saw everyone else overcome with grief. "I decided if this had to happen to anyone, it was best that it happened to me, because nobody else could have handled it." She smiled sadly. "A very ego-boosting kind of thought." Nevertheless, one thing didn't quite sink in immediately. While her parents did not have to live without each other, she had to live without both. She threw herself completely into the business of avoiding this thought. Less than a week after the deaths, she returned to finish the summer session at Dartmouth. "It was really funny," she explained to me. "My father spent three hundred dollars for me on the course, and I didn't feel it was right to let it go to waste."

Returning to Barnard for sophomore year, she tried to pretend that everything was the same, and she avoided anything that might remind her of the tragedy. She stopped playing the cello—to this day it lies with a broken bridge under her piano. Alone in the apartment, she became utterly fanatical about keeping it clean. Her mother's spotless household loomed constantly before her, and she tried to keep the apartment as it was when Anna was still alive.

As she sketched the whole tragic story, I grew silent. I knew what it was to lose one parent—let alone two simultaneously. I knew all too well what it was like to grieve. Hesitantly, I inquired how she had dealt with the deaths on a purely emotional level. But try as I might, I couldn't make this young economist delve beneath the rational. "I remember thinking in the beginning, 'Well, it's just like they're away on vacation.'" She was speaking perfectly normally, with a hint of practicality in her voice. Clearly, her reluctance to let them go led her to live as though they were anything but dead. "You keep on thinking they're going to come back. And then the longer they're away, the easier it is to cope with."

Unfortunately, her valiant attempts to be the perfect hearthkeeper led to a drop in her grades. Temporarily, she had lost sight of her own future. She even began having difficulty with math courses. She explained her new burden to a professor; he suggested—not facetiously—that she hire a maid.

More and more, she strove to pattern herself after her parents. Their conservative moral codes "reigned supreme." Still, fate had taken her by the hand and gradually she adjusted to being alone. She began, at long last, to establish her independence. Casually, she began dating again. Then, in the late winter of her senior year, two years after the tragedy, she began her first real relationship. Yoav Galed was an Israeli medical student taking his degree in New York and she saw him frequently throughout that spring and summer. For the first time in her life, Judy fell head over heels in love. Yoav was handsome, intelligent, physically strong. And, clearly, his nationality was a strong reminder of her parents' immigrant heritage. She was sure that Anna and Tony would have been thrilled with her choice had they been alive.

Finally, at age twenty-one, following her graduation from Barnard, she decided that sleeping with him could not offend the dead.

As the end of college drew near, career was becoming an all-important issue to her. She realized that she lacked the originality to make a career out of pure mathematics; she tried student teaching, and found it unchallenging. Instead, her logical, quick mind found itself drawn to business, law, and government. Throughout the spring of senior year, she vacillated back and forth. Then, finally, Yoav urged her to go to the one place that had intrigued her most—the Fletcher School of Law and Diplomacy in Boston.

In September, then, he cheerfully packed Judy off to New England. And as soon as she was safely out of the city, he shattered the relationship by never once either writing or calling her. The loss was crushing—briefly. She was alone again, living for the first time away from her parents' apartment. Gone were the familiar rooms in New York; she knew not a soul in the Boston area.

Despite it all, she threw herself into the program at Fletcher, slowly putting loneliness behind her. Living close to the campus, she made a huge effort to get to know her fellow students, and intellectually she felt right at home. Soon she belonged to a regular crowd—a clique, at long last— and went to parties every Saturday night.

Not surprisingly, given her background, she chose international law as her academic specialty—a decision made not on a farsighted basis but from pure interest. Forty percent of the students in her department were foreign; she could call upon her knowledge of Europe and her fluency in several languages. "I didn't know what I was going to do with it," she recalls. "But I was fascinated." It was hardly a traditional field for a woman, but it drew out those ambitions Anna and Tony had so carefully encouraged in her.

Originally, she had planned to spend a year getting an M.A. before looking for a job in New York. She spent the summer of 1974 in relatively mindless work as "corporate value indexer" for a large conglomerate: day after day, she slogged through domestic and international contracts, preparing data so that the company's legal department could computerize it. She was bored silly. Opportunities the following fall looked little better; the market for international law specialists was largely in government, and she found the pay quite unappealing.

Eventually, after consulting trusted professors, she returned to Fletcher for another year. Instead of a plain M.A., she would now have an M.A.L.D.—Master of Arts in Law and Diplomacy. But this experience was not nearly so positive as the first year had been. Many of her friends had graduated, and she was frustrated, trying to write a thesis. In fact, for the first time, she found herself having difficulty academically, taking a third year to complete it.

In the fall of 1975, still working on her magnum opus, she spent three days a week doing market research on Africa and Asia for a Fletcher professor, who was also employed by a Boston electronics firm. Finally, the hard work paid off: in September 1976, she was put on the permanent full-time marketing staff. When I interviewed her two years later, she had won several substantial pay raises, and the company held her in increasing respect.

Over these past few years, however, her job has become more familiar—and inevitably more routine. When we met, she was thinking of looking elsewhere, afraid she had reached a "dead end." Her immediate boss is a feminist, interestingly enough, and Judy is more keenly aware of women's issues than ever before. But even as a working woman who is not exactly being promoted in leaps and bounds, she does not feel discriminated against. In fact, the Women's Movement has made her only more aware that she has never faced real prejudice.

In April of 1977, she began dating Halim Habib, a Jew from Lebanon. Halim has a position slightly higher than hers in the same company. Warm, intelligent, he brought great companionship to her life—as well as a serious conflict. This time, at last, a serious lover withstood the test of a first anniversary. Soon thereafter they became engaged.

Her wedding with Halim was very traditional—including a reception at the Essex House in New York, where her relatives threw a sit-down dinner for 120 people. The food was kosher.

Although she and Halim share small household chores, theirs is a distinctly old-fashioned relationship—one very similar to her parents'. She has even changed her last name. When I called to schedule the interview, she first checked with her husband to be sure he approved of the date and time. Suddenly, she has discovered, there are complicated issues in her life that are as yet unresolved. Once again, as I found over and over during research for this book, children loom as a major problem; the ideologies of two worlds come together in Judith's life over this single issue like thunder-clouds meeting head-on. She may be intent on career, but the man she has chosen is not willing to assume any day-to-day responsibility for child care—he gladly bows to what he feels is a woman's natural expertise. If a sacrifice is to be made, she is the one who must make it. Only now does Judith comprehend the enormous energy her mother needed to do everything all at once. She loves the idea of working and has always geared herself for it, but she often ponders the sheer logistical problems of coordinating a career and a two-year-old.

Hypothetically speaking—of course—Judy guesses that Halim would not object to her leaving work to become a housewife and mother. "We've talked about it a little bit," she admits grudgingly. A pause. "I think he'd like to see that at some point." As I tried to pin her down, she became more and more irritated. "I'm not willing to say that I'm going to stop working, period," she said carefully. "Nor am I will-ing—" She stopped for a moment to think. Then, in exas-peration: "I don't know what we're going to do." On the one hand, she is now somewhat bored with her job; on the other, she is fully aware that stopping work for a few years to have a child—even if she then hires a full-time nurse—will inevita-bly hinder her career advancement.

Judith is now at a turning point. Halim wants to start a family within the next three years and she basically agrees with the timing. She clearly recognizes that shortly she must decide, but she does not yet understand that sheer inertia and a refusal to look squarely at her choices will soon decide for her. Already, at age twenty-six, she finds her job boring, and is slow to do anything about it. Failure to choose soon will be tantamount to career sabotage.

Currently, her greatest fear is losing her husband—a new emotion for this independent woman, but not too surprising for someone who has suffered so much loss. Like her mother, Judy considers career and marriage equal—but finds some things are more equal than others. Her uppermost goal is to maintain a solid marriage and to raise their children. "Career will need a lot of work at certain points in time," she rationalizes, "but I think the marriage will always need effort and work."

Carefully, step by step, Judith Habib is eliminating any complication that might tempt her to choose work over family. She never consciously envisioned having to make such a choice, but there it is. Her career requires far more responsibility and time than her mother's work as an office manager ever did—and that is the trap. As she moves further and further away from a decision for her profession, Judy is simply following the lesson she was taught on Anna's knee: family first.

Ten

Elaine Magdaal

The January morning was eye-achingly bright, with the kind of snap to the wind that numbs your cheeks right away. Still, I strapped on my hat and scarf, deciding to walk the fifteen long New York City blocks to Elaine Magdaal's apartment near Sutton Place South. Actually, I wanted more than a simple stroll—I was looking for some time to gather my thoughts; the only thing I knew about Elaine Magdaal was that she was a high-powered advertising executive with a prestigious New York agency.

Somewhere in the recesses of my inevitably prejudiced mind, I imagined her a small, dumpy woman with glasses and a three-piece suit and I nearly recoiled in shock when she opened the door. Elaine was at least five foot nine, statuesque, with long dark hair, almond-shaped brown eyes, and high cheekbones. Even a film star couldn't have been more striking.

The foyer of the building was quite posh—including a fancy doorman; the apartment itself was a spacious bachelorette. However, unlike Judy Habib's place, this had no warmth or ambience of home. Two big modern sofas and a rug were color coordinated in soft oranges and yellows; but the walls were stark expanses of white unbroken by a single picture or ornament. Most striking of all, everything was military-clean—so immaculate and empty of detail that I instantly suspected—correctly—that she spent very little time in the apartment.

Looking back, I find it almost ironic that Elaine was the one who introduced me to Judy: the differences between their lives did not end with interior decorating, and the sharp contrasts proved quite illuminating. They had met as graduate students at Fletcher School of Law and Diplomacy: Judy had loved the school, Elaine hated it. At the time, both were ambitious—and had been since childhood. Now, however, Judy is considering compromising her career for her personal life and Elaine flatly rejects the idea. In short, while Judy married Halim, Elaine married the advertising business. A difference in the example their mothers set proved to be one key to how they wound up in such contrasting situations. Perhaps they have only two things still in common: both are women, and both are faced with making choices—difficult choices—that until now were never considered part of the game plan.

Elaine was born in Holland in 1952, the first daughter of Ulrich Magdaal, a Dutchman, and Raika Suhartra, an Indonesian. In 1960, the family of four moved to the United States, settling in California. The emigration forced changes in their lives: Ulrich, who had been comfortable enough abroad, found he had to start over again at the bottom. To help bolster the budget, Raika went to work as a secretary in his office.

Nevertheless, despite their immigrant status and the tight financial circumstances, Elaine found childhood a secure and happy time. Ulrich and Raika had been foresighted enough to make certain that the Dutch-speaking Elaine began English lessons well before they moved to the States. As soon as they were in America, like many immigrants in previous eras, they stopped using Dutch in front of the children. Overall, home was a secure, loving place.

Elaine recalls that right from childhood she saw her father's honesty, intelligence, and strength as qualities she wished to emulate. His Horatio Alger story set an example she would never forget: starting again from scratch in a country where he had trouble with the language, he rose from an accountant to a vice-president of a large corpora tion. He was a traditional male to the core, hiding certain feelings from his family—feelings he deemed inappropriate. "As I was growing up," she told me, "he was never verbally loving, the way a mother might have been, the way my mother was. But you always knew he cared." She looked at me with a grin. "If the family was watching a sad movie, he was the first to cry and the only one to get up and walk to the bathroom."

But Ulrich deviated from a traditional role in one crucial way: he expected great things from his daughter. Emigrating had hampered his own opportunities, he felt, and he wanted Elaine to excel. Early on, she carried a sense of responsibility for fulfilling her father's expectations. She was Ulrich number two—the son he never had. That she was a girl did not perturb him in the slightest—at least, not until much later.

In sharp contrast, Raika offered her daughter little encouragement scholastically—she had had little herself, and did not miss it. Family came before all else—it should be a woman's whole world, if possible. Raika worked only because she had to.

Elaine identified with her father and could never accept her mother's way of life for herself. Raika was a "working woman"; Elaine wanted to be a "career woman."

The Magdaals had a traditional marriage, with traditional roles. "As my father says, there can only be one captain on a ship," she comments. Like so many other mothers of women I interviewed, Raika made her wishes known, and had her way, only through careful manipulation of the more powerful patriarch.

From the beginning of grammar school, Elaine was a different sort of girl, a girl who worked hard for the future. She had a natural ability for mathematics and conceptual thinking, an ability that would stand as the basis for much of her later learning. School became a playground for expanding her mind—she learned English, made friends, and became used to a new country. Still, she was different from her peers in a second way, one that could never be hidden or avoided: her skin was dark. Often, neighbors or other children confused her with the Mexicans who were considered second-class citizens in California. From the ordeal, over the years, came an important lesson from her father: it was good to be different. Ulrich told her not to assimilate completely into American life, not to minimize her differences. "It's good to be the black sheep," he would say. "Don't follow the crowd. . . . Be yourself."

She was. As an adolescent, she watched westerns and police shows on television, and loved war movies. She did read Nancy Drew, but the Hardy Boys were special favorites. Her idols were professional men—particularly those in the political arena, like Jack Kennedy, or geniuses like Mozart and Liszt. She admired doctors, especially those "making great cures."

The men in her real life interested her much less. Boys, after all, were just boys. She felt self-conscious—and too tall—and she avoided anything that even resembled a dance. Besides, while her young friends talked about getting married by the time they were eighteen, she felt different, thinking hazily of twenty-five or thirty as a deadline.

In her early teens, Elaine decided she wanted to be a doctor and turned to her father for support. Ulrich gave it five-hundredfold. Every night after school, they discussed her plans in great detail. "I figured out my life. . . . I would get out of residency when I was thirty-two, I had the whole thing packed in. And, of course, I [would go] through college in three years. That was the way I planned things at the time." She spent her summers working as an aide in a hospital where her father had connections. "I respected [those doctors], their lives meant something. They were contributing something to society."

By high school, Elaine began to blossom physically, finally thinning out. Suddenly, she was more and more popular, and even joined a sorority—the height of social convention. Nevertheless, she kept up her solid A average, never lowering her sights on the future. With her assertive, arrogant nature, she seemed to fit in—at charity car washes, skiing, beach weekends, and slumber parties. She was a girl who knew her own mind; surprisingly, she found, people respected her for it. It was the late 1960s: suddenly, to be different was a good thing.

Still, like almost everybody else, she did begin to rebel against parental authority. She smoked cigarettes, and a little pot; she occasionally chugged beer or cheap wine. Despite these peccadilloes, she never did anything that might jeopardize the future she and her father had planned, and kept relations with him on a pretty even keel. Refusing to tie herself down to any one man, she played the field, dating boys with two things in common: they were "gorgeous" and—more important—"dumb." At seventeen, right after her high school graduation, she lost her virginity to a man she describes as a "muscle beach construction worker." Making sure her dates were intellectually inferior was her way of remaining aloof. It was a pattern that would repeat itself for years to come.

Gradually, a special interest in social studies and politics came to the fore—the result, no doubt, of her dual citizenship and skin color. She loved to argue issues, and developed a strong friendship with a teacher who led keenly competitive discussions on current events. Unlike most other women I spoke with, she read the local newspaper religiously. Little by little, politics began to appeal more than medicine. With President Kennedy as an idol, she decided she wanted to study international affairs. In 1968, she spent much time working for Bobby Kennedy's presidential campaign.

Her college applications reflected this new orientation: she begged Ulrich to let her apply to Columbia—the eastern heart of political activism. Firmly, he said no. Instead, despite her strong protestations, he restricted her to California schools. Finally, she chose USC: a political science teacher told her that international affairs was one of the school's strong points, and her father endorsed it because it was quite close to home.

Thus, unlike most of the other women I interviewed, Elaine had a post-college plan even before her graduation from high school: graduate school in international affairs, then a diplomatic career. Her father, in the meantime, disapproving of her left-wing politics, kept stressing that if she went to business school, she would be certain to have a job waiting for her at graduation. But Elaine's ideals were loftier. Looking back, she realizes she wanted to become Henrietta Kissinger. Ending racism appealed most of all. "I wanted to go to South Africa, fight with the blacks—the liberation movements."

Late in high school, she first heard about the Women's Movement. Feminism picked up where Ulrich left off, daring her to be different. She embraced its precepts in a way he did not: her father was turned off by what he viewed as the "non-feminine" stridency of the movement. She often argued with him about this. Ulrich had pushed her toward a career, but had always assumed she would get married as well. He had told her to keep her virginity for a husband. But Elaine was beginning to realize that she didn't need to marry to enjoy a relationship with a man. As she swung her orientation from the traditional concepts of marriage toward the idea of having several long-term affairs with different men, children simply floated out of the picture. "I always felt that you couldn't really do a good job of seeking a career and establishing yourself, plus working on a relationship, at the same time." Her obvious conclusion: concentrate on career in her twenties, and then—if she felt the need—form a relationship with a man in her thirties. Not really wanting children removed the biological urgency of making an early commitment to a man.

She entered the University of Southern California in February of 1970, already planning to graduate a semester early. Elaine did indeed major in her heart's passion—international affairs, with specific concentration on Africa. She was somewhat disappointed with her professors, and longed for a real intellectual center like Columbia. Still, she dug in her heels, and by junior year had honed her general interest to a sub-specialization in arms control and disarmament. Very serious about her future, she worked like a dog and attended dozens of extracurricular seminars.

She found it challenging to be a woman in this ultra-male field—the kind of challenge only a "black sheep" could fully enjoy. Besides, she had always identified with male professionals—for the most part, she had never met a woman who held a position to which she aspired.

A generation before, such elaborate career planning would have made Elaine an oddball. But in the early 1970s, such foresight was fashionable for a woman. A high point of her years at USC came when Jane Fonda spoke at the campus and then Elaine met her personally. The movement had become more and more a support system for Elaine, and she read the main canon of feminist literature. Basically, she agreed with the movement's ideals, but found few of them original: all had been part of her life since she had been very young. Additionally, she was disturbed by feminism's man-hating elements; for this reason, she loved *The Female Eunuch,* which expressed the view that a woman could be liberated and still remain sexually attractive.

More important as time went on, however, was her strong inability to identify fully with the feminist watchword of oppression. She couldn't help but feel that hard work could always overcome prejudice in the workplace. It was more important for a woman to get mobilized, she felt, than for her to attend a political meeting and complain. Still, despite her reservations, Elaine considered herself a "women's libber" and, in keeping with her political nature, followed the movement closely in the news media.

Because career was uppermost in her mind, she refrained from heavy socializing, sticking with a few deep friendships with women. Her relationships with men continued to follow the carefully prescribed pattern: she only dated and slept with those to whom she felt superior—those who were safe.

She could not afford a complicated affair; a certain part of her heart must remain cool and untouched so that she could pick up and go wherever a career might take her. The caution ultimately paid off when she defied her current boyfriend's anger and applied to graduate schools in the East—Harvard, Fletcher, George Washington. When only Harvard rejected her, she broke off with her steady and headed for Fletcher. Priorities couldn't have been clearer.

But soon she hated the school. At Fletcher, the faculty was narrow and right-wing, and many of the students were foreign, from rich, aristocratic backgrounds that made her uncomfortable. Still, she let down her hair and had two serious affairs with men from the Third World. Both of these lovers were clearly unsuitable for her in the long run, but they represented a shift in her dealings with the opposite sex—they were her intellectual equals. On the first day of school, she met a dark, short, intense Ceylonese, and soon, a "rocky romance" developed. He was very much like her father, a sharp deviation from her former pattern: powerful, intelligent, controlling, full of ambition for her career—a demanding perfectionist. But it soon became clear that he was more like Ulrich than she had ever bargained for. He had precise, traditional ideas of how a woman should comport herself. He wanted her to be a "lady" *and* a career woman—a combination that confused her. She wasn't used to deferring to men, and she wasn't about to do it now—at least, not for long.

After three months, she began dating yet another foreigner, behind the first one's back. Her Persian was considerably safer than the Ceylonese had been: from an aristocratic family, he could never have made a permanent alliance with a middle-class American. He too tried to control her, but it mattered little this time. She had chosen him because she knew they could never get tangled up in a real commitment. Still, she loved him. In June, she received her M.A. and took off for Europe with Samon. Then, upon her return to New York, she decided she must end this "number-one affair" of her life. It was a simple act of self-protection: she could not afford to begin her career in the shadow of Samon's enormous emotional demands. "It was taking care of myself," she remembers. "It was really, I guess, *everything I had been taught.*"

Here it is in black and white, I thought as I listened to her, here it is—the choice I had always feared, the choice Katharine Hepburn had warned about—the main subject that I was investigating. This woman was not only choosing career over men, she was accepting the necessity for choice—accepting it with unhappiness but nevertheless with clear resolve. Digging in, she set her priorities more firmly than ever. Still, she didn't quite grasp the idea that she was setting a pattern: year after year, her life would revolve around such mandatory severances.

"How did you feel?" I asked.

She looked at me, suddenly sad, where before she had been matter-of-fact. "I was miserable," she said. "I went through hell that summer."

Putting distance between them, Elaine went back to California. To make things worse, she was extremely ambivalent about her Fletcher experience and hated every job interview in her specialty of nuclear disarmament. For the first time in her life, she was having a crisis over her career, her direction—the very center of her life. As a respite from immediate decision making, she took a position in trade promotion with the Dutch Chamber of Commerce. "A bullshit job," she says, "except that I got into marketing a little bit. And I got into business, because I had to deal with businessmen."

After a year and a half, she decided it was safe to return east. Government employment still seemed totally unappealing—her strengths were organizational and mathematical, not diplomatic. She wanted to be able to speak her mind, not live in a world of tact. She wanted to be a businesswoman—ironically, exactly the profession her father had projected all along.

She got her present job not by lucky break or academic

credential, but—taking a page from her father's book—on sheer force of personality. In New York City, the day before returning to the West Coast, she skimmed the list of advertising agencies in the Yellow Pages. Persistently calling the first one she recognized, Elaine finally got beyond the receptionists and secretaries to the head of account management. He put her off, saying they only hired people with M.B.A.s. Undaunted by her lack of the correct degree, she demanded an interview anyway: by five o'clock the following afternoon, she had a position as assistant account executive. Being a "black sheep" had given her the confidence and courage needed to snare the company's interest. "It was pushy-broad time," she said, smiling—everything Ulrich had trained her for.

Only a year later, in May of 1977, she was promoted to junior account executive. She now has a crucial function as liaison between the creative admen and one of the agency's most profitable accounts. She loves the work, she loves the responsibility she has acquired—and is nakedly ambitious for more. A six-figure salary seems within reach in the not too distant future.

Elaine does not feel that being a woman has hindered her per se. But—like Judy Habib—she does complain that she has to work much harder to get noticed than a man would. Nevertheless, she doesn't hesitate to work a fourteen-hour day—in sharp contrast to Judith, who despises and avoids the idea of working that hard. Elaine sees it as her father undoubtedly did so many years before—it is the only way to get to the top. Accordingly, she plans her personal life around her professional life, keeping personal commitments to a minimum so they do not clutter up her business day.

As she nears thirty, however, Elaine begins to feel increasing parental pressure to stop being a workaholic and to begin making those personal connections. Her father, to be sure, is very proud of her work. But, although he often brags about her to his friends, he is worried that the demands of her job eliminate any possibility of marriage and children. He never quite anticipated that she would have to work *this* hard. "I have done a lot of things that he wanted me to do," she told me, squirming uncomfortably on the couch. "But I haven't lived my life as a woman the way he wants." She is angry: her father is changing his tune about her career and she feels caught in the middle.

Clearly, Ulrich's ambivalence is now forcing her to consider issues that she avoided before. I asked her if she really believed a woman could realistically balance career, marriage, *and* motherhood. "Yes," she answered. Then, carefully: "But I don't think you can have the kind of career I'm talking about *and* have a happy marriage *and* have good children." And so, again, she sets priorities: "Marriage is more important to me than children."

But even a childless marriage seems like an imposing—and perhaps impossible—commitment, and so she continues to pick men who will not threaten her. For now, she has switched from foreigners to married men—the most recent a forty-nine-year-old who lives in the suburbs with his wife and three children. Basically, she admits to a fear of intimacy; gradually, she has been trying to keep her eyes peeled for men who are more eligible. But still, she continues to set up impossible requirements: she wants someone who will support her work, not demand too much, allow her to be independent. He must be strong, successful, intellectually very bright, open, sensitive, in touch with his emotions, flexible—in short, perfect. "Where is this man?" she asked me plaintively. "*My* Dashiell Hammett!"

Elaine is not sure that in the long run a permanent commitment is worth the career sacrifice. She is still basically uncompromising. "If I fell in love with a guy who wanted to go to Boise, Idaho, I'd say goodbye," she told me emphatically. Nevertheless, despite the fact that she lives her life according to the feminist dream, she no longer feels a strong affiliation with the Women's Movement. While it gave her some peripheral support, it was never essential for the survival of her identity. She believes she would be where she is now with feminism or without it. As in everything else, in the long run she is committed only to herself.

Sometimes, Elaine Magdaal dreams about giving up her career, getting married, and writing that spy thriller she's been talking about for years. Ultimately, though, she recognizes that it is only a fantasy. "I'm a career woman now, and there's no reason for me to give it up," she told me firmly. Very much a product of her father's careful modeling, she was one of the few *true* "career women" I met. An uncompromising attitude, powerful ambition, a strong self-image—all these are assets required for a climb to the top of the corporate heap. Unlike Judith Habib, her priorities remain clear and uncluttered—even though this enormous investment in her profession may well cost her the rewards of marriage or motherhood. While she never envisioned being in a position where one aspect of her life would cancel out the other, she now acknowledges—with reluctance and a little despair—the need for sacrifice. As I left her apartment that evening, I believed Elaine Magdaal makes this choice with her eyes wide open.

Eleven

Alexis Whitmer

Elaine Magdaal's willingness to make major sacrifices for her career contrasted sharply with Lexi Whitmer's quandary over precisely that issue. Like Judy Habib, Lexi is confused and ambivalent about just how far she is willing to go for her professional life. An executive producer for a local television station, she is thirty-one and still single—just a little farther down the same line Elaine has always traveled. For years, she too avoided complicating her life—by choosing a succession of inadequate men. But now she has really made a "mistake," really gotten herself in the thick of it, by becoming seriously involved with a man ten years her senior, a man she loves, a man who is pressuring her to marry and have children. She is terrified: her mother was one of Friedan's "walking dead"—a woman who gave up a career and then turned into an alcoholic. But, on the other hand, Lexi is lonely and tempted. What to do?

Born in 1947 to a movie actress named Margot Ray and her husband, Phillip Whitmer, young Alexis was caught between career and family warmth from the very start. She came into her parents' lives atypically late—when both were in their early forties. Margot was a successful woman, and her career had always been the top priority for her. While Phillip served as dean of students at a prestigious college near Los Angeles, she commuted regularly between the New York stage and Hollywood.

Lexi, as she was nicknamed from an early age, grew up mostly in Pasadena, in a comfortable house paid for partly by her mother's earnings. With four bedrooms, many baths, a pantry, and maids' rooms, it was nothing if not spacious. The backyard was lush with gardenias, roses, camellias. Trees surrounded the house: magnolia, poinsettia, lemon, pear, orange, avocado. Although Margot was more extravagant than Phillip, their two substantial incomes made almost anything possible. It was an early lesson for Lexi on a woman's financial power.

But the family paid dearly for all the extras Margot's career brought them. She was emotional, high-strung—onstage not only at work but at home as well. The constant pressure of long hours and commuting to Pasadena took its toll. Finally, when Lexi was about ready to go to school, Margot succumbed: she gave up her work to take care of Phillip and the children. It was a sacrifice for which the entire family would suffer: quickly, Margot became frustrated and turned to alcohol to while away her boredom. It was a clear lesson on what motherhood could do to a woman.

Phillip, on the other hand, remained reasonable and stable. As a college dean who had graduated from Harvard and MIT, he devoted special attention to his daughter's education—attention her mother was incapable of giving. As time passed, Lexi drew closer and closer to him and he became her mentor. Clearly, he expected much from her. It pleased him no end that his daughter loved grammar school; not surprisingly, his own field—English literature—was Lexi's special forte. Trying to impress her father, she struggled through Hemingway, Fitzgerald, Elizabeth Bowen. Her young intellect bypassed the Nancy Drew stage completely.

When brother William, two years her senior, left for boarding school, Lexi became a second son to Phillip. They often spent afternoons reading together in his office; he took her to the movies, or even to church. They discussed literature and matched wits on trivia. Occasionally, the relationship became even more Freudian: on Saturday nights in the TV room, she would lovingly iron his shirts.

With two career-oriented parents as examples—Margot,

her own ambition shelved, now lived vicariously through her daughter—Lexi set her goals high. Margot emphasized the need for a woman to be independent, to have her own purpose. In keeping with this idea, Lexi repressed any desire for marriage and motherhood. Nevertheless, down deep, she liked the warmth and intimacy that went along with family living—her relationship with Phillip had shown her the kind of love only relatives could provide. And so, throughout her childhood, she daydreamed—ambivalently, to be sure—about her family of the future. There was no need for a husband in this fantasy, no need for complication, no need to give up a career—and no need even for pregnancy. The kids "would just be there in position [magically] when I was twenty-four," she said, laughing.

Adolescence brought little change to her life. She remained oriented toward a profession, backed solidly by her father's pride and her mother's deterioration into worsening alcoholism. Margot's illness plagued Lexi; afraid of having friends drop by casually, she would ask them over only when there was a reasonable certainty that her mother would be sober. Embarrassed, insecure, she felt she kept a "dark secret" concealed at home.

Worse, Phillip had begun to drink heavily too—an act of real betrayal as far as Lexi was concerned. "I remember feeling rage," she says, "as he poured the drink that I knew would put him over the line." Disgusted, she began to turn to her peer group for close friendship. Red-faced, awkward, she envied her mother's looks and the social success they had once brought. There was nothing else to do but fall back into a clique where the important thing was intelligence, not beauty. She and her friends weren't asked out much during the first few years of high school. Instead, they were "buddies" with the boys in the class.

Gradually, however, she put shyness aside and grew more popular with the opposite sex. Her rebellion began during a family summer vacation on Cape Cod when she started going steady and began to sneak out the back door to meet her boyfriend in the moonlight. Turning her back on her hard-drinking father, she chose exactly the sort of person he would hate—a wild, rambunctious youth who was forever getting into trouble in school. Jimmy was someone with whom she could have fun, and experiment, without getting serious; he was intellectually far beneath her, and his parents lived in Massachusetts.

Back in Pasadena, on the other hand, she felt a need to be more decorous. A steady there might grow to be serious—and threatening to her ambitions. Besides, at home she was still primarily under her father's wing. Phillip would interview young men from eastern prep schools; then, the next year, when they enrolled as freshmen in his college, he would introduce them to Lexi. He wanted her to see the proper sort of boy: blond, preppie, straight, serious about work—someone too busy to distract her from her own studies.

It was on a date with just such a person—bland, unexciting—that Lexi touched a man for the first time. It was the night before her high school graduation. Her initial reaction was horrified surprise—proof positive of how much Margo and Phillip had kept her in the dark about sex. "Oh my God, what is that?" she thought. Now she laughs at her naïveté. "I didn't know which way it went, up or down," she told me, laughing. "In pictures it hangs down, but when it's doing its thing, then it's up. He wanted me to touch him and to stroke him, and I was stroking him backwards. He started squirming around; I must have been driving him absolutely nuts. I was quite bewildered about which end was the business end." All in all, this purely extracurricular experience left her virginity and her ambition unscathed. She still wanted a career far more than any man.

Continuing to push her, Phillip suggested that Lexi shoot for prestigious eastern colleges, such as the ones he had attended. She worked hard at her high school courses: predictably, humanities were still her forte and she dropped math as soon as the school allowed it. On the college boards, she was thoroughly her father's daughter, with a near-perfect 798 in French.

Finally, she chose to matriculate at Vassar. The college appealed to her in several ways. Set on a lush campus, it seemed glamorous—a romantic boarding school. It was considered academically excellent. And, of all the prestigious Seven Sisters, it had a rather risqué reputation—undoubtedly deriving in part from Mary McCarthy's sexually explicit novel about Vassar alumnae, *The Group*. Vassar, like Lexi, was a combination of the academic and the daring, for the career woman and the socialite. It fitted right in with the dichotomy of her life.

As a freshman, for the first time ever, Lexi had trouble making friends. Never before away from her parents, she was lonely, uncertain of how to best fit in. Finally, she drifted with a group of "hippyish" girls with whom she had little in common. Staying on the periphery, somewhat aloof, she thought of herself as the group's "straight mascot"—even distinguishing herself from them by daring to wear skirts occasionally instead of blue jeans. She was somewhat happy.

But being away from Phillip and Margot's influence had a more serious effect in that it allowed her ambition to soften. While Lexi had ostensibly gone to college for an education and to find a profession, she gradually began to get sidetracked, letting other things—to her parents' horror—dominate her life. Career became more and more secondary. She majored in English and minored in French, and it required little effort for her to get terrific grades. Slowly, she began depending on what she already knew, coasting on native intelligence and her previous laurels.

In short, being three thousand miles from her professionally oriented parents released that part of her which had always enjoyed romantic Ginger Rogers movies and dreamed of intimacy. Rob Manly, a sophomore English major from Yale, became her major concern. "I fell in love for the first time," she explained simply. "He became my constant preoccupation for the remainder of my college career." She began cutting classes to stay with him during the week. When she did return, she found it more and more difficult to face her friends: like her mother, they thought she was compromising herself and her future. During freshman year, she had begun extracurricular work—for the campus tour service, as a baby-sitter, office clerk, or hospital aide—but soon her affair replaced these activities, too. "I stopped practically everything," she says sadly, "except seeing Rob, doing [a minimum of] work, and washing my hair."

It was Lexi's first intellectual relationship—and her first completely physical one. After six months of sharing the same Holiday Inn bed on weekends with Rob, she finally gave in. Several months later, she grew frightened of playing with fire—like Dottie in *The Group*—and went on the pill.

But despite the length of this liaison, Rob was not really a long-term prospect for Lexi. A poetic, romantic young man, he was intensely intellectual and very well read, but, like Lexi, he could get by without devoting much time to his studies. Lack of ambition and career drive were fine for a college beau, but not for a husband; her parents disliked him, hating the way he drifted with the wind. They worried about Lexi closing out her life to others.

Distracted by Rob, Lexi paid little attention to the growing Women's Movement—an ever-increasing topic of conversation during her Vassar years. Besides, she'd already heard everything that Betty Friedan and Gloria Steinem were talking about—years before, from her mother. Despite the women's lib furor and Margot's increasingly concerned phone calls, Lexi successfully managed to avoid thinking about her future at all. She would worry about career later: college happened only once, and should be fun.

But as graduation neared, she began to get panicky—like many women I interviewed. The only thing that really intrigued her was the idea of going to England—where she had once spent a summer. During her senior year, digging

around Vassar's guidance office, she discovered that the college annually sent two of its graduates abroad to be BBC
interns. She had had no prior experience in broadcasting and
certainly no prior interest, but an internship would get her to
Britain. With the future looming, she had switched back to
her earlier strong ambition. In response to the message coming down loud and clear from Margot, Lexi told Rob he
would just have to wait until she returned. Ambition was the
only thing that would get both her mother and her peers off
her back.

She won the fellowship and headed for London in September. Soon she had fallen into a happy routine. Her job
turned out to be quite interesting—she worked on a science
radio show with real professionals, people who taught her a
great deal. It was all exciting, challenging. Maybe her mother
was right, she thought.

Nevertheless, ambivalent, she fantasized endlessly about
Rob, dreaming of life together with him, wanting marriage.
But when Rob did come to live with her the following June,
she felt "invaded"—a reaction that shocked her. "This was
my life, my independent life . . . even if it was lonely," she
told me. Her job was just more fulfilling than he was—
precisely as Margot had always maintained. Additionally,
she felt the strain of trying to work and maintain a relationship simultaneously—something she had never attempted at
Vassar. She would come home from a long day, tired, and
Rob would be raring to go out and hit the town.

Confused, she continued to evade planning for the future.
Knowing her job would be over in October, feeling threatened by the proximity of decision making, she arranged to
take a trip to Greece in November—after Rob went back to
the United States. But her lover rebelled at the idea. He'd
already been waiting a year for her. She understood her
choice: if she didn't come home, she would lose him. She
acquiesced resentfully.

By the time Lexi returned to the States in the fall of 1970,
she had a firm goal: a career in broadcasting. Priorities were

once again clear and Margot and Phillip were once again happy. At a dead end with Rob, although still unable to admit it or deal with the idea of being alone, she started looking for a job without worrying about its location. He was teaching English at a private school near New York; Boston, New York, Washington, and San Francisco all seemed possible to Lexi. "I was ready to take off," she says. Finally, a radio station in Boston offered her a position as a production director. She didn't hesitate for a second.

Her work began with editing tapes and other "pickup stuff," but the boss was grooming her to be his right-hand man, and her ambition grew quickly. Soon she was in a managerial position—scheduling facilities and staff as well as producing an arts program. She had her own office and her own secretary. It all gave her a new wave of confidence. Before long, a co-worker at the station seemed interested in her. In February of 1971, bored with Rob, she finally broke it off.

By April, her new relationship had gone down the tubes, and a month later, again tired of a solitary existence, she called Old Faithful. "We stayed together for another three years," she told me wearily. Having left his teaching position, Rob briefly worked for a real estate agency but soon had no job at all and came to live with her for six months. Essentially, he was a deadweight around her neck: he let her support him, let her be the aggressive breadwinner in the family. For Lexi, he was only a security blanket: all her energy and intellect went into work. Overall, it was a pattern which would dominate the next six years of her life.

In 1972, her hard work paid off and she was finally able to move up into television—still at the same station, where she was soon promoted to associate producer. Now she dealt more with the content and structure of shows rather than simply with the nuts and bolts. In full swing, she set her sights on becoming a full-fledged producer within two years.

Meanwhile, the relationship with Rob was going nowhere fast. He was unemployed and totally dependent on her, and she was getting tired of being a nursemaid. He had outstayed his welcome. Finally, following a new teaching job, he moved back to New York City, and they saw each other only on weekends.

In 1974, Lexi went home to California on vacation. On a visit to San Francisco, she met Art Starton, a writer working on his first novel. He had graduated from Yale in 1967, started medical school, dropped out, taught English, and gone to China—all in search of direction. He was a quiet, brooding young man, and he appealed to her in some of the ways Rob had at the beginning. "He was very smart, but very gentle and lost." And so Lexi repeated the pattern over again. She returned east; they began corresponding; he came to visit for a weekend. Jumping from one iceberg to the next, Lexi now broke off with Rob for good, and Art's short visit lasted for three years. Her fantasies of having a dependent child had come true. Art became very domestic, doing the household chores while she worked, making it easy for her to put all her energy into TV. Once again, she was the dominating force in the relationship. She needed not to be alone, while simultaneously needing to put her career first.

In 1975, her father died of a heart attack, and Margot became extremely dependent on Lexi. Only with concerted effort could she cope with both the death and her mother at the same time. Now she relied even more heavily on Art for companionship and friendship. She also began to push him, trying to make him more successful, more aggressive, more strong. Finally, Art found a job working for a local newspaper; nevertheless, it soon became apparent that they were in a rut—the same rut she had been in with Rob. Accordingly, she began to require he be more like Phillip—be more the kind of man she had been brought up to marry. "I got more and more strident about what I wanted," she says. "What I wanted him to do [was] to make me happy." Increasingly mismatched, they finally broke up in May 1977. He moved to another city.

Now, for the first time in many years, Lexi was really

alone. Although she dated casually, she was determined not to get involved too fast again. Just as Art left, she got her first real production assignment and gave it her all: the effort paid off when the show won accolades on all fronts and she was granted the title and salary of a full producer.

The new job has been a big responsibility for her, and she loves it. She now oversees her shows from the germinal stage right through the nitty-gritty of programming, staffing, budgeting, shooting, editing, publicity, and airing. Her annual pay has been increased to $18,000.

In the summer of 1977, she started dating Aaron Fletcher, a forty-year-old executive producer at her station. Aaron contrasts radically with the men Lexi generally chooses; he is also the very first man she has realistically considered marrying. "He is very directed," she says. "And ten years older, very conservative."

Nevertheless, he is several rungs above her at work, having been there ten years longer, and she admits that often he controls the relationship. She alternately likes this and is bothered by it. Aaron wants her strong, but not strong enough to push him around. He offers her security and stability—but she pays the price of a certain degree of domination. He respects her career, but his job is clearly more important to him than hers is; he is perfectly willing to support her. "He seems to have a lot of scar tissue from women who have been on his case to be more liberated," she says, laughing. "He is looking for [a] strong woman who will not hesitate to take on some of the more traditional trappings of wife and motherhood." Currently, he is pressing Lexi to marry him, settle down, and have his children.

At this point in the interview, Lexi began shifting about in her chair, her replies became more and more terse. Irritation seeped from every pore, a clear by-product of her current crisis, her current indecision. "When it gets right down to it, something in me is terrified of that because it's giving up or giving in." She remembers her mother's early example. "I don't have any sense that there is life after marriage and children. . . . It's like going off into never-never land. Very scary." She looks around at her friends, and they all agree that leaving work to have children seems lonely. "Being very afraid of that isolation, [my friends] are saying, 'Well, I'll have [a baby] if you'll have one.' "

In short, despite a firm commitment to her work, the part of Lexi which once designed houses and installed children in them has not been totally squelched. In fact, she is deeply ambivalent about whether or not to continue working: sometimes marriage and motherhood seem an attractive alternative. "I've joked with a friend of mine, 'I just want my slip to come in the mail at work, saying, . . . "OK, you've proved you can do it. It's OK—you can go home now." ' " When it gets down to brass tacks, Lexi is proud of her achievement—but knows she will continue to sacrifice a fulfilling personal life unless she sets different priorities. Reaching the age when her mother married her father, she is now taking the time to stop and look around, to see where she is going. Never, as a child—never before, in fact—did she think she would have to make such a conscious and restricting choice. But now she recognizes that she will not have the four children she once dreamed of—in fact, unless she is willing to make some big compromises, she may never be a mother at all.

Lexi does not yet know which choice she will make. In fact, she—as are many of her friends—is knocking herself out to avoid the finality of such a choice by frantically "credential piling," as insurance against the day she may want to re-enter the job market.

One aspect of Lexi's story continued to puzzle me until I wrote up this chapter: what had changed within her to allow such serious consideration of the traditional life-style she had discarded years ago? Thinking about it, however, I remembered that after Phillip's death in 1975 Margot underwent a mastectomy. She became dependent on Lexi—completely. During this traumatic time, Lexi found the strength to rise above their child-parent relationship—to mother her mother.

Seeing a psychiatrist, she was able to separate herself emotionally from Margot. "I no longer saw us as being the same person," she told me, "but [saw] that somehow we really are different." As a result, I felt, Lexi gradually began to define how much of her ambition was actually her own. Like Margot, she has launched a successful career, but now, in her early thirties, she begins to think it may not be enough, and allows herself to feel concomitant needs for security and stability.

I asked Lexi to list her current major goals. She hesitated. Her head bent under the lamplight, I could see gray hairs glisten against the brown. Then she looked at me directly. "I guess, in general, it's just to get some peace and quiet," she said. "To get off this fence I'm on." Another pause. "And I guess, specifically, it's to have a family." Although Lexi Whitmer may find it difficult to face, she sounds as though she has already made her choice.

Twelve

Rachel Fielding

"She's twenty-eight years old, a clinical psychologist, and she's pregnant," my friend Laura Kelly told me excitedly. "I met her on the subway."

"The subway?" I queried skeptically. "Do you really know this woman well enough for me to call her?" But I was intrigued, I had to admit it. For several months, I had hoped to find a career-oriented woman who was going to have a baby. I was dying to find out how she planned to manage a sleight of hand my other interviewees had said was impossible. In particular, I wanted to see the role her husband would play. From Laura's description, Rachel Fielding was very ambivalent about her unplanned pregnancy, worried about how she would maintain her psychological practice while raising the child. Her juggling act promised to be fascinating. I called.

When I arrived at her home on a weekday afternoon, her husband answered the door. The Fieldings lived in the cozy top floor of a big old Cambridge house. The rooms were small, full of nooks and crannies; the windows were of odd size and intricately shaped. Though inexpensively furnished, it was quite comfortable. Before settling down in the sunny living room with Rachel, I had a long discussion with Michael on the merits of their new food processor. He was clearly the cook in this home.

In fact, as I learned later, Michael was a very liberated young man, who worked his schedule as an attorney around their home life; he even planned to assume an equal part of the child care. This was the first time I had encountered a husband willing to break free of traditional male roles in a way that would actually mean rearranging and restructuring his own career. Most women I had previously interviewed—Lexi Whitmer, for example—had partners willing to help out with the chores—as long as it was convenient and cost them nothing.

My first reaction was disbelief, then surprise, then envy. But as we talked, I began to see something new—and unexpected. Young women I had spoken with had often complained that the modern male had not changed fundamentally in his expectations for women. Here, however, was the imagined ideal—a truly flexible man. Nevertheless, the Fieldings had major role problems. Why? Eventually, I was to discover that the *woman's* expectations for the man had not fundamentally changed, despite her altered expectations for herself. While Rachel was grateful that Michael so willingly took on both child-care and household duties, she nevertheless still assumed he would also play a more traditionally male role. Raised in a home with a father who was an abundant provider, she inevitably expected the same from her husband. Her feelings underscored yet again just how much we internalize the role models we are weaned on in childhood—regardless of how we may later resist. Rachel Fielding's background illuminated sharply why she was still experiencing difficulties in what most women imagined was the best of all possible worlds.

She was born in 1950, the first child in a strictly traditional Jewish family of five. Her early environment reinforced this sense of convention: Louise and Bernard Fischer raised their children in a growing Jewish suburb of Boston, a community whose houses were small, brand-new, and set tightly together. Here everyone was on their way up—hardworking husbands with supportive wives who kept clean homes and made lots of babies. Rachel's street, consequently, was brimming over with other children her age.

Childhood was a time of security and love. At first, money

was a little tight: with Louise at home with the children, the family was dependent solely on Bernie's income. But it didn't really matter. The family was bonded closely together with a love money could have never replaced. Nevertheless, Rachel's parents made sure their children did not worry about finances; they never fought over it—or any other issue, for that matter.

Bernie ruled the roost, a traditional male, a little chauvinistic, very dogmatic. Nevertheless, his attitude toward Rachel was substantially different from his attitude toward her mother. Like many fathers in "Mavericks," he encouraged his daughter to have ambitions—often treating her like a son. He admired her stubborn and independent spirit—even while he was trying to get her to think like him. Simply put, they were a great deal alike.

Watching her parents interact, Rachel could see that her mother had her way only by being devious. "She got things around the mulberry bush," she remembers. But Louise was not particularly happy in her role as the acquiescent homemaker. Educated at Smith, she felt restless and did not know how to break free; consequently, she encouraged her daughter to excel in school, to extend herself, to think broadly of the future—much as Sarah Diamond's mother had. But Rachel did not desperately seek intimacy, as Sarah did. With a secure home base behind her, Rachel could think about her own future in other terms.

Encouraged by both parents, Rachel distinguished herself from the start as a top student. She did exceptionally well in traditionally male subjects like math and science. One day she would definitely have a career, she knew, although she was unclear on which one. Marriage seemed a possibility, too. "But I didn't see that as the only thing in my life," she was quick and emphatic to point out to me. "I think that had to do with my father. . . . I saw him as always having a major focus of activity outside the house. . . . My mother had a lot of doubts about what it meant to be female, and she had a lot of trouble mirroring [a female image] back to me. So it was easier for me to get a mirror from my father about what one could do and what one could be."

In fact, during these years, she would rather have been a boy. "I thought they could do more," she told me with a grin. "Men were always much more energetic, involved, doing things that seemed interesting." Her school experience reinforced this notion: wanting to be the head of her class, she continually found herself competing with a boy. She loved sports and soon identified herself as a tomboy.

When Rachel was in the fifth grade, the Fischers moved up a notch to a much fancier Boston suburb. Bernie's business was improving, his expectations were rising. Rachel switched schools but continued to excel. In 1965, she entered high school, but dropped math and science—as girls traditionally did—in order to pick up a second foreign language. Shooting toward college, continuing to be at the top of the heap, she was obsessed about homework.

But while secure with her academic status, she was not nearly so pleased with herself socially. Her looks were a sore spot. Neurotic about her skinny frame, she avoided being weighed in gym class, and although she did belong to both a popular, fast-paced clique and a more intellectual one, she simply felt inadequate. The socialites were exacting in their requirements, with an enormous emphasis on clothes, money, cars, and boys. They were the trend setters. "It was a Jewish version of being cool," she says now. Innumerable color-coordinated Villager and John Meyer outfits were requisite, and a girl had to smoke Marlboros and go drinking on Saturday nights.

Bernie did not like to see her involved with this fast crowd, and here the first signs of family discord began to simmer. He and Louise urged Rachel to concentrate on her studies—which she did easily. Nevertheless, she found it fun to be part of a gang—even if only on the periphery. In an effort to control her, Bernie refused to let her drive the family car after she got her license. Because teen-age social life revolved around cars, she felt stigmatized. She couldn't bear being treated like a child.

By contrast, boys were not something they argued about. For one thing, although her mother had married at twenty-one, Rachel continued to identify mainly with her father and did not contemplate getting married until her early thirties; thus, boys were somewhat useless for a while. Moreover, she simply felt very uncomfortable with them, still viewing herself as a tomboy, although she knew it was no longer appropriate. She wasn't sure where to fit in.

Still, unless you intended to live on Mars, you had to date. And so, in the ninth grade, holding her partners at arm's length, Rachel accepted the inevitable. By junior year, she had even acquired a steady: since image was more important than substance, she chose a "desirable" member of the football team who drove a classy MG. The relationship itself left a lot to be desired, but that didn't matter too much to Rachel because she wasn't serious about it anyway. It was all for show. Needless to say, sex didn't even enter her mind.

Sexual peer pressure *was* a very complicated issue, however. It was chic not to be a virgin—and yet most "good" girls in Rachel's crowd still claimed to be one. For her own part, Rachel never even let her steady get close enough to be a threat to her chastity. Kissing alone was bad enough. Over the ensuing years, this self-protective aloofness would prove an able defense against all men who expressed real interest in her.

Instead, she devoted all her emotion to planning for the future. In many ways, her ambition cut her off from her peers—most girls she knew did not plan to have careers. Following a class trip to Washington, D.C., she had a vague dream of being a senator. Soon, though, thinking realistically, she decided that a career in the field of health might be more attainable.

College was a certain and immediate goal, and she ended up at her mother's alma mater—Smith. As a man might, she mapped out a strategy for the coming years. Like Elaine Magdaal, she had already decided to aim for a graduate degree, wondering whether to stop at a master's or shoot for a Ph.D. The major task before her was merely to define the field. But, although she viewed college mainly as a place to study, she became dismayed by the insularity of a rural, all-girls school from the moment she set foot on the Smith campus. Something she craved was missing, a certain "all-around element." Even someone as private as Rachel Fielding felt cut off from a social life here. "It was just too academic," she told me. "I wanted to become more of a whole person. I felt that Smith was kind of an ivory tower. . . . I missed . . . the whole counterculture revolution." A fairly unorthodox girl to begin with—by her peers' standards, at least—she was beginning to feel the urge to take part in what her generation was becoming famous for. It was 1969.

Acting quickly, she transferred to Stanford for sophomore year and jumped right into the middle of the big pond. Here there was the Haight-Ashbury drug scene, the Grateful Dead, Grace Slick, and the Airplane. Here were riots over Cambodia and Kent State. All of it appealed strongly to a girl who had never been particularly traditional, who had never quite fitted in with fraternity dances and fast cars. She came into her own, put on weight, streaked her hair, and took up a California girl image. As she relaxed more and more around men, her social life improved: here at Stanford, intelligence added to a girl's appeal. Most important, she felt at home: it was expected that one was aiming for a career. She wasn't weird anymore. As Rebecca Madison discovered when she came from Wyoming to Radcliffe, Rachel finally found other women who shared the same feelings she did.

To her delight, many people told her she looked like Gloria Steinem; still, though the Women's Movement was certainly a common topic at Stanford, she felt its impact only slightly. In fact, there had been more intense debate at Smith—where she had first encountered feminism—because the school was considering going coed. Feminism endorsed her desire for career, but she felt little need for such support—she had always got plenty from her parents. Additionally, she had never felt oppressed. Still, she did read the standard feminist literature and found guidance from a feminist woman professor. Symposiums on day care and related issues drew her attention, but mostly out of principle, rather than need. She wasn't worried about children—yet.

Although Rachel was dead set on having some sort of career, she was still confused about which direction to take. The need to decide began to press with increasing urgency as her time at Stanford passed. Of course, few of her peers knew exactly what they wanted, either—although they were all intent on careers—but this was little consolation. In her senior year, she took law and business entrance examinations, and GREs as well, in an effort to keep all options open.

Marriage was certainly not an alternative. All through college, she had continued to keep men at a distance emotionally, and especially sexually, because to Rachel sex implied commitment. As a self-protective measure, she decided marriage might never be a part of her life, because men and sex were just too complicated, and took too much energy away from serious things.

Slowly, the idea of practicing clinical psychology began to seem like a definite possibility. She was majoring in the field, and had enjoyed her work with autistic and schizophrenic children in day-care centers and summer camps. But she felt a strong lack of guidance. All of Stanford's tenured psychologists were experimentalists, extremely disdainful of clinicians. "I had no role model," she recalls. "There was no one for me to talk to." Nevertheless, after much soul-searching, Rachel decided to take the plunge. She was overjoyed when Columbia accepted her as a Ph.D. candidate, and ecstatic when the federal government gave her a stipend under the National Association for Mental Health.

New York City was exciting—but lonely—and Rachel concentrated hard on her work. It was an intense program with a clinical internship in the third year and a dissertation in the fourth. She planned to receive her degree by 1977. Bernie and Louise were thrilled for her. Louise, once again, took vicarious pleasure in her daughter's success. Bragging about her to all her friends, she seemed to deal with Rachel almost as an extension of herself. In short, Louise could now consider herself a completely successful mother: her daughter had fulfilled her every expectation. Just as she had hoped, Rachel found the work both fascinating and fulfilling. Her future looked bright in a field where there were many opportunities for women. More self-confident, with her career seemingly well on its way, Rachel gradually felt she could afford more close contact with the opposite sex. She dated many different types of men—and finally let herself become sexually intimate with a few. Then, during the summer of 1973, she met Michael Fielding. "It seems to me that we were star-crossed lovers," she told me, a puzzled expression on her face. "It was almost as if he fell off a cloud." She laughed. "This is one of the few things in my life I still do not understand at all." In reality, prior to Michael she had never allowed herself to open up, wanting to find the right sort of man first—one who wouldn't cause complications with her career.

They met through friends. Her first impression of him, in fact, was not complimentary at all—despite what she told me initially. With his cuffed narrow pants and penny loafers, she thought he was a "drip." But, assessing him again, she decided that maybe he was "cute"—and even a little endearing. Though he was a first-year Harvard Law student and lived in Boston, they began dating.

He was hardly the most clearly directed person Rachel had ever met, and that was really fine with her. Michael had done undergraduate work at Yale and spent three years in the Peace Corps in an effort to "find himself." Coming from a family of Western European Jews, he placed great stock in intellectual pursuits, and common interests in academics sparked their relationship. He seemed like a flexible young man—attractive, intelligent, easygoing—and not surefooted enough in his life plans to threaten her. In fact, he wasn't particularly ambitious at all. Coming from a family of strong women, he was not interested in a conservative wife any more than she was interested in a conservative husband. Later that year, Rachel managed to take her internship at a well-known mental hospital near Boston, and she began living with him.

In keeping with his laid-back "liberated" character, Michael was willing to do all the housework and cleaning, and this arrangement suited her just fine, because she had no intention of ever being subservient to a man. "I had a lot of conflicts about being the woman in the relationship," she says, "and I would not do anything. I didn't cook. I didn't clean." Meanwhile, hating law school, Michael took a year off—again in search of his identity—to work as a carpenter. Her parents, thinking he was a bum, pressed Rachel to get out.

But she was serious about him—and, besides, she loved their unorthodox arrangement. Being the pacesetter, the breadwinner, was exciting. In the summer of 1975, they married.

But then Michael's lack of direction and his discontent with his chosen field began to create problems. Slowly, Rachel began to feel he lived vicariously through her career—just as her mother did—pressing his ambitions for her as a substitute for his own. He urged her to drive herself hard, to forge ahead. Soon she found that this emphasis on her career rubbed her the wrong way. Further, to her surprise, she began to feel angry that she made more money than Michael—despite her liberated attitudes. It was a problem rooted not in finance but in emotion, an anger that she could not shake, no matter how much she rationalized. "It's a neurotic issue," she admits, "but I think he should be able to take care of me."

Rachel fights these feelings—she recognizes that they are unreasonable. But she has discovered that some of her expectations were formed so long ago that even she, a professional psychologist, is unable to reverse them easily.

Eventually, Michael did finish school and began practicing public-sector law. While his salary is adequate, Rachel likes the luxuries their two incomes provide and so continues to wish he would go into private practice, so that, if need be, he alone could support her in the style to which she is accustomed.

Since finishing her dissertation and receiving her Ph.D. in 1977, Rachel has been practicing clinical psychology in a private group, and teaches graduate students part time. She enjoyed this routine for a year; ultimately, though, she preferred to work in a university or medical center. And so, in July of 1977, she received a postdoctoral fellowship and got ready to pick up stakes and move to a different city. Michael, ever flexible, was willing to follow her.

But fate intervened. She was pregnant, victim of a failed IUD. Her first thought was abortion, but when, during an ultrasound X ray, she saw the amniotic sac, such drastic action seemed less simple. Not simple at all, in fact.

Finally, Michael and she decided it would be immoral to snuff out a life just because it was inconveniently timed; they had planned to have a baby in several years anyway. Still, Rachel is not happy, and she has not embraced the idea fully. Turning down her fellowship was crushing. "I was pretty depressed for a while," she told me, sighing, "because it became apparent to me that I could not do two things at the same time that were that time-consuming. A fellowship is full time." Currently, she plans to work part time for the first year, having a nurse for the time she and Michael are busy. She feels trapped, worrying that the baby will cut deeply into her private practice for many years to come.

"Is there any chance you might *like* staying at home?" I asked tentatively.

"Yeah, I'm sure that's a possibility," she said quickly. "But that makes me real nervous. A lot of people have suggested that I might like it at home—and every time they say it, I feel like jumping out the window."

Rachel dreams of recapturing her fellowship in 1979. Even though these positions are full time—as she herself admits—

she hopes that she can swing it by working only four days a week, with Michael doing the same. Of course, she is the first to acknowledge that this may well be impossible. In any case, she now feels that her ambivalence about the baby has provoked a delayed identity crisis. "It's very scary to me. I never thought that would happen. I sort of cruised through graduate school while everyone else had self-doubts." Now, with pregnancy making her think deeply about all her choices, she begins to wonder exactly where in her field she can find a niche, given the restraints of having a child. "My major goal [for the future] is to decide what it is I really want. So that I can focus on the one or two things and not feel that I have to go around plugging all these holes in myself." Trying to balance everything has suddenly made her aware that the choices she makes now will shape the rest of her life. Looking around the field of clinical psychology, she sees no one to whom she can turn for an example. "The women in my field traditionally are not married and don't have kids," she explains.

As each day goes by and her options seem more and more restricted, the Women's Movement appeals increasingly to Rachel, and her outlook becomes more radical. "I'm really hysterical about what I want, what's morally right and what's not morally right. [There should be] nationalized day care and all that stuff. I have an axe to grind." Her own needs have finally made feminism relevant to her in a way it wasn't during those days when career seemed uncomplicated.

Rachel's peers—professional women—pressure her to keep working, urge her not to remain in the home with her child. Her parents, on the other hand, despite their previous support for her career, have now begun encouraging her to take time off and be with the baby. Like Elaine Magdaal, Rachel finds her parents' switch in attitude very confusing—and threatening.

Overall, the idea of becoming at all like her mother terrifies her, yet she recognizes that to be fair to her child she must incorporate at least part of Louise's strategy in her present life-style. Having patterned herself upon her father's example, such a concession comes hard, and she is desperately trying to reconcile and integrate what looks like two totally opposite ways of living. This crisis, this juggling act, is something she never anticipated, and she feels totally unprepared to deal with it, unprepared to make the necessary compromises. Finances aside, even working part-time strikes her as a big psychological sacrifice—a detour around a large lake when she had been charging down the open highway at ninety miles an hour.

In the long run, she and I agreed, being caught in the middle like this puts her life on a desolate, lonely plateau. As she admits, she does not want to believe that choosing one thing or the other may be her only release. Rachel Fielding is running scared.

Part V

Self-Made Women

*I risked everything I believed in and everything
I thought I had—all my intelligence, and whatever else—on the possibility that there is such a
thing as starting over.*

—CHRIS HASTINGS

Unlike the women in the previous sections, who at least identified with either their mothers or their fathers, the group I have called "Self-Made Women" identified with no one at all. Right from the start, they rejected the role models their childhood environments proffered to them.

Growing up under extraordinarily difficult conditions—emotionally, materially, or both—they became far more concerned with their present than with their future, using all their stamina simply to stay alive from day to day. Many of them, unlike those in other sections, had no choice but to work to support themselves. Stressed hard early in life and continuing to be stressed, they coped not merely with a single disaster but with a multitude of disasters. Life itself was a holocaust.

But like hothouse seedlings, these women were forced to a painful and brilliant maturity. Using no role model, no mentor, they began to shape and guide their own lives, dragging themselves upward by their bootstraps, daring to dream dreams they had never heard of or seen before. They forged whole new identities for themselves in a world where they had been rudderless. Eventually, they developed a peculiar sense of vision and direction. They came, early on, to live and deal with risk, and it was the development of a skill, a capability that would pay off in a big way later on. In many ways, they became like the self-made men of years gone by, making and breaking their own luck.

For the most part, I found these women to have become quite successful within their chosen fields; they showed a dedication which rivaled that of those who modeled themselves professionally from the start. But instead of viewing choice as an ironic curse, this group has found it a sought-for and unaccustomed luxury. Their early expertise at creating choices and then handling them has proved invaluable in both their professional and their personal lives. Once they lived in a world with no future, little choice. Now, through careers, they sit in positions with many alternatives on all sides.

Each of these women reached a crisis point sometime in her mid-twenties when she had to make plans that would inexorably direct her life for years to come. She accepted the need for sacrifice and sought a mentor—a search that often ended in the ranks of the Women's Movement.

As a result, these women turned out to be the most devout feminists I interviewed. If they champion liberation ardently, it is because they need to. Feminism has become more and more a bulwark in their struggles upward; they feel the movement provides them with examples of women who make their own successes happen—and this, after all, is their trademark.

As I talked with these women—three of whom are presented here—I could feel their tangible strength. There was pride built on real career achievement; there was a keen sense of self-awareness, of limitations tested and known, a quality of balanced humility. Are they better off? Not necessarily, for they still have to make the same painful choices as everyone else. But, in the long run, of all the women I talked to, these were the most able to choose realistically between alternatives, to accept the sacrifices—and the consequences.

Thirteen

Amy Wheeler

Amy Wheeler had insisted on coming to where I was staying in New York, uncomfortable with the idea of talking in her own apartment. I didn't like it—when a woman takes you into her home, I felt, she lets you into her life—but quickly I understood. Amy's whole life story was characterized by her fiercely self-protective instincts. Independent, self-sufficient, self-reliant, she had learned these attributes the hard way. Sent at the age of twelve to live with her father, rejected by a mother who didn't want her—and who let her know it in no uncertain terms—she was a survivor. Her father hadn't wanted her, either, she told me, her clear blue eyes mirroring that old pain. "When I was twelve, I knew what the hell was going on. I knew what it was like to have been bounced. I knew I was going to have to do it on my own."

She was born in 1949 to Sally and Bob Wheeler, who had married in the nick of time—a mere six months before her arrival. It was not the best of circumstances from the start: Sally was a bitter woman with two daughters from a previous marriage that had ended in divorce. She did not welcome Amy's arrival—or that, in 1952, of yet another baby girl. Hating every minute of homemaking, she gave away most of her responsibilities as fast as she could; from an early age, the children were saddled with the cooking and cleaning, while their mother loafed in bed until noon reading dime-store novels. "When my little sister was born," Amy remembers, "I was three years old, but it was my responsibility to do things like laundry, and watch her, and take her for a walk in the park."

They lived in a tiny town in Idaho, population three thousand—a town of provincial, ordinary middle-class Americans. Bob Wheeler was a mechanic who owned a service station, a tough customer determined to rise above his low-income background. But it wasn't easy—not with so many mouths to feed. He worked sixteen hours a day, seven days a week. Still, they barely scraped by.

With her father gone nearly all the time, Amy remained primarily under her mother's erratic rule. Sally was hardly a good example of the joys of motherhood—or of being a wife, for that matter. Right from the beginning, the children knew how miserable marriage could be, and how shabbily a man could treat his helpmate because Bob Wheeler constantly ran around with other women.

Finally, when Amy was five, whatever security she had was shattered with her parents' divorce. It was an ugly time: full accounts of her father's peccadilloes were published in the local newspapers, with pictures of the family on the front page. And then, like a wounded cobra, Sally struck out at Amy, blaming her for all the trouble—if she hadn't gotten pregnant with her, she wouldn't have married Bob in the first place. Calling the five-year-old child into her bedroom, she broke the news viciously by telling Amy, "Your father hates you so much he's leaving—for someone else."

"That really hit me hard at the age of five," Amy told me nervously. "I really felt terribly responsible."

In the backwaters of Idaho, in the middle 1950s, a woman's only alternative to homemaking was a menial job. With nothing more than a high school diploma, Sally went to work as a telephone operator. Less than a year after the divorce, still miserable, she remarried. The message was obvious: a woman either does shit work for shit money, or she does shit work for no money. Ned Tyler was a divorcé with three children: the family numbered nine, and Sally was still miserable.

So was Amy. In this huge new family, she just couldn't seem to find a niche. She felt lost, an outsider—a feeling that would plague her for many years to come. "I was no longer special," she says, "living day to day with all those other children." She had been Bob Wheeler's favorite; she missed him terribly and began to resent her stepfather.

Now, on the third time around, Sally was simply desperate to make *this* marriage work. Even though she still abdicated many of her responsibilities, she tried to create family unity by forcing religion and home study down everybody's throat. Each evening was spent in the living room, reading the Bible, or meeting with other Jehovah's Witnesses. Amy, like the other children, despised it all. "There was never anything fun," she told me, grimacing. "If it sounded fun, you couldn't do it . . . it was the Lord's will." The family didn't celebrate Christmas, allow Halloween, or exchange birthday presents. They really didn't do anything but study Scripture.

In short, Sally made home a prison. Any outside intrusion seemed to threaten her world. The seven children were literally not allowed to cross an imaginary border drawn around the house—on pain of a severe spanking. Amy was not allowed to play after school at someone else's house, nor were her playmates allowed to come home with her. Overnights were out of the question. Needless to say, all these restrictions obliterated any possibility of making friends. "We were expected to find our friendships within the family," Amy recalls with great anger. "I didn't like that, and since I was the recalcitrant, I was shunned." Her isolation was complete.

Amy's mother and stepfather backed up their dictums with an old-fashioned heavy hand: if her childhood was marked by feelings of loneliness, it was equally punctuated by a great deal of fear. Neither Sally nor Ned hesitated to beat her brutally when she dared challenge their authority. "He really gave me black eyes," she told me. "They thought . . . they were going to knock some sense into me." It took remarkably little to set them off. "One time I happened to tell a girl in school to 'shut up.' 'Shut up' was a no-no word in our household. My sister happened to hear me and told my parents. I really got zonked . . . really hit a lot. I couldn't go to school because of [a broken] nose and stuff."

She often missed school because of the bruises. Still, when she could attend, she made sure to distinguish herself. School was an escape from abuse, one place she could find positive feedback. Very early on, she was a top student in her class: excellent at math and science, she also won several prizes for English papers.

At home, however, her scholastic achievements were ridiculed—or disbelieved. Once, when she brought home an A on a composition, Sally accused her of plagiarism. Another time, she wrote an article that the school wanted to publish in its newspaper. "My mother wouldn't let me. She said she thought I'd copied it from some church book."

In short, Amy's parents felt that school didn't matter, that being smart wouldn't help her do anything. She was destined to nothing more than following in her mother's footsteps. Clearly, too, Sally and Ned felt Amy might learn something that would threaten her devotion to God. "Education was never held out to us as a thing to strive for. . . . We were always expected either to become very involved in the religion or get married."

But Amy wanted no part of this claustrophobic world—as a child or as an adult. She dreamed of adventure, of escape from a mechanized, automaton-like existence. Books were her bridge into fantasy, and she sneaked forbidden volumes into the house: Trixie Belden and Nancy Drew mystery stories; Rudyard Kipling and his strange new worlds; *Redbook* magazine for romantic intrigue. Her appetite was voracious.

When Amy was ten, Sally and Ned packed the entire family into the car and drove to New York City for a convention of Jehovah's Witnesses. Here, like Dorothy seeing

Oz for the first time, Amy found her dreamworld: the craggy skyline, the crowded sidewalks, Yankee Stadium, Staten Island, Carnegie Hall, the subway, the Automat. Stunned, she imagined giving a piano debut at Carnegie and living in the big city. Naturally, she hid these heretical fantasies—as she had always hidden her real thoughts—but that didn't matter for now. At last, her dreams of escape had found something concrete to give them focus. Inadvertently, Sally and Ned had provided fuel for her fire.

As Amy Wheeler entered puberty, her blond hair and pretty smile began to draw notice from boys. She loved it; here, finally, someone was paying attention to her in a good way—with a kiss instead of a slap. Naturally, however, Sally slammed the door tight on dating, and allowed no phone calls from boys, no mixed social events. It was part of her religious neuroticism: she soon became convinced that her daughter's good looks were gifts from Satan. "Whenever she would catch me looking at some guy in church," Amy says, "I would get taken to the car and yelled at. She would accuse me of sleeping around—even when I was twelve!" Sally was obsessed with fear that Amy would get pregnant out of wedlock—as she herself had—and constantly called her daughter a tramp.

When Amy was in the sixth grade, the Tylers moved to Florida, where Ned had been offered a position as a technician at an Air Force base. But the job had evaporated by the time they arrived. For a full year, he was unemployed and the family almost starved, reduced to eating "really crazy things, like hominy grits three times a day." Occasionally, when there was absolutely no more money left, a check would miraculously arrive—"from the Lord," Sally would claim. But Amy knew perfectly well that only a child-support payment from her real father could send her mother to the store to buy neat treats like bologna sandwiches.

It was a period marked by increased beatings from Sally and Ned, who had grown more and more frustrated with their own lives. Sally was still unable to deal with either her daughter's irrepressible personality or her blossoming good looks. Still, even in these most wretched times, Amy managed to flirt, because a social life was her only escape from home. Finally overwhelmed, Sally packed Amy off to Bob Wheeler—but not before terrifying the twelve-year-old girl by calling her "a wicked child" and warning that Amy was being sent away to her real father so that he could punish her with unprecedented fury.

The fear was devastating, as was the sense of complete rejection. When Bob Wheeler picked her up at the airport in Idaho, he found a petrified girl who shied away from his touch. Immediately, however, he demonstrated that her life was about to change, by buying her a whole new wardrobe and showering her with words of affection. Warily, Amy decided that things might be all right.

Bob Wheeler had come up in the world, and was making a lot of money in real estate. When he saw how much his daughter liked her new things, he advised her to plan on marrying a college man. She listened hard: never before had anyone given credence to her secret fantasy of moving up in the world. In addition, her father lavishly praised her intelligence and high grades in school. With his support, she began to dream a young man's dream: to leave Idaho someday and make her fortune. Still, in keeping with her background, these dreams centered on catching one particular kind of airplane ticket—a man.

Now, for the first time, she was allowed to invite other girls home, and even to date. But learning to trust others was difficult for a girl who had wrapped a protective cocoon around herself. While she did make friends, she could never bring herself to trust them, convinced they were talking behind her back.

Still, she was quickly part of the "in" clique at school. Smoking, drinking, and swearing were musts, and she participated eagerly. Nevertheless, with her background, she found it hard to bring off the proper air. A popular girl was supposed to smile at all times and never, ever, talk of depressing things. Amy, on the other hand, found it impossible to suppress her "serious" personality: on their first date, one young man told her that, for a fourteen-year-old, she had more problems than anyone he'd ever met.

Before too long, however, her new bubble burst. Like his ex-wife, Bob Wheeler became convinced that his daughter was promiscuous. God help her if a boy made the familiar adolescent mistake of bringing her home late. "Fourteen years old, in a dress, and my father would beat me up in the front yard," she told me bitterly. "In front of my boyfriends." She sighed. "After that, they'd never want to go out with me again."

Soon, with boys her age afraid to date her, she began hanging around with older men—men who brought the inevitable sexual complications that her father had been so anxious to avert. All along, Amy had been determined to avoid the trap that had caught her mother, the trap Sally had predicted would be her fate. She intended to be a virgin when she married. Unfortunately, Sally, who preached purity but had conceived out of wedlock, was really a miasma of contradictions, and Amy was hopelessly confused—to say nothing of being completely uninformed. "The first time I had an orgasm," she told me, "which was only by petting, I remember saying to the guy, 'Oh, gosh, will I get pregnant?' "

At sixteen, she fell hard for a twenty-two-year-old sawmill worker who was saving his money to become a hairdresser. To Amy, any man who ambitiously saved his money was a step up. Nevertheless, she refused to sleep with him; he dumped her. A week later, she called him back to acquiesce. "We went out in his car, and parked on some farm road," she told me with distaste. "I remember thinking, 'God, is this what it's all about? It's so icky!' "

Desperate to find a man to run off with, she naïvely assumed Roger would want to marry her. It was a rude awakening. Before long, he was going out with other girls, and she felt crushed, used, "sold down the river." The general pattern was one often repeated in the next few years. "I was always bonkers over *somebody*—and I would expect them to be crazy about me because I was risking my life to be with them."

Even though Roger didn't stick around long, his example taught Amy that if you worked hard and saved your money, you could get out of Idaho—and away from all it represented to her. Always the enterprising type, she had picked strawberries, ironed shirts, and worked as cashier in the school cafeteria for extra money. Now she began to bank it.

She was determined not to close any door which might aid her escape and so poured herself into studying. Business courses were her special forte—shorthand, typing, business math, and management. During junior year, she even won a contest for being the fastest shorthand student in the state. Nicknamed the Brain by her crowd, she began to win respect for her intelligence instead of just her looks. Unlike many of the women I talked with, she kept herself well informed during these years—reading the Idaho *Daily Statesman* and her father's *Wall Street Journal.* All this made her even more certain: she *had* to get out.

Bob Wheeler's fury over his daughter's imagined promiscuity made their relationship unbearable. Finally, at sixteen, she got a job after school as a waitress, left home, and found her own room for fifteen dollars a month. Bob hit the roof at this rejection of the life he offered—and tried to get her fired. But she was good at her work, and the manager of the restaurant refused to cooperate. In accordance with her plans, she opened a savings account and lived frugally.

In the spring of her senior year, she met Cal Stuart, a college man who immediately seemed to be that airplane ticket she had been searching for. Amy was swept off her feet by his good looks and excellent prospects, and soon they were talking about getting married. A Mormon, Cal felt that he and his wife should be virgins on their wedding night. She did not dare tell him about Roger.

He did more than simply offer to marry her. Almost as important, he encouraged her to apply to college herself—a new and startling idea that she seized excitedly. She talked with her high school guidance counselor and sent away for catalogues. "I was going to be a doctor," she told me. "I worked at my job till midnight, when the restaurant closed, and saved all my money." She even won a state scholarship to help with finances. Things were finally shaping up.

But fate intervened. One winter night while Cal was on National Guard duty, Amy got drunk with one of his best friends, and they ended up in bed. Before long, she discovered she was pregnant. Now she was a typical small-town girl caught in a typical American tragedy. Abortions were illegal in Idaho in 1967, of course, and she "couldn't even get the name of a quack." Nor would she have had the money to pay one. Nevertheless, despair was overtaken by determination. She simply was not going to let this destroy her life. She seduced Cal, faking the pain of losing her virginity. Several weeks later, she "discovered" she was pregnant with his baby.

In February 1967, Amy's seventeenth year, they were married. Now she was afraid: she was about to be a young mother, trapped just as her mother had been. Still, she concentrated on being a good wife and making the best of her situation. Her husband was in college: she willingly put aside her own ambitions and found work to support him.

But before long Cal dropped out of school—money was tight, and a baby was on the way—and he went to work as a butcher. In a subtle way, her esteem for her husband began to fall. Perhaps it was that he had left college without a fight, without being willing to live on a shoestring—as she had for years. Or maybe it was that he had been so easily duped about her pregnancy. At any rate, she was already fed up with him. "That day I had Tim in the hospital," she told me, "it hit me: 'You really don't need him anymore.'" Baby or not, she was going to get where she wanted to go.

Three weeks after giving birth, she went back to secretarial work in a computer center. Nights were spent in the Laundromat doing diapers; it was, as she had feared, a carbon copy of her mother's life. She had herself sterilized so she could never get pregnant again. For the first time, convinced that a man wasn't a ticket to anything, she signed up for a course in computer programming, determined to create her own opportunities.

Over the next several years, her respect for her husband continued to wane. She had a number of short-term affairs with college students; Cal could never seem to gather the discipline necessary to return to school. Then, penny-pinching, he stupidly canceled Tim's health insurance—over Amy's vociferous objections—just before the baby caught pneumonia and had to be hospitalized. Now they were in debt up to their eyeballs, and college was out for good.

And, finally, she simply decided she didn't want to be married anymore—at least, not to him. She asked him for a divorce.

Alone with Tim in their small apartment, she continued caring for him and working full time as a secretary. Child-support checks came infrequently at best; her difficult life had never been so hard. Unpaid debts mounted before her eyes like a tidal wave—especially Tim's old hospital bill, that bitter pill. To her dismay, she discovered that a secondhand Volkswagen Cal had "bought" her was actually mortgaged. "The payments were thirty-five dollars a month," she remembers. "I was only making four hundred a month—clearing exactly three hundred. I paid one thirty-five in rent, a hundred for the baby-sitter. I was so poor that first year I didn't have a television, ... I had to disconnect the telephone, ... I had to wear nylons that had runs in them." She laughed sardonically. "And my father, all this time, said, 'Don't ask for a cent. You made your bed—sleep in it.' "

I was stunned. Even more remarkable, during these desperate days Amy Wheeler showed the extent of her determination and finished her high school credits by taking classes one evening a week. I began to see that the worse her life was the more she accomplished. At work, she quickly advanced from a secretary to a marketing assistant, adoring her new job. After a while, her boss had so much confidence in her that he left things in her hands during his frequent business trips.

Then complete disaster struck. While Amy was away at work one afternoon, Tim doused himself with a caldron of scalding water. He was in the hospital for three weeks, as the doctors struggled to save his life with numerous skin grafts.

She had had the foresight to get medical coverage as soon as Cal left, but it didn't begin to cover the bills. Her paycheck was docked each day when she took the baby to the doctor. But money was only the least of the horrors. "I couldn't pick him up because he was burned from head to toe. I'd hold him by his feet and his hair . . . and he would cry all night long." She looked at me hard. "I have to tell you, if there was anything that ever made me strong, it was getting him through that."

She ran herself ragged, shuttling between work, home, and Tim's doctor. Her friends thought she might have a nervous breakdown. But she didn't. Instead, she poured all her tension, all her nervous energy, into one object: work. It was the one place she felt in control. Every afternoon at five o'clock, she punched the time clock, hating to have to go home.

A year later, in November 1970, Tim had finally healed. Amy knew that this was her chance to make her exodus—to really get out of Idaho. Looking at a map, she arbitrarily picked San Francisco, printed up a batch of résumés, and began submitting them to marketing companies in the area. Using vacation time, she went down for a few interviews and finally landed a job—as a real estate secretary. It was a comedown—but at least it was in another state. The psychological lift was enormous. Packing all her belongings into a U-Haul truck, she drove with Tim to California and settled in a suburb; quickly, she was bored at work. Then, out of the clear blue, a coffee company that had interviewed her when she first came to San Francisco offered her a job as a marketing assistant. Suddenly she was on top of the world again. "It was so super!" she said, grinning at me. "I got to walk into meetings with yellow pads instead of shorthand pads!"

By now, it was abundantly clear to Amy that she did not really want a job—she wanted a career. Enterprising as ever, she began to look for mentors—for women who could show her the way. Not surprisingly, she began gobbling up the feminist literature, and going to hear feminists like Gloria Steinem speak. She liked what she found; becoming more assertive, she goaded all the secretaries at work into refusing to get coffee for their bosses.

In 1972, Amy finally concluded—women's lib or no women's lib—that she needed a better education to move up in the business world. Though still moonlighting as a waitress, she enrolled in night college. At home with Tim less than ever, her guilt level reached an all-time high when friends predicted that he would be a disturbed child. "Everyone I knew used to say, 'You really ought to be at home with that baby. You ought to go on welfare!' " But she ignored the warnings, determined to go it alone. Using feminism as a moral support to ward off the guilt, she finished her two-year program in only eighteen months by attending four nights a week and every weekend. Her motivation was immense. She got a new job that helped with tuition and transferred to a four-year school. In the summer of 1975, she graduated cum laude from California State. With bright eyes, she told me it was her greatest achievement. I couldn't help but agree.

Meanwhile, she was designing marketing programs for a financial corporation, and had won raises that brought her salary to twelve thousand a year. "That's when you know you've arrived," she said with a grin. "When you can quote it in annual fees instead of [weeks]." Things were improving in other ways, too. She began seeing Lou Pagan, a self-made engineer who owned an equipment-manufacturing company. He was two years older, educated, very bright; after the miles of meaningless sexual relationships, here was a man who really cared for her. He even adored the baby. Best of all, Lou could teach her a great deal about business. He supported her college efforts, sometimes taking care of Tim while she was at school; and often picked up the tab for extras—easing her financial burden without threatening her autonomy.

But in accordance with her pattern, she soon felt he did not suit her rising image. Ambition dictating her tastes and needs, she wanted a man who exuded success—a man in a three-piece suit. Gradually, as she had with her husband, she began to feel that Lou could no longer keep pace and she dropped him.

For a while, she was fiercely lonely: she had grown dependent on Lou, and missed his support and cheerful face. But instead of feeling sorry for herself, she picked herself up, shook herself off, and accepted a new job in Chicago that paid eighteen thousand a year.

The job lasted four months. She set up a new marketing department for a family business that was about to go big time. Now her résumé listed her as a marketing manager with an impressive salary. A succession of short-term jobs in marketing and selling over the next two years won her the plum she'd been waiting for ever since that Jehovah's Witnesses convention years before: New York.

Her present job is with a well-known marketing agency. Earning $40,000 a year, only twenty-eight years old, Amy Wheeler was the best-paid woman I interviewed. She particularly likes the autonomy and power that work brings. "When I'm pitching my program to someone, I'm asking them for anywhere from a quarter of a million dollars up to three-quarters of a million," she says with pride. Nevertheless, just as a man might, she views her current position as only one more step up the ladder. Her plan is to be an independent entrepreneur within five years, with a company of her own. Right now, she is building a network of skills, associates, and contacts. Her motivation, plain and simple, is money. That is the only kind of security she has ever known.

Unlike her career, her social life leaves much to be desired. She finds she often intimidates men her own age because of her successful career and earning power. A ten-year-old son doesn't heighten her appeal, either—an ironic twist for a woman who once thought her future doomed to only marriage and motherhood. Ultimately, her life-style would require an extremely liberated man, anyway; she would not consider moving to another city, preferring to commute by plane if there were a job conflict. She certainly does not envision herself in the role of homemaker.

Besides, there is little chance of finding the time a relationship needs because she sees Tim little enough as it is. "I just couldn't justify coming home from a business trip and then going out on a date," she says. She has often turned down dinner invitations to be present at her son's school plays or other important activities. She refuses to believe that he has really suffered from her career. "It's not easy," she says, "but you *can* do both. You can. It just depends on your attitude. I had to be willing to sacrifice a lot."

Her abundant love for her son is evident in another way: during their first month in New York, in a life or death situation, Tim was her first thought. At three in the morning, she woke in her bed to find a man holding a knife at her throat. He cut her breasts a few times; but she forced herself not to scream because Tim was in the next room; she didn't want him to wake up and let the intruder know he was there.

Then the man raped her. "He spoke Italian. I tried to talk to him, but I couldn't communicate with him and that was just the epitome. . . . His first intention was just to rob me, then when he found I was home he figured he would take what he could get." Her voice was very controlled and tight. "I thought to myself, How the hell did I get myself into this mess and how the hell am I going to get out? I really don't want my child to die." She looked at me and said violently, "I can tell you, *I* don't die. I'm a survivor!"

A woman who makes and breaks her own life, Amy has particular trouble dealing with someone forcing his will upon her. Since that episode, she has become stridently feminist in her views on punishment for rapists. "When I think of sex right now it makes me want to throw up," she says. "Until they make the penalty for rape like they do in Saudi Arabia for shoplifting—I mean, until they start castrating people who do things like that—I think women will have to live in fear."

Nevertheless, she is basically certain that stridency itself will get the movement nowhere. "I don't think men have planned from the early ages to treat women like chattel. . . . They aren't really malicious when they say, 'Get coffee.' It's that their mothers have taught them that. And they don't want it rubbed in their faces that they're wrong. I think there's a way to lead them from that thinking into a more positive vein, rather than pounding on them." She laughed. "That was my mistake at the coffee company. I ended up creating a lot of enemies. . . . It's hard for men," she reflected. "I think the most we can do—and what I am certainly teaching my child to do—is to do his share of dishes and to look upon women as equals."

Despite her joy with her son and with her career, Amy Wheeler broods. "I hate to think what I have sacrificed," she said with real regret. She has proved to herself that she can live alone but hopes it will not always be so. "I can't tell you how happy it would make me to live with someone and have a good solid thing. And it bothers me. Sometimes I think I have made a very dear choice. My career is very very important to me, and I could never give it up. I can never have another baby. . . . Tim will be going to college in eight years. What will I do when I'm thirty-five?"

The idea of being thirty-five and still alone would not appeal to many women. In fact, it does not appeal to Amy, either. Nevertheless, her priorities are clear. Though lonely, she has fought too hard for too long ever to consider giving up what she has. As she left me that evening, I was filled with awe. Never before had I been so thoroughly convinced of a woman's commitment to her professional life. The contrast between her and the many ambivalent others I had inter-viewed was sharp.

Later that night, I found myself reflecting that career was never an easy or an obvious step for Amy Wheeler. Her background had placed every conceivable stumbling block in her path; nobody showed her how to shape a career, nobody gave her an education, or financial aid, or even a helping hand. In fact, the more I thought about it, the more I felt its very impossibility was the key. Rarely are we appreciative of what comes easily. Sacrifice itself is the ingredient which makes Amy Wheeler so certain of her choices.

Fourteen

Brenda Cyndar

In 1958, when she was twelve, Brenda Cyndar came home from summer camp to an empty house. Her father had died three weeks before, but no one had bothered to tell her. She hadn't even been invited to his funeral.

Having been motherless for a decade, she was now fatherless too. Isolation locked tightly around her: not a single relative wanted to take over her parenting. But Brenda wasn't particularly surprised. Like Amy Wheeler, she'd been preparing to be on her own for as long as she could remember.

Like many young couples, MaryEl and Norman Cyndar made a hasty marriage in the middle of World War II, never really getting to know each other. When Norm came back from overseas a paraplegic, MaryEl felt her life saddled with a responsibility she had never bargained for, tied to a man she barely loved. In 1948, worn out, she deserted her crippled husband and their two-and-a-half-year-old daughter to run off with another man.

Despite her young age, Brenda understood much of what was going on. Thirty years later, she can remember her mother screaming at Norman that she didn't want "his child." The tiny girl took it to heart; it was the first bitter rejection in a long line.

Still, her father wanted her—and, more important, needed her. After the divorce, they moved to a small city in New Jersey, where they established themselves in the home of Norman's aged and feeble parents and his sister. Here, as before, Brenda had no woman around her with whom to make a healthy identification: her grandmother was in her late seventies, an infirm and crotchety old woman; her father's sister, a spinster, was severely schizophrenic. Ultimately, Brenda would reject these examples—and her mother's as well—when it came to planning her own future. But that wasn't until years later.

Instead, her life revolved around her father—a warm and loving individual who gave to his daughter as best he could, under the circumstances. He worked at home, as an accountant; he looked forward to Brenda's noontime recesses, when she would walk home from school to make his lunch and keep him company. Little by little, she assumed responsibilities her mother had abandoned. Norman treated her like an equal, including her in discussions with his friends, and this, too, encouraged a premature adulthood. She was never asked to leave the room, regardless of how inappropriate a conversation might be for a child; she gradually became his confidante, almost his wife.

But in spite of their intense intimacy, Brenda could not really identify with her father, or even think about emulating him. He was crippled. Worse, he was dying—a new disaster that placed even greater responsibility on her shoulders, although she had more than her share already. She was five and a half when Norman crashed into her bedroom in the middle of the night, hysterical, to say that he had developed glandular cancer. "He burst into tears all over me," she remembers. "I was really tiny for my age. I remember not being able to get my arms around his neck, and I had to stand up and just hold him. I was very very strong. I did not cry until he left the room."

For the next seven years, she lived in fear, watching the slow process of her father's dying. She did all the family cooking, relying a great deal on peanut butter. She bathed him, changed his sheets, cared for his paralyzed body. And, as his accounting business disintegrated over time, she took baby-sitting and odd jobs to supplement their income and help pay for food. She had no bedtime hour. When she began to menstruate at age eleven, it was Norman who taught her how to insert a Tampax.

Norman worried terribly about how she would cope after he was gone. She would need to be independent, completely self-reliant. Starting when she was six, he began putting her on buses in the middle of the city, giving her money and a map, and letting her find her own way home. By the time Brenda was eight or nine, she was making day trips into New York City by herself.

Additionally, he felt a need to educate her about the world. She should not grow up in a vacuum, he insisted, no matter how poor they might be. And so, in much the same way she had learned to care for her father, Brenda also learned to care about the lives of those less fortunate than herself. Together, she and Norman watched the evening news and discussed it in detail. The neighborhood they lived in was itself a perfect topic: small, lower middle class, industrial, full of "racist whites" who felt threatened by the two black neighborhoods that pressed in on either side. Norman, very liberal, tended to root for the underdog—a throwback to the Judaism he no longer practiced. Horrified at McCarthyism, he had been a full supporter of the Rosenbergs. Even his best friend was black. Over and over, he made sure that Brenda understood that it was her responsibility to help the downtrodden. These exact concerns took seed in her early life; years later, they would lead to a career.

The conservatism of the neighborhood came home to Brenda on a purely personal level as well: no one wanted his children playing with this curiously disturbing little girl who had no mother. Brenda's precocity was downright alarming— her independent ways and ideas might be a dangerous influence on others. Consequently, she had great trouble making friends, and learned that people were often closed-minded and insensitive. She could not look to others for warmth, sympathy, or compassion. There was only herself—and Norman, for as long as he lasted. Soon she identified more with the local street-wise blacks than with the sheltered whites. "Most kids were frightened of me," she told me sadly. "I was very serious. I never smiled or laughed a lot. And that set me apart. I was never silly." Marilyn Monroe, Doris Day, Cary Grant—the idols of her childhood peers—held no magic for her. To Brenda, they seemed phony, full of hot air: what did they have to do with the real world?

A desire to please her father and her high native intelligence guided her easily through the early years of grammar school. But Brenda Cyndar's life simply did not center on the normal signposts of childhood: after all, she was watching her father die. As much as possible, she drove the dreaded specter of the future from her mind. It was too painful and lonely to deal with. Instead, she lived from day to day, spending much of her time in the hospital, reading Dickens and Hardy aloud to Norman and buoying his spirits during chemotherapy treatments. Nevertheless, she did have one fantasy about the years to come, a fantasy she could face because it would postpone the inevitable loss: she dreamed of becoming a doctor and curing her father.

As the pain increased, Brenda administered Norman's Demerol injections at home. Soon he became addicted to the synthetic morphine, and the doctor wouldn't give him sufficient prescriptions. It became her responsibility to go to different drugstores and charm pharmacists into giving her illegal doses. At this, as in everything else, she was adept. She had to be. She was keeping her father alive, and he was all she had.

Then, in the summer of her twelfth year, she was packed off to camp and came home to find her father's room empty. Norman was long dead and buried. Loss—and a sense of failure—overtook her. His death had been expected, expected almost since she could remember; still, the shock reverberated through her violently. With neither a funeral nor the standard trappings of death as a vehicle for her grief, she began sneaking out of the house in the middle of the night to hitchhike to Norman's grave, where she would sleep until morning. "I never worked out his death," she told me simply. "So I had to establish a contact. Of course, we didn't talk to each other or anything. I mean, he was dead. But I still didn't want to let him go."

Even in the early days, Brenda's grandparents had been too old to cope with anything. Over time, they had receded further and further into the background. But after Norman's death, Brenda had to remain with her elderly relatives, no matter how inadequate they might be. Soon, aimless, all alone, she became uncontrollable and rebellious. It was a declaration of rage against society, God, her relatives, her peers—and herself. Cracking the whip, her grandparents tried to exert their long-invisible influence, tried to fit her into their conception of what a young girl should be like. But Brenda had never encountered such boundaries before, and she was damned if she would let someone else run her life. Instead, desperate to keep control of a world where no control was really possible—after all, her father had died despite all her efforts—she refused to eat. Her body, at least, was hers.

Soon her distaste for food had grown into the illness known as anorexia nervosa: she stood five foot four and weighed only fifty-eight pounds. "I looked like a concentration-camp victim," she says. Now she—and she alone—would decide whether she would live or die. It was an expression of her fury at this ultimate desertion by her father—a betrayal which only reinforced that of her mother ten years earlier.

Eventually, her grandparents hospitalized her: the disease has a mortality rate of about 10 percent, and Brenda was losing ground fast. The doctors began feeding her intravenously and threatened to tie her into bed if she tried to rip out the tubes.

Months later, after many ups and downs, the doctors won. They were making her accept blood transfusions and nutrients against her will. Finally, in a true and predictable gesture of control—and just before it was too late—Brenda started to eat.

When she emerged from the hospital, Brenda's grand-parents felt they could no longer cope with her. She was dispatched to live with other relatives. But no one wanted her—especially after they discovered she was penniless. Although Norman had given his sister-in-law, an attorney, numerous cash payments to hold in trust for his daughter, her aunt later denied ever having received the money. Once again, it was a devastating betrayal.

Shuttled from house to house, always sleeping on couches and never fitting in, Brenda went to over a dozen different high schools in three years. Finally, at fifteen, she tried to take control of her life, and headed for Chicago. Somehow, she would find her mother. But when MaryEl discovered she had no inheritance, she kicked her out, too.

Over the years, Brenda had built a tough outer wall around herself; now MaryEl added the final brick. Brenda Cyndar vowed never to depend on anybody for anything. She was no longer as vulnerable as she had been when her father died. Self-reliance and independence were now attributes as necessary to her soul as bread and water were to her body. She lied about her age and got an apartment in the black ghetto on Chicago's South Side. It was something out of a Richard Wright novel—no radio or telephone, alcoholics as neighbors, cracks clear through the walls, knife fights and murder in the halls. Still, given her early training in social awareness, she fitted right in with the neighbors—more so than she ever had before in any white area.

She supported herself by working nights as a nurse's aide, starting school after her shift was over—at seven in the morning. But nothing there really intrigued her: life was too hard and she was too tired. Besides, with Norman dead, she had no one to whom she could bring home a report card; math, once her forte, now netted her a steady supply of C's. Overall, then, personal survival was the first and only priority.

Life was very different for Brenda than for her teen-age peers—so different that she continued to feel uncomfortable with them. Having girlish crushes on boys or making a date for the movies seemed puerile to her. Besides, burned by her mother, her aunt, and her grandmother in turn, she didn't trust other women. Nor would she play up to men by trying to look sexy—she shunned makeup and let her curly hair frizz. "I wanted people to see me for what I was, instead of being pretty and prim," she recalls. "I didn't want a guy to like me because I had big breasts." In reaction, she stubbornly wore a bra several sizes too small, masking her bust.

Most of her energy, in short, was concentrated on her job—something that once again set her off from her peers. Working in the hospital, she began to think about her future for the first time, deciding that maybe she really could be a doctor; even with Norman dead, she could dedicate her life to helping others. In 1964, armed with a high school diploma and a firm sense of purpose, she moved back to New Jersey and entered Fairleigh Dickinson, a community college. She took a job as ward clerk in a local hospital and attended classes in the evening.

But night school was a terrible disappointment. She wanted to be stimulated, excited—not subjected to a boring extension of high school. And, as usual, she felt completely isolated; there was no time to talk to anyone or make friends, even if she could have let down her guard. The burden of daily living wore her down, and her outlook became more and more negative. She paid thirty dollars a month for an apartment with broken windows and no heat, and slept on the floor with the stove turned on. Medical school gradually seemed further and further away.

After a year, she gave up and transferred to a nursing school in New Haven. Here, again, it didn't take her long to establish a reputation as an oddball: she moved out of the dorm and into a commune—something strictly forbidden by the administration. Though white, her new brothers and sisters chose to live in the black section of town as a political statement. Nothing could have appealed more to Brenda, who loved to be in the midst of underdogs. She identified with them, after all. She always had.

She was drifting, however, completely unsure of the future. Gradually, she cut more and more classes, and was finally booted out of school. She moved in with an artist-in-residence at Yale—a man for whom she felt real empathy because his father had died when he was very young.

Not her first sexual relationship, it was nevertheless her most fulfilling. Jason was intelligent and fun, but he was forever tripped out on drugs, not the type to make a commitment to a woman. That was fine with Brenda: she trusted only herself. Still, she found a job as a lab technician in a hospital and supported herself, while providing her lover with extras—just as she had once helped her father financially. The overall pattern would repeat again and again throughout the ensuing years.

In her spare time, Brenda now taught ghetto kids as a volunteer—and loved it. Little by little, she began to consider having a real career in community service work. Finally, she was facing the future directly and beginning to make plans. She became tired of carrying the temperamental Jason—whom she now viewed as a drag. In early 1968, after a year with him, she took off for Boston.

Jobs came hard, and she could only find work as a lab assistant at a large teaching hospital, but she was persistent. A year later, she finally lucked into her heart's dream: working in the Roxbury ghetto. Her teaching experience had paid off—she was hired without a college degree. It was to be the first in a long line of community-oriented jobs which she got by hook or by crook.

Her title was "youth coordinator" for the Office of Economic Opportunity. She found jobs for the junkies, the pushers, the unwed mothers, the criminals, the teen-age alcoholics. She immersed herself in the Roxbury community—and felt at home, for the first time in a long time. In effect, she had found herself a new and needy family.

But to Brenda, placing her charges in government-subsidized employment didn't seem like the answer. And so she took it upon herself to found an alternative school, a school where kids with unorthodox backgrounds could get a little unorthodox education. Once again she used her own limited funds to support it. She tutored, she counseled, she tried to keep her young protégés out of the gutter. Perhaps here she could succeed in changing the course of life—as she had failed to do for her father.

Newly confident, politically radical, she was a natural for the feminist movement. She devoured de Beauvoir, Millett, Friedan. The movement seemed to affirm the freedom she'd always needed—and always managed to get. Moreover, within its ranks, she sensed a support system never before tapped. In years to come, it would provide her with a sisterhood, a new radical family—the family she had never really had. Finally, her life seemed to be falling into place.

In 1971, the OEO discovered her alternative school: disapproving of the project, they quickly closed it down. Transferred to another job-development program, resentful, bitter at the American government, she felt her freedom had been taken away. Her life was directionless again. Before the year was out, she had taken off for Europe, and flew to Italy, then Greece. There, as it turned out, she would meet a man and a way of life that radically altered her thinking and her image of herself.

She was certain she was being followed. Every time she turned around, the dark, good-looking stranger with piercing eyes was watching. Finally, getting up her nerve, she approached him and told him to get lost. But instead of making the expected sexual advance, he drew a map and asked her to meet him, for a mysterious reason, in a cave on a nearby Greek island. Her spirit of adventure was aroused—but caution got the better of her. Still, she gave him her itinerary and told him to write.

Next stop: Munich. Brenda got a job as supervisor in a factory that printed art books. Her salary was surprisingly large—confident of her ability, she had lied on her job application, claiming to have a B.A. from Boston University.

Meanwhile, postcards began to filter in from the peculiar Greek. Finally, intrigued, she agreed to meet him in the secret cave. There, she discovered he was a member of the Greek underground, looking for an American passport runner. Although scared, she jumped at the chance anyway. Here was something to believe in, here was direction: most of all, here was a chance to help oppressed people. It was even more exciting than working with ghetto kids—a spy novel but with real live danger. Traveling back and forth to England, she began picking up fake passports and delivering them to certain Greek intellectuals trying to escape the country.

The peculiar young man turned out to be intense and well educated, with a degree in architecture and a Ph.D. in math. It didn't take long for Brenda to fall in love with him. For the first time, she was not taking care of her man—the job gave her enough purpose in life. Instead, Dimitri became a joyous part of her life and a mentor. He encouraged her to consider getting her college degree—she shouldn't have to waste her talents on jobs with little real responsibility. But being a secret agent was challenge enough for now.

Six months passed. To cover her illegal activities, Brenda tutored Greek children in English. Then, one day, Dimitri was arrested. Hysterical, Brenda tried to get him help, but the underground packed her off on the next ship out of the country. "Everybody's life was in danger," she told me tautly. "They didn't want me to talk if I was tortured."

The trip gave her plenty of time to think. She had to regain control and put her life back together. Dimitri had made her very conscious of her lack of education; now he might be dead, and his advice even more precious. She wanted to follow in his footsteps. Social protest was the province of intellectuals, she felt; only when educated could she effectively help a cause. Firmly, she decided to get the best job possible and then enroll in a good school.

In late 1972, back in Boston and lying again about a B.A., she began work as a psychiatric social worker. The job carried a lot of responsibility: in addition to running group therapy sessions, she did some staff training. She also started a women's group that would last for over four years—a group that talked about goals, dreams, and the politics of being a woman. Gradually, it all gave her a tremendous sense of fulfillment. She worked lovingly with impoverished mothers; she began reading aloud to prison inmates; she helped set up an abortion service for pregnant adolescents.

Now she was convinced: helping the disadvantaged would be her life's work. The whole experience in Greece had given her a sense of her own power, and all she needed to do now was act. A degree—a *real* degree—would be vital. Never before had she thought so concretely about the future.

She was now beginning to trust people for real—the result of her beloved women's group, the result of working in danger with the underground in Greece. Then, in 1972, she met a man who seemed to fit into her future. Randy Peakes was a conscientious objector doing biology research at Harvard, the son of a southern tenant farmer—a real underdog. Even better, he wanted to return one day to his native state to help the folks he'd left behind. In short, Randy was a great deal like Brenda, and the love between them grew.

And so, when Randy left Boston to attend medical school in New York, Brenda commuted to see him—commuted religiously. As the relationship deepened and weekend travel became impractical, she moved in—over the vociferous objections of her women's group—and landed a job in a hospital on Long Island. Then, six months later, she made good on her promise to herself and enrolled at Sarah Lawrence College—this time, as a day student. Her priorities were well established and clear.

Supremely confident, she was set on getting through in two years. The course load would be heavy, but it would be worth it, and credits from Fairleigh Dickinson would help. Absolutely set on a career, she supported herself—and, once again, her lover—by working two part-time jobs in psychiatric social work. Every spare minute was filled; she clockworked her day so that sleep only absorbed three or four hours a night.

In 1976, receiving her B.A., she eagerly went straight into a graduate program in public health at Yale, determined to equip herself to design health-care plans for the poor. But she was sadly disappointed, finding that Yale mostly taught hospital administration. "[Yale] is health for business," she told me disdainfully. "I'm health for change. I would be talking about communities and they would be talking about dollars and hospital beds per person." Disillusioned, she began taking supplementary courses at Harvard for her second year, and has found more compatible programs filled with students from impoverished countries who intend to return to their homelands. "They have a world perspective," she says contentedly.

Brenda would undoubtedly have been happy to continue living casually with Randy. But he is far more conservative than she. Eventually, he asked her to marry him—provoking an enormous crisis. He wants permanence, stability, and, eventually, children. She is torn: happy years spent with him have softened her insistence on self-reliance; once, before even reaching puberty, she vowed never to marry, and never had to consider revising that plan until now. But she has been with Randy for five years, and she looks on it as a trial marriage—with a successful result.

Furthermore, as she approaches the age of thirty-five, she feels pressured to make a decision. She can now see a great and long latent desire within herself to have a family—the same desire which led her to mother the homeless kids of the Boston ghetto.

For now, their relationship is an equal partnership that does not threaten her in any of the traditional ways. Even though he works impossible hours as a surgical resident, Randy does all the cleaning in their apartment. Nevertheless, Brenda recognizes that his schedule will not allow him to participate fully in child care. Besides, with her psychological training and her "orphan's" background, Brenda is convinced that the mother's presence is all-important to a child in the first two years of life. She strongly believes that a parent must be willing to make some sacrifice if she is going to bring life into the world.

She now plans to be home with her children full time

through the first year and part time through the second. While some of her dedication stems from a sense of responsibility, a great deal also comes from her own very real desire to watch her babies grow. "If you don't see your child develop in the first few months of life, you are missing something," she pointed out assertively. She realizes that time away from her career will set her back, but she is willing to make the sacrifice. For many years, she was a girl who had practically nothing: now, as an adult, she does not expect to have everything.

Despite Brenda's growing desire to place a family above her own work, she still considers herself a feminist, and is certain she will return to her career after an initial period of child raising. Her goal is to find work in international health—preferably to set up health clinics in Africa. Randy, conveniently, is willing to move with her: because neither seriously wants to be rich or famous, they are both flexible and adaptable.

Brenda Cyndar forged her own destiny, with no one to guide her, no one to give her shelter, no one to offer her a helping hand. Aimless, drifting, she eventually found goals—goals that came from deep within her and which were supported by her feminist peers. Consequently, she is sure of herself, sure of what she wants. Like Amy Wheeler, she has accomplished nothing except by dint of hard work. All this has enabled her to make choices, to acknowledge that sacrifices are necessary—after all, they have always been necessary for her. She is not alone anymore. Now, for the first time, she eagerly anticipates the future.

Fifteen

Chris Hastings

Heroin, speed, and LSD had taken over. Chris Hastings was hearing things and seeing things—things that weren't really there. Lying in bed one night, she heard her lover and his friends return after a night out. In the back of her car was a deer they'd hit on the road. They dragged it inside and cut its throat. A bloodbath. They tore out its heart with their hands and offered it to Chris. A hallucination? She thought not. The stench of blood was overpowering.

Finally she knew. This was no dream: she would die if she stayed there much longer. But she had nowhere to go, no one to be with. She wasn't even sure that she could remember her own name.

Like Brenda Cyndar, Chris had been fighting for a foothold on life since she was a young girl; over the years, she had tried on a thousand different faces. The heart of the deer was simply the last chapter on the lonely road downward into her own private hell.

She was born in 1950, the first child in an Episcopalian family of four who lived in Buffalo, New York. Mark Hastings was low man on the totem pole in a law firm; Anne Hastings, not the typical 1950s housewife, was a professional painter and artist. On the surface, all was well. In reality, however, the household was composed of people who never really connected with each other. Mark worked constantly and just wasn't around very much; Anne had ambivalent feelings about having children and let them know it from an early age.

In short, a taut silence prevailed most of the time. Anne's portrayal of adult life was nothing that would make a child eager to grow up. She was unhappy as a parent, unhappy as a wife, unhappy as a career woman. Gradually, she withdrew into a deep depression. To escape reality, she developed a marijuana habit and grew her own crop in the backyard. Being stoned distanced her from her own feelings—and from the children as well.

From an early age, Chris began to find fault with herself, taking the blame for her mother's lack of interest. She loathed her dark hair and ruddy complexion; worse, nearly blind in one eye, she was required to wear a patch over the stronger one to strengthen the weaker. Rendered virtually sightless, she was always bumping into things and looking clumsy. Anxiety became a keynote of her childhood, and when she graduated from the eye patch to ordinary glasses, she continued to be extraordinarily self-conscious about them, feeling ugly. Anne threatened to nail the glasses into her head if she didn't stop taking them off, and Chris took her seriously.

As a result, she wished she were someone else, someone her mother could love more. A little girl across the street became the object of her fantasies. Over and over again she stole this girl's party shoes, worshiping them, convinced they would transform her into a golden-haired perfect child that her parents would adore.

Mark Hastings wasn't much of an alternative to his wife. A junior partner, he spent most of his time at the law firm, and at home, he was hardly an example of healthy adulthood. His major activity was drinking with Anne: cocktail hour often lasted until nine o'clock at night, and only afterwards would the children get dinner.

By the age of five, Chris was making the first in a series of desperate attempts to impress her presence upon these oblivious adults. Sneaking up behind her mother in the kitchen one afternoon, she assaulted her with the family hammer. Sadly, her parents were too self-centered to get the message; after all, she had been too small to inflict real damage.

A year later, internalizing the anger, Chris tried to commit suicide by drinking a bottle of Anne's perfume. It was an ultimate way of getting attention, but she was also serious—she no longer wanted to live. Although the attempt failed, she would spend the next eighteen years of her life trying to die.

Or worse. No one ever touched in the Hastings household, and Chris began to rely on herself for physical contact. Not surprisingly, considering her self-image, this contact took the form of punishment, not love. "I did terrible things to myself," she told me, voice low. "I dug holes in my skin till it bled."

As a little girl, Chris became involved with friends who reflected the negative and sadistic atmosphere she found at home. Her gang specialized in mini-vandalism, and her inner feelings of rage were an asset on the streets, where violence ruled. They tested new kids on the block by throwing rocks at them; she found her best friend when a newcomer threw a rock back. "I knew she was a person of equal caliber," she said, laughing.

Finally, when Chris was in fourth grade, her parents woke up to their daughter's rapidly deteriorating condition. They enrolled her in an unorthodox private school on a rural farm. Here, for the first time, Chris got positive feedback and encouragement—and the sense of community and family that home had always lacked. She took shop and ceramics; she learned painting and silk-screening. At last, she felt worth something.

Still, each day after class, she had to go home and the dream would end. Increasingly, she and her brother, two years her junior, began to rely on each other for the support and love their parents did not provide. It was barely enough. Fighting to stay emotionally stable from day to day consumed all her energy.

While her peers read Nancy Drew and other girls' books, Chris remained untouched. It was too painful to learn about what others had when she had so little. She was confused, rootless: she didn't want to grow up, but she didn't want to stay where she was, either. Looking back, she feels her total negativism about life stemmed from a complete lack of a healthy female—or male—role model. "I had no idea of what a sane adult woman looked like," she recalls. Chris never thought about growing up to be a wife, or a mother, or a career woman. She had no dreams at all, and she could only identify with stories in which animals were cruelly treated—stories with turnabout happy endings.

The onset of adolescence brought her troubles to a crisis: her first period was a major trauma. "I knew it was the end of the world," she remembers. "I had no idea of what was going on." Anne had never bothered to educate her only daughter about the facts of life; to Chris, the flow of blood seemed somehow connected with death. She fantasized that her mother had "murdered" her.

In fact, there was a homicide, albeit strictly psychological, because Anne had no intention of making room for a new woman in the household. Instead, she upstaged her daughter with a nervous breakdown and took off for a sanitarium. By the time she returned, Chris had the problem of menstruation under control: severely anorectic, she had lost enough weight to ensure that her period would not return. "There wasn't room in [my mother's] little girlhood for my adolescence, so I erased it. . . . There wasn't room for my own femaleness." [15] To substitute for the normal cyclical bloodletting, she began her own symbolic ceremony—with a razor blade. It was pain she could regulate in a world where so little—especially pain—could be controlled. Tragically, as before, her parents didn't even notice.

There was only one high spot in her life: school. Here she could watch normal people functioning, and slowly, her circle of friends became more and more a family. She worked hard and did very well. Nevertheless, Chris's lack of identity kept her from extracurricular activities that came easily to everyone else. She could not try out for plays for fear of losing herself completely in portraying someone else. Modern dance, once a passion, became too threatening because of the emphasis it placed upon the body—she felt it high-lighted her ugliness.

While craving the attention her anorexia and physical trauma might draw from her parents, Chris protected herself from the watchful eye of the school authorities by hiding underneath baggy clothes and long sleeves. Her body became a hated object, something she despised, and her father's subtle hostility toward her budding sexuality exacerbated the situation. In his eyes, a girl should look like Marilyn Monroe—blond, blue-eyed, voluptuous. Unknowingly, he fueled her fire of self-hatred with such attitudes. "I was encouraged [by my father] to hate my body," she told me, "and therefore to hate myself."

Further, Mark warned that she shouldn't be such a good student: boys were attracted to beauty and charm, not brains. He did not encourage her to have a career; in fact, he informed her early on that he would never pay for a graduate school education. He seemed to fear she would be like her mother—educated and bright on the surface, but crazy and helpless underneath.

Despite him, however, Chris aimed for college, because college was school and school was safe. "It was easier to plan for college than for life," she told me seriously. In accordance with high grades and board scores, she applied to Sarah Lawrence, Vassar, and Bennington. Anne and Mark expressed no opinion on where to go and probably couldn't have cared less. Still, forever trying to please, she decided on Bennington, her mother's alma mater.

In 1968, therefore, she traveled off to Vermont. Quickly she found Bennington very familiar. With its small student body of six hundred women and its open curriculum, it reminded Chris of the private school which had sheltered her for so many years. But here she began meeting a new breed of women—women who were more interested in their careers than they were in men. Suddenly, it wasn't a sin to be ugly and smart. Chris started reading the standard feminist literature and was soon fascinated.

In high school, she had been completely aimless, with no

ambitions at all. Her father rejected careers for women; her mother's example had convinced her that marriage was "death by alcohol." But Bennington provided myriad examples of healthy adult women—people she could emulate. The seniors were especially impressive—many were headed for law or medical school. "They were the first women I knew who wanted to have professions," she remembers bitterly. "My mother's work I didn't consider a profession—because she didn't take it seriously."

Before long, she felt more at home than ever before. But old problems still plagued her. The feminist identity so clearly espoused by Bennington built upon an individual's sense of herself—and Chris's self-image was terribly weak. She related to her peers but felt outdistanced, different. Her emotional problems were far too deep for feminism to give her such an easy way out. Years of suppressed rage at her parents and at life in general continued to be expressed self-destructively. The last straw came when, during her freshman year, her parents decided to divorce. In reaction, Chris flailed away in undirected fury. "Why should they get to dissolve a home of which I never got enough in the first place?" she demanded.

As usual, she turned the emotions inward. Dieting in earnest, she ate only one hard-boiled egg a day. She resumed slicing up her arms with razor blades; she drank herself into oblivion with alcohol. Frightened, her roommate dragged her to the college's health services, and Bennington's dean called Mark and Anne to warn that Chris was highly disturbed; she would not be allowed to return to school without a clean bill of health from a psychiatrist. Typically, the Hastingses sent her to Anne's therapist—who gave her an easy, disinterested permission to go back. Once again, the message came through loud and clear: no one cared.

Back at Bennington, she stopped emulating the career women and became enmeshed in the spaced-out atmosphere of non-reality so pervasive in the late 1960s. It was the perfect setting for her anger and loss to fester. The routine of drugs and little work provided a natural escape from the emotional pain that hammered away inside. Dispassionately, she had sex with several men. By the end of freshman year, she was using marijuana and speed frequently but complained that neither got her high enough, and soon began a lengthy intense love affair with LSD. It wasn't long before she was mainlining heroin, becoming a dealer to support her habit. "I loved danger," she remembers. "I hoped to be killed, I believe. It was suicide by attrition."

Mark and Anne had provided her with no real family; "hippie" culture did. Suddenly, a whole community of brothers and sisters provided instant friendship, instant love, instant sex, instant highs. There were no limits or boundaries—all a girl needed was a backpack and a thumb. "Being a child of the sixties was that you go on the pill and you go on the road."

Five hazy years passed at Bennington, with time off in the middle. She did almost no work, taking only those courses which she had easily passed in high school. But by the end of 1973, she had begun to panic. The end of college was drawing very near, and she had postponed leaving for as long as possible. Where would she go now? She had no goals, no direction. "It was death, I just knew it. I couldn't imagine living outside that environment." In a desperate search for purpose, she did some student teaching in a private school—but was far too shaky to consider a career in education, even though she basically liked the experience. "I knew somehow that I couldn't be an adult—by which I mean have a professional identity *and* be suicidal *and* be so desperately needy. I couldn't do both."

She tried seeing a psychotherapist. For her first session, she arrived dressed not as herself but as the Mexican revolutionary Zapata. As a further way of expressing her ambivalence—and real fear—about therapy, she repeatedly got too drunk to drive to appointments.

Graduation arrived. With nowhere to go, Chris was painfully open to suggestion, and so accepted her current lover's exhortation that she live in New York with him for the summer. But although this man was a dance teacher at Bennington, he was hardly a model of mature adulthood. "He was almost as destructive as I was. He was like Charles Manson. . . . He was artistic, and brilliant and crazy, an alcoholic. Just perfect for my purposes. . . . We took speed and heroin and nearly starved to death—which was fine because I enjoyed being very thin." Quickly, she took up stealing to support them.

In the early fall, Chris got blood poisoning after walking on broken glass. Five feet eight, only ninety-five pounds, her body simply couldn't fight the infection. Finally, she limped with her lover back to Bennington. She could feel the world closing in. "I didn't know where I was. Going around in circles. I was in the process of having a nervous breakdown. I knew I was psychotic. I was losing spatial orientation."

Then came the watershed night when her lover offered her the heart of the deer. Some survival instinct in Chris told her she was in real danger of dying, and so she told her lover she was leaving; with a shrug, he told her he didn't care. Hysterical, she drove to Cambridge, talking to herself and seeing things on the road. "I kept . . . telling myself I was all right," she told me in a low voice. Finally arriving at a friend's restaurant, she "staged" her nervous breakdown in the kitchen. At last, they took her to a therapist at Harvard University—the same one she had rejected earlier in the spring. Looking at her hands, once again covered with razor lacerations, he asked, "Oh, are those messages for me?"

It had taken twenty-two years, but finally someone had noticed her pain.

At a private mental hospital, she and her therapist began to untangle the strands of her life and look squarely at the damage. Because he took her seriously, she was able to trust him like no one before. In many ways, Chris began again, as a new person. "When I think of my life," she says thoughtfully, "I think of the times I spent dying and the times that I haven't. . . . I risked everything I believed in and everything I thought I had—all my intelligence, and whatever else—on the possibility that there is such a thing as starting over." Like the other "self-made women" I describe in this section, Chris Hastings dared to change the course of her life—and won, despite great odds.

Chris's parents were not pleased with her choice of hospital. After all, Anne reasoned, why should her daughter have more expensive treatment than she had had? "My father's attitude," Chris says sadly, "was that 'if you want to be in a hospital, you have to be in a state hospital.' . . . They were going to see I was punished and put in a snake pit." But, fortunately, her grandparents—previously not particularly close to Chris—came to her aid financially. As a result, she was able to remain despite Anne and Mark's efforts. Her grandparents came to visit her often in the hospital—something her parents could not muster the courage to do even once.

At this most desperate time of her life, Chris reached out to her grandmother—finding her strong and ready to give. During Chris's childhood, the distance between Buffalo and Washington, D.C., had made sustained intimacy difficult. But now she began examining her grandmother's life, looking for a viable and mature role model. Louise Graves was a remarkable woman, vital and energetic; educated at Oxford, she had made a career of teaching art to high school girls, and, for her generation, had been quite an ardent feminist. Her belief in Chris's intellect and stamina was strong, and she encouraged her granddaughter to hope for the future, to have ambition, to make plans. Never before had an adult reinforced her in such a positive and dramatic way. "[My grandmother] said you can have a career and a brain, *and* a man with a brain," Chris told me, with warmth. "And that if you love once, you'll love again; and that there's always a first time to start. If the heart of the deer was the bottom, then what she offered as a living ideal [was the top]."

Most important, because of therapy, Chris was finally ready to hear her grandmother's encouragement, ready to dare. After six months, she left the hospital for a halfway house. She had totally discarded drugs, anorexia, and self-destruction. Here she gradually became involved in the outside world again. The home itself was a nurturing environment, providing her with an immediate family of others who were just coming from hospitals. She found work as a bartender in a popular Cambridge restaurant, and even this gave her a sense of purpose and identity: she had responsibility, she was useful. Before long, she was promoted to manager.

But the road to recovery was not easy, and some days, she felt too depressed to get out of bed. Time passed, and little by little she gained strength and a growing sense of herself—who she was and whom she wanted to be. Then, in the fall of 1976, she found a job which captured her heart and gave her a true sense of purpose: teaching English at an exclusive girls' school near Boston. As a gesture of newfound autonomy, she moved into her own apartment, alone. It was a risk, but she took it eagerly, getting only a guinea pig for company. She picked up modern dance again, something she had dropped at puberty.

Two years later when I interviewed her, Chris was still adoring her work—teaching seventh through ninth grades. "It is enormously fulfilling," she told me, a real excitement in her voice. "A stunning experience. When I go to school in the morning, I'm loved by kids and respected by colleagues." Her students' love shines from the walls of her apartment, every available surface covered by the drawings and artwork they've made for her. She puts her heart into her work—and it is noticed. She is admired, finally, for who she is. Her clearly defined role in the school is a tremendous relief for the girl who never had a sense of her place in life. The rewards are built in: when she does her job well, she can watch her students improve.

Chris Hastings now believes her role as teacher extends far beyond simple instruction in English composition. Having completely lacked role models herself, she fervently hopes to provide her girls with a good example of a healthy and happy adult woman. Being a feminist is also a strong part of Chris's new identity. "When I present literature now to my classes, I have lots of discussions about the role of the women in the book," she explains. She tries to motivate her charges, to encourage them to shoot for careers. But to her consternation, she has noticed a newly reactionary trend in her school. She feels the Women's Movement has stalled, has pulled up short before reaching the newest generation. She wants to light up the fires once again. "I feel some responsibility, as an educator of young women, to speak directly to what I was taught in college by my peers as being women's issues. . . . I just finished teaching *Far from the Madding Crowd* to my eighth grade—and they'd never heard the word 'sexism.' "

As an added bonus, the matriarchal structure of the school itself has given Chris a full fleet of her own role models—career women who guide her in her own endeavors. It is a "mothering"—a shared interest—which she never received from Anne.

Somewhat after beginning to teach, Chris felt certain enough of herself to take another sort of gamble: love. Allowing herself to become seriously involved with Daniel Rifkin, a professor of political science at a local university, she hoped that her identity was strong enough to permit development of a healthy relationship. Because he was married, with two young daughters, she tried to be reasonably self-protective, and refused to be pushed around or treated like "just a girl friend." Even when Daniel separated from his wife in 1977, Chris insisted on maintaining her own apartment. She would not forfeit her hard-won autonomy.

The man she has chosen has—not accidentally—a great deal of respect for her. He openly returns her feelings for him, and they often share their work. He is the first really stable man she has ever dated, and over the past two years, they have come increasingly to consider marriage. "God forbid I would have ever thought of it," she said, laughing. "But this is an extraordinary man. I like him and I respect him. He's sexy and very very smart. . . . I'm amazed that after all that I've been through and after all the fear, I find that I'm really romantic and I really love loving."

Because Daniel already has two daughters, he is not interested in more children. For Chris—surprisingly—this constitutes a matter for considerable thought. "I'm not convinced that for me having children would be the best way to love, to be a loving person in the world," she told me. But she is still exploring the idea in her own mind, not wanting to be bullied by Daniel's definiteness. Still, she fears she might not make a stable mother—a fear that is clearly a by-product of her anger with Anne and Mark. "They fucked up by not knowing themselves well enough to know that they were not candidates for parenthood." She has accepted the possibility of remaining childless and instead concentrates on planning her own future: "My responsibility as a woman . . . is to figure out what's the most responsible and true way to be a loving participant in the real world. And for me, that may not be raising small children. It may conjure up too much."

Career is a number-one priority, however. Although she adores her job for now, she recognizes its eventual limitations and hopes to enroll soon in a Ph.D. program in clinical psychology. For the next two years, she will work part time toward a master's degree in education at Harvard. At this point, she is still not ready—nor distanced enough from her own therapy—to withdraw the support system her job offers and work full time toward a degree in psychology.

Daniel gives her a great deal of support for her ambitions and plans. As an added boon, he willingly helps with housework in both their apartments. Daniel's children do fix him to living in Boston, however, and this may yet prove a serious stumbling block. When they first began dating, Chris made it clear that if she wanted to get a Ph.D. at Berkeley, she would go to Berkeley. She still feels that way. Her sense of self is very dear to her now, and she is not about to give it up. "Daniel knows that a relationship with a man is not the first priority in my life. And I think he loves me for that," she says. Unlike many women her age, she has fought so long and hard for career and independence that she will not compromise them. Just as clearly, she understands the need for choice and is willing to sacrifice personal life for professional, if necessary.

Having finally achieved a sense of self-esteem, Chris Hastings can now afford to look back and evaluate her past. In the long run, she believes that her suffering and sense of "corelessness" were not especially instructive. "I wouldn't want to grow up in heaven," she claims. "Heaven would be as dull as hell—hell would be exciting. [But] you don't have to slash your wrists, you don't have to have anorexia nervosa, to know that adolescence is hell. You don't have to feel like you're nobody to know what it's like to be small and dependent. . . . It didn't teach me anything—I only had to learn my way out."

Nevertheless, after having listened to thirty life stories, I could not help but feel that the horror Chris endured has aided her in developing an ability to make choices, to make sacrifices. Her life is in control, for perhaps the first time, and there is no question who sits in the driver's seat. She lived for twenty-four years with no direction, no role models, no future. Then, friendship with her grandmother, feminism, therapy, and her own strength helped her define what she wanted. Her strong career drive is an affirmation of her new self-respect. She has courageously risked giving up mental illness, drug and alcohol habits, to enter the world of productive adults. Right now, she has little problem with the idea of choice. She has fought hard for the dreams and goals many of us take for granted—fought too hard to be confused. She takes life one day at a time, and her commitment to herself stands firm.

Part VI

Taking Risks, Making Choices

The motion of generations is pain.
—MARIA KATZENBACH
The Grab

The femin*ine* mystique preached that women didn't need a variety of choices because biology predetermined their realm of expertise; the femin*ist* mystique said that women didn't need a variety of choices because choice in itself was unnecessary, limiting, and defeatist. In the long run, then, there was only one difference between the two: one gave birth to boredom—for those not suited to housewifery—and the other to exhaustion—for those not geared to "Superwomanhood." From the women I interviewed, one message stood out clearly: blind acceptance of the femin*ist* mystique is as much a decorous observance of a new tradition as blind acceptance of the femin*ine* mystique was a decorous observance of the old. Once again, a problem has arisen because a system of values has been applied en masse to an entire population.

A few months ago, in the midst of my writing, an acquaintance told me a story that seemed to sum up some of the problems faced by our generation. She had recently become a mother, while simultaneously teaching full time at a nearby university. Using a day-care center—which she had applied to months in advance—she clockworked her schedule down to the minute. Racing between home, the university, and the center, she managed to keep it all together; both she and her husband worked four days a week as a compromise. But now, even looking back on that time makes her feel exhausted. In retrospect, she realizes that her attempt not to shortchange the needs of her baby, her husband, or her career resulted in shortchanging the most important needs of all—her own. She had proved she could do it, but at what cost to herself?

Finally, then, the oversimplified tenets of women's liberation have been no panacea. The movement promised that if women worked they would be happy and fulfilled. But as more and more of us have ventured out into the business world, universal happiness has not descended. Universal confusion has, however. As Hallie Parrish told me in Chapter One, women are finally beginning to wake up to an intrinsic truth, a truth men have taken for granted and accepted for generations: work is *work*—not play. Work is not always fulfillment: it is 90 percent drudgery and 10 percent illumination—like motherhood. Its satisfactions are not sufficient for everyone.

The Women's Movement has made great strides in winning the equal rights women deserve as a group. But it has failed as a miracle drug—it has not cured the malaise of all individual American women. Before we are women, after all, we are people: many of our discontents can only be solved by us alone, for ourselves alone. Even when a woman subscribes wholeheartedly to feminist doctrine and makes no choice between parenthood and career, even when her husband rearranges his own career, there is still a price to be paid. And, ultimately, it is the woman herself who bears the cost.

With nearly all doors open to us, with increasing legislation in our favor, with more and more of us flowing into the job market at one time or another, are we more content, more fulfilled than our mothers were? I think not. If the fifteen women in this book represent the difficulties of this generation, then they are, in fact, proof that women's liberation has not been a cure-all. I think it would be accurate to say we are overwhelmingly confused about who we are—just as confused as our mothers were, if not more so. We are trapped between one mystique and the other, and the way to freedom is not at all clear. Even worse, we are often ashamed to voice our feelings of conflict because we live in a time when women are supposed to be free of conflict. We already cringe at the inevitable male backlash: "The messiah has come and you're still complaining?"

We are the products of two vastly different worlds, forged in the fire of dissent and strife. While it is difficult to generalize about fifteen women so very different as those presented here, one feeling common to them all is frighteningly clear: wherever they come from, whatever they do, whoever they are, they all feel an increasing need to choose between the two worlds, to simplify their lives, to stop straddling the fence. I see a new and painful light dawning in the eyes of my compatriots, a new acknowledgment of the need to choose. Some realize it with horror, as it increases the immediate pressure, while others realize it with heartfelt relief because facing it releases some of the tension.

Each and every one of us finds the idea of making choices frightening: to make a choice is to take a risk. Studies [16] show that women are generally risk-averse—they see risk as a possibility only for loss, while men tend to see it as an equally balanced chance for loss *or gain.* Now, for the first time in history, an entire generation of women is being asked—as men have been for years—to choose their destiny, to take risks. Now, even if a woman elects traditional family-oriented life, it is a *choice,* a gamble—not a passive assumption of the inevitable. Contrary to what the Women's Movement says, it matters little which kind of choice we make, so long as we take the risk of making that choice for ourselves. The opportunity to choose is that which, in the long run, feminism has really given us. This is what we have gained—and it is both a blessing and a curse, both liberating and painful, but never, as we were taught, easy or natural.

Of the women in this book, those presented in the last section are the least confused and frightened about their futures; simultaneously, they are the least risk-averse. Their lives have been filled with risk, and they are not leery of it. Each in her own way was an underdog, a loser, someone who learned to seek out the risks which might eventually bring her greater fulfillment as an individual. I believe we must look to women such as these—women who finally insisted on doing things their own way—for our own futures.

In the long run, then, we must defy the pressures emanating from both mystiques to choose according to their rules. To subscribe to dogma is a living death of our individuality. Each woman must decide which risks are to be her risks, which choices are her choices—and so direct the course of her own life according to her needs, goals, and ambitions.

The liberal panache of those of us who came of age in the 1960s placed a high premium on homogeneity. The unisex, blue-jean generation looked alike, talked alike, and thought alike—just as the housewife generations did. Fighting the stereotype of our parents, we developed one of our own. Now we must dare to be different, dare to be business-women, dare to be wives and mothers. It will not be easy.

There are, I believe, many of us spread far and wide across America who all feel a little lost and insecure about where we are headed, about where we have been. As two warring worlds give birth to a new composite, confusion is inevitable. Sooner or later, we all wind up beached on the island of indecision. I take solace in the notion that if we stop to listen, if we stand still, quiet, under the dark night sky, we will hear a cacophony of voices, the cry of others who have learned that to choose is to live.

Appendix

The following table shows the pertinent biographical data on all those interviewed. Because no names are included here, none of the information is fictitious. The fifteen interviews in the book were drawn from this group of thirty. The table is included solely for the reader's interest.

DISTRIBUTION DATA

Number	Age	Birthplace	Religion	Marital Status	College	Occupation
1	31	Czechoslovakia/Maryland	Jewish	married/no children	Radcliffe	writer/poet
2	29	New York	Jewish	married/no children	Mills	housewife
3	25	New York	Jewish	single	Connecticut	floor manager, Bloomingdale's
4	24	California	Buddhist/Catholic	married/no children	Wellesley	Ph.D. candidate in botany, Berkeley
5	29	New York	Jewish	single	Syracuse	museum administration
6	26	Holland/California	Catholic	single	USC	advertising, account executive
7	24	New York	Jewish	single	Radcliffe	art gallery: selling
8	27	New York	Jewish	single	Brockport State	secretary

Number	Age	Birthplace	Religion	Marital Status	College	Occupation
9	28	Ohio/California	Catholic	married/divorced	Berkeley	M.D. candidate, Harvard
10	26	New Jersey	Protestant	single/engaged	Skidmore	Ph.D. candidate in oceanography. Harvard
11	28	Massachusetts	Protestant	married/2 children	Connecticut	housewife
12	26	Wyoming	Protestant	single	Radcliffe	Ph.D. candidate in history, Harvard; currently doing adminis-trative/clerical work
13	27	Massachusetts	Jewish	married/pregnant	Smith/Stanford	clinical psychologist
14	30	Indiana	Protestant	single/engaged	Radcliffe	art gallery: selling. administration
15	28	Chicago	Protestant	married/divorced	Boston U/Hunter	TV production. entry level
16	32	New York (upstate)	Protestant	single	Syracuse	sales representative computer services
17	26	New York	Jewish	married	Beaver	piano teacher/housewife
18	28	Idaho	Jehovah's Witness	married/divorced/1 child	California State	sales: management level

Number	Age	Birthplace	Religion	Marital Status	College	Occupation
19	28	New Jersey	Catholic	married	Mundelein	M.B.A. candidate, Harvard
20	27	Nebraska/California	Protestant	married/divorced	Boston State	secretary
21	25	Massachusetts	Protestant	married	Boston U	painter
22	31	New Jersey	Protestant	married	Middlebury	university administration (unemployed)
23	26	New York	Jewish	married	Barnard	international marketing specialist
24	31	California	Protestant	single	Vassar	TV production
25	28	New Jersey	Catholic	single	Fairleigh Dickinson/Elmira	medical illustrator
26	32	New Jersey	Jewish	single	Fairleigh Dickinson/Sarah Lawrence	M.A. candidate in public health, Yale and Harvard
27	29	Ohio	Jewish	single	Wisconsin	Ph.D. candidate in English, Brown
28	28	New York (upstate)	Protestant	single	Bennington	high school English teacher
29	24	North Carolina	Protestant	single/engaged	Hollins	secretary
30	29	Massachusetts	Protestant	single	Smith	high school French teacher

Notes

1. Betty Friedan, *The Feminine Mystique* (New York: W. W. Norton, 1963), pp. 342, 375.

2. *Ibid.,* p. 305

3. Kate Millett, *Sexual Politics* (New York: Avon Books, 1971), p. 47.

4. *Ibid.,* p. 175.

5. Shulamith Firestone, *The Dialectic of Sex: The Case for Feminist Revolution* (New York: Bantam Books, 1972), p. 72.

6. "Math Mystique: Fear of Figuring," *Time,* March 14, 1977, p. 36.

7. Lorelei Brush and Grace Baruch, "Women + Math = ? : Encouraging More Women to Study Mathematics," *Radcliffe Quarterly,* June 1977, p. 7.

8. *Ibid.*

9. *Ibid.*

10. Friedan, p. 367.

11. *Ibid.,* p. 374.

12. Caroline Donnelly, "A Word to the Wives about Part-Time Jobs," *Money* magazine Guide to Jobs and Careers (reprinted from September 1975 issue), p. 28.

13. *Ibid.*

14. Salvador Minuchin, *et al., Psychosomatic Families: Anorexia Nervosa in Context* (Cambridge: Harvard University Press, 1978), p. 8.

15. *Ibid.,* p. 381. Minuchin *et al.* further identify the psychosomatic family which breeds anorectics as one where the members are unable to deal with anger. Instead of confronting problems openly, they drive tension underground; argument is avoided at all costs by walking out or changing the subject. "Normal families are able to disagree."

16. See excellent discussion of women and risk in Margaret Hennig and Anne Jardim's *The Managerial Woman* (New York: Doubleday, 1977).

Bibliography

The following bibliography is a compilation of books and articles I read while working on *Between Two Worlds*. I was particularly interested in watching the media portrait of today's young woman; additionally, the interviews themselves began to lead me in new directions, not only within the realm of women's rights, but also in that of psychology, human development, and history. The sources below are not intended as a definitive listing on feminism and women's history, but as a catalogue of the writings which helped shape and influence my ideas and thought during work on the book.

Abernathy, Virginia, M.D. "Feminists' Heterosexual Relationships," *Archives of General Psychiatry,* 35 (April 1978).

Amdur, Neil. "Are Women Geared for Distance Running?" *New York Times,* April 25, 1978.

Baker, Russell. "Sex Objects Finish Last," *New York Times,* April 25, 1978.

Beauvoir, Simone de. *The Second Sex,* ed. and trans., H. M. Parshley. New York: Bantam, 1968.

Bennetts, Leslie. "Feminist Drive Is Likely to Persist Even If Rights Amendment Fails," *New York Times,* May 31, 1978.

———. "The Type of Attack Affects Rape Victims' Speed of Recovery, Study Shows," *New York Times,* April 14, 1978.

Brody, Jane E. "Teenagers' Use of Contraceptives Is Found by Survey to Be Effective," *New York Times,* June 7, 1978.

Brownmiller, Susan. *Against Our Will: Men, Women, and Rape.* New York: Simon & Schuster, 1975.

Broyard, Anatole. Review of Natalie Gittelson, *Dominus, New York Times,* May 24, 1978.

Brozan, Nadine. "Training Linked to Disruption of Female Reproductive Cycle," *New York Times,* April 17, 1978.

―――. "Women Who Waited: Starting a Family after the Age of 30," *New York Times,* September 23, 1977.

Brush, Lorelei, and Baruch, Grace. "Women + Math = ? : Encouraging More Women to Study Mathematics," *Radcliffe Quarterly,* June 1977, p. 7.

Chafe, William. H. *The American Woman.* London: Oxford University Press, 1972.

Coles, Robert. *Privileged Ones: The Well-Off and Rich in America.* Children of Crisis, Vol. V. Boston: Little, Brown, 1977.

―――. "The Die in Dieting," *New York Times,* May 28, 1978.

―――― and Coles, Jane Hallowell. "The Maid and the Missus," *Radcliffe Quarterly,* June 1978, p. 4.

Collins, Jean E. "Publishers Depict Women in New Ways," *New York Times,* April 30, 1978.

Cott, Nancy F., ed. *Root of Bitterness: Documents of the Social History of American Women.* New York: Dutton, 1972.

Davidson, Sara. *Loose Change: Three Women of the Sixties.* New York: Doubleday, 1977.

Donnelly, Caroline. "A Word to the Wives about Part-Time Jobs," *Money,* September 1975.

Dullea, Georgia. "A Lack of Sexual Desire Emerges as a Contemporary Condition," *New York Times,* May 1, 1978.

Erikson, Eric. *Childhood and Society.* New York: Norton, 1963.

Ephron, Nora. *Crazy Salad.* New York: Bantam, 1976.

Firestone, Shulamith. *The Dialectic of Sex: The Case for Feminist Revolution.* New York: Bantam, 1972.

Fiske, Edward B. "Colleges Try Hard Sell as Fewer Seniors Apply," *New York Times,* April 24, 1978.

Flexner, Eleanor. *Century of Struggle: The Women's Rights Movement in the United States.* New York: Atheneum, 1974.

Frankfort, Ellen. *Vaginal Politics.* New York: Bantam, 1973.

French, Marilyn. *The Women's Room.* New York: Summit, 1977.

Friday, Nancy. *My Mother, My Self.* New York: Delacorte, 1978.

Friedan, Betty. *It Changed My Life: Writings on the Women's Movement.* New York: Random House, 1976.

―――. *The Feminine Mystique.* New York: Norton, 1963.

Gallese, Liz Roman. "Moving Experience: Women Managers Say Job Transfers Present a Growing Dilemma," *Wall Street Journal,* May 4, 1978.

Harvin, Al. "Rugby: Women Join in Traditions," *New York Times,* April 17, 1978.

Haseltine, Florence, M.D., and Yaw, Yvonne. *Woman Doctor.* Boston: Houghton Mifflin, 1976.

Haskell, Molly. *From Reverence to Rape: The Treatment of Women in the Movies.* New York: Holt, Rinehart & Winston, 1973.

Hennig, Margaret, and Jardim, Anne. *The Managerial Woman.* New York: Doubleday, 1977.

Henry, William A., III. "The Roots of Feminism," Boston *Globe,* August 14, 1978.

"HEW Rules That Girls Must Have Equality in Sports," *New York Times,* January 25, 1978.

Hite, Shere. *The Hite Report.* New York: Dell, 1976.

Howard, Jane. *A Different Kind of Woman.* New York: Avon, 1973.

Hunt, Morton. "Today's Man: Redbook's Exclusive Gallup Survey on the Emerging Male," *Redbook,* October 1976, p. 112.

Kelton, Nancy. "A New Mother's Confessions of Ambivalence," *New York Times,* April 26, 1978.

King, Stanley. *Five Lives at Harvard: Personality Change during College.* Cambridge: Harvard University Press, 1973.

Klemesrud, Judy. "A Criminologist's View of Women Terrorists," *New York Times,* January 9, 1978.

————. "Are Mormons against Feminism? Not Exactly," *New York Times,* May 5, 1978.

Kneeland, Douglas E. "Backers of Equality Amendment Making Illinois a Prime Target," *New York Times,* May 30, 1978.

Knight, Michael. "Harvard MBA: A Golden Passport," *New York Times,* May 23, 1978.

Lovenheim, Barbara. "Admen Woo the Working Woman," *New York Times,* June 18, 1978.

Low, Natalie S. "The Power of Money in Marriage," *Radcliffe Quarterly,* June 1978, p. 10.

Lyons, Richard D. "Another Sexist Bastion Falls," *New York Times,* May 13, 1978.

McManus, Otile. "Money . . . the Third Partner in Marriage," Boston *Globe,* July 11, 1977.

"Math Mystique: Fear of Figuring," *Time,* March 14, 1977, p. 36.

Mellen, Joan. "Hollywood Rediscovers the American Woman," *New York Times,* April 23, 1978.

Millett, Kate. *Sexual Politics.* New York: Avon, 1971.

Minuchin, Salvador, Rosman, Bernice L., and Baker, Lester. *Psychosomatic Families: Anorexia Nervosa in Context.* Cambridge: Harvard University Press, 1978.

Mittenthal, Sue. "After Baby, Whither the Career?" *New York Times,* February 14, 1979.

"New $1 Coin Is Backed, but Symbol Provokes Debate," *New York Times,* May 24, 1978.

New Yorker. Talk of the Town, May 15, 22, 1978.

O'Brien, Darcy. "A Generation of 'Lost' Scholars," *New York Times Magazine,* March 18, 1979.

Oelsner, Lesley. "What Rights Amendment Could—and Couldn't—Do," *New York Times,* May 29, 1978.

Quindlen, Anna. "Flight Attendants: An Old Stereotype Is Given the Air," *New York Times,* April 24, 1978.

———. "Women in TV Ads: The Old Image Lingers," *New York Times,* May 16, 1978.

Rankin, Deborah. "Business of Women Is Business," *New York Times,* April 30, 1978.

Robertson, Wyndham. "Women M.B.A.'s, Harvard '73—How They're Doing," *Fortune,* August 28, 1978.

Sheehy, Gail. *Passages.* New York: Dutton, 1976.

Singular, Stephen. "Moving On: Reaping the Rewards of the Women's Movement," *New York Times Magazine,* April 30, 1978.

"Study Looks at Feminism and Sexuality," *New York Times,* April 25, 1978.

"Top Women in Big Business, The," *Fortune,* July 18, 1978, pp. 58–64.

Tyson, Molly. "Two Rhodes Converge," *Womensports,* September 1977, p. 28.

Weaver, Warren, Jr. "Court Ruling Lets Girl, 9, a Victim of Sex Assault, Sue a TV Network," *New York Times,* April 25, 1978.

———. "Supreme Court Bars Higher Pension Costs for Women than Men," *New York Times,* April 26, 1978.

Weinraub, Judith, and Nellis, Muriel. "In Her Own Words: Twice as Many Women as Men Are Addicted to Drugs and Alcohol," *People,* May 8, 1978.

White, Robert W. *Lives in Progress.* New York: Holt, Rinehart & Winston, 1975.

———. *The Study of Lives: Essays on Personality in Honor of Henry A. Murray.* Chicago: Aldine-Atherton, 1971.

Wicker, Tom. "He, She or What? " *New York Times,* April 18, 1978.

"Women and Success: Why Some Find It So Painful," *New York Times,* January 28, 1978.

"Women Gain Job Status, but Slowly, Study Says," *New York Times,* May 23, 1978.

"Women's Cause Gets a Lift on Pension Plans," *New York Times,* April 30, 1978.

"Women Who Rank Highest," *U.S. News & World Report,* April 18, 1977, p. 38.